Sustainable Learning

Inclusive practices for 21st century classrooms

Sustainable Learning provides readers with the knowledge and skills to be confident and effective inclusive teachers. The authors show that these skills are essential to quality teaching – teaching that is evidence-based, purposeful, relevant and responsive to students' needs.

The book employs three overarching frameworks to examine inclusive practices in education: equity (learning for all), relevance (learning that matters) and sustainability (learning that lasts). It encourages teachers to see all students as learners and to consider the complexities and diversity of learning in the 21st century.

Chapter features include:

- 'Think and do' exercises to promote reader reflection
- Tables, figures and diagrams to help readers visualise core ideas, theories and themes
- Examples to illustrate the links between theory and practice, and showcase contemporary research in the field of inclusive education.

Lorraine Graham is Professor of Learning Intervention at the University of Melbourne, Victoria.

Jeanette Berman is Director of Educational Psychology at Massey University, Auckland, New Zealand.

Anne Bellert is a Lecturer in Primary Education at Southern Cross University, New South Wales.

Sustainable Learning

Inclusive practices
for 21st century
classrooms

Lorraine Graham
Jeanette Berman
Anne Bellert

CAMBRIDGE
UNIVERSITY PRESS

CAMBRIDGE
UNIVERSITY PRESS

477 Williamstown Road, Port Melbourne, VIC 3207, Australia

Cambridge University Press is part of the University of Cambridge.

It furthers the University's mission by disseminating knowledge in the pursuit of education, learning and research at the highest international levels of excellence.

www.cambridge.org
Information on this title: www.cambridge.org/9781107695955

First published 2015

Cover designed by Marianna Berek-Lewis
Typeset by Aptara Corp.
Printed in Singapore by C.O.S Printers Pte Ltd

A catalogue record for this publication is available from the British Library

*A Cataloguing-in-Publication entry is available from the catalogue
of the National Library of Australia at* www.nla.gov.au

ISBN 978-1-107-69595-5 Paperback

Lorraine Graham
Thankfulness, Bernice.
Sustainable love and hope
Joy, Sorcha, Jamie!

Jeanette Berman
For my mother, my husband and my children

Anne Bellert
I acknowledge the support of my family, friends and colleagues. Thank you.

Foreword

The adjective 'sustainable' is perhaps one of the most important words we can apply in the field of contemporary education. For more than fifty years I have argued strongly for the use of sustainable teaching practices that will bring about optimum and enduring learning in all our students. Underpinning my argument is a firm belief that sustainable learning can only be achieved through effective and *sustainable teaching*. In addition, sustainable learning can only be achieved if the school curriculum and the methods of instruction are compatible with, and relevant for, the culture and society in which the students grow as members. This book has addressed both these aspects in a very constructive and practical way.

Sustainable learning is evident when students feel good and confident about the knowledge, skills, attitudes and values that they have acquired, and can apply them effectively and build upon them as they continue to learn across the life span. A particularly strong perspective that Lorraine, Jeanette and Anne have all presented here is that sustainable learning is essential for an individual's future life in an ever-changing world. They eloquently argue this point when they remind us in chapter 3 that students in our classrooms today will still be active and influential in the 2070s. For these students, and all others who come after them, sustainable learning is an essential attribute for adaptive living in the years ahead. As the authors stress throughout this book, *learning that lasts* is meaningful, intentional and future directed. This applies to all students, including those with differences, disabilities, learning difficulties, or other special needs.

This book presents a well-argued case for viewing sustainable learning as an essential component and goal of successful inclusive education. Although inclusive education has been advocated and practised worldwide for more than 20 years, it is still very much a work in progress. Teachers are still challenged every day to decide how best to achieve sustainable and relevant learning for all students, regardless of their ability or disability. One solution is differentiation of teaching method and curriculum content; but this approach is far from easy to sustain, as the authors point out in chapter 7. But without differentiation, adaptation and culturally responsive teaching some learners will fail to reach their potential.

The authors here argue that what is required is *responsive teaching* that can address the needs of all learners. Figure 3.1 in chapter 3 provides a good reference point for teaching that is indeed responsive. For our teaching to be responsive to individual differences among students it is necessary also to be skilled in formative assessment processes and strategies. Chapter 5 provides a comprehensive coverage of this important topic.

Overall, this book should provide beginning teachers with a good understanding of the issues involved in achieving sustainable learning across the ability range.

The format of the book, with its clearly stated 'intended learning outcomes' (objectives), 'big ideas' and embedded activities in each chapter certainly makes it a user-friendly resource.

Although the text often refers specifically to inclusive education in the Australian and New Zealand contexts, the principles of using responsive teaching to support sustainable learning has universal appeal and wide application. Sustainable learning is learning that lasts. It is achieved through well-structured and responsive teaching for all learners.

Peter Westwood

Contents

Contents

List of figures and tables

About the authors

Lorraine Graham is professor of learning intervention at the University of Melbourne. She has been an active researcher since the 1990s, with positions as associate director of the National Centre of Science, Information and Communication Technology, and Mathematics Education for Rural and Regional Australia, co-developer of the *QuickSmart* literacy and numeracy programs, and professor of inclusive education and psychology in the School of Education at the University of New England. Lorraine is a fellow of the International Association of Research into Learning Disabilities and recipient of the University of New England's Team Award for Excellence in Research. She has dedicated her career to creating relevant and responsive systems of strategy and instructional support.

Dr Jeanette Berman is director of educational psychology at Massey University, Auckland, where she teaches undergraduate and postgraduate courses and provides continuing education for practising psychologists and teachers. She has previously taught special and inclusive education in teacher education programs at the Australian universities of New England and Canberra. Jeanette continues active practice as a psychologist in schools, is registered in both Australia and New Zealand, and is a member of the Australian and New Zealand Psychological societies. She is also a member of the Australian Psychologists and Counsellors in Schools, the International School Psychology Association and the International Association of Cognitive Education and Psychology and has presented at conferences around the world. Jeanette has a special interest in understanding learning and teaching through assessment and has researched and applied dynamic assessment within her practice. She also has a strong focus on Indigenous education and has been the school psychologist in an independent Aboriginal school for many years. Jeanette is an artist, calligrapher and photographer.

Dr Anne Bellert is a qualified primary-school and special education teacher and consultant who has worked in a wide range of school settings since the late 1990s. As well as teaching, Anne has worked closely with classroom teachers, school executives and family members of students with disabilities or learning difficulties to promote inclusive practices and approaches. Anne was involved in the development of the *QuickSmart* programs and pursues research and publication interests focusing on learning difficulties in basic academic skills, literacy, numeracy and, more recently, the potential role of cognitive neuroscience in 21st century education. She is currently a lecturer in education at Southern Cross University.

Chapter 1

Introduction to sustainable learning

Intended learning outcomes

Engagement with the text in this chapter will enable readers to do the following:

- understand the framework of this book and its overall focus on sustainable learning as a way of bringing together inclusive teaching and learning practices in contemporary classrooms

- delineate important concepts associated with special and inclusive education and effective teaching and understand how these are related through sustainable learning

- be familiar with key terms used in this text and understand their derivation

- understand how relevant legislative frameworks apply to educators' responsibilities and education provision to students with disabilities or learning difficulties

Big ideas

- Sustainable learning is learning for all, teaching that matters and learning that lasts. Its foundation is effective classroom practice, and its goal is to provide for the learning needs of all students throughout their school years and into **lifelong learning**.

- Effective teaching occurs within a series of nested frameworks. Legislative frameworks define teacher responsibilities.

- Teaching for sustainable learning pays attention to students' cultures and their relationships with places, families and communities. Such teaching is responsible, relevant and intentional and focuses on the key capabilities of human performance.

- The key capabilities of human performance can be summarised using the acronym **ATRiUM**, which stands for **Active learning**; Thinking; Relating to others; Using language, symbols and information and communication technology (ICT); and Managing self.

Introduction

Sustainable Learning presents a new way of looking at effective **inclusive practices** for contemporary classrooms. As authors, we bring a blend of classroom, specialist and consultative experience in education and school psychology to the task of exploring in detail what teachers need to know and do to be confident, effective and inclusive. Throughout this text, we focus on practices and strategies important in engaging diverse learners and present these within a coherent framework built on what we consider to be the most important factors in understanding learning and teaching.

Our ultimate goal is to guide appropriate instructional **differentiation** according to students' needs so that at least three conditions are satisfied. First, quality learning experiences should be available to all students. Secondly, to accomplish this, all educators need to focus on acquiring the skills underpinning teaching that matters. (By this we mean teaching that is evidence based, purposeful, relevant and responsive to students' needs.) Thirdly, students must be able to demonstrate that content is mastered and learning maintained to the extent that, as far as possible, they become independent learners throughout their lives. Independent and active learning is fundamental to meeting contemporary challenges; we contend that it is not enough to have only 'taught' content.

Sustainable learning is learning for all, teaching that matters and learning that lasts. Figure 1.1 shows how these key organising ideas are all involved in sustainable learning. Effective, responsive teaching supports learning for everyone – learning that is maintained and lifelong. All three dimensions of sustainable learning are interlinked and unfurl during and after the school years.

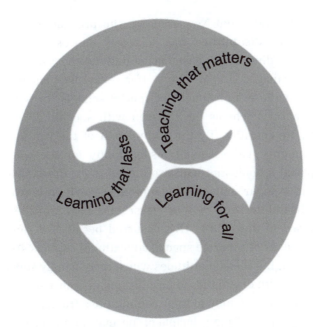

Figure 1.1: *Sustainable learning: learning for all, teaching that matters, learning that lasts*

Learning for all

As it is described in this text, sustainable learning is an approach to inclusive education that aims to secure a fair society into the future by equipping teachers with ways to respond to the increasing complexity and diversity evident in contemporary classrooms and with the skills and resources to be able to teach every student in a way that is 'sustaining, tenable, healthy and durable' (Sterling 2008, 65). The presentation of Māori and Aboriginal models and terminology in pertinent sections of this book, for example, aims to incorporate valuable perspectives relevant to inclusive practice and to respect the cultural and language contexts of learners.

The last 50 years have seen significant progress towards primary education provision for every child on the planet. The UNESCO Education for All initiatives in emerging nations have been grounded in the knowledge that education is a key driver of economic and social progress, particularly the education of girls (Ischinger, cited in Asia Society 2011, 5), which has been identified as one of the best investments a society can make in terms of future social and economic benefits (Boserup, Tan and Toulmin 2013).

There is clear evidence that in the effort to increase equity and enhance educational outcomes globally, enabling young children's participation in pre-primary programs is effective, alongside intensive support programs (for example, in literacy and numeracy) targeting key skill development by learners at risk, parental involvement and close ties between schools and communities. A further vital factor is the development of teachers' capacity and motivation to deliver better instruction to every student in the classroom.

Disability often results from an impairment that may be physical, cognitive, sensory, emotional and/or developmental.

Integration is the placement (permanent or non-permanent) of students with disabilities or learning difficulties in mainstream, or regular, educational settings.

Learning difficulties are problems with basic academic skills encountered by learners, which often have social and emotional dimensions. In New Zealand, the term 'named learning difficulties' is used to encompass attention deficit hyperactivity disorder, autism spectrum disorder and dyslexia.

Inclusion in education is the provision of educational opportunities that meet students' learning needs within their own communities.

In Australia and New Zealand, the provision of education to students with **disabilities** has followed the usual pattern of gradually expanding from basic schooling to the education of students with particular impairments (for example, visual and auditory) and then the establishment of special schools. In the first half of the 20th century, schools for children with specific disabilities were run mostly by charities. By the second half of the century, most regional governments had assumed responsibility for the education provided by special schools and had also moved to establish special educational units in 'regular' schools (Angloinfo 2014). The **integration** of students with disabilities into regular classrooms began in the mid 1970s and increased in the 1990s. This occurred because of concerns about the effectiveness of separate special educational settings and in conjunction with changing societal attitudes which increasingly supported the rights of people with disabilities to be educated in their neighbourhood schools and to contribute fully to their communities (Konza 2008).

The impact of the principle of 'normalisation' also contributed to the rise of integration in schools and the participation of people with disabilities in their communities (Bank-Mikkelson 1969; Nirje 1970). The term 'normalisation', coined by Wolfensberger (1970), underscored the right of all individuals to be valued and to participate meaningfully in their communities, including attending local schools. Konza (2008) characterised integration (or mainstreaming) as the schooling of most students with disabilities in regular classrooms for part or all of the school day. Integration, as an educational policy, still includes the provision of separate specialised settings as an option for students with severe disabilities.

The period from the 1970s to the 1990s saw more and more students with disabilities or **learning difficulties** educated in their neighbourhood schools, but because of a lack of resources, the provision of appropriate access and materials (such as ramps, modified toilets, audio loops and large print or Braille texts) was not always widespread. This meant that many students were still not able to attend their local schools.

Since the mid 1990s, however, the **inclusion** philosophy has been influential in changing education provision for students with disabilities or learning difficulties. Inclusion is about more than the location of education; it requires the provision of an educational system that can meet the needs of all learners and include their families as part of local school communities. It involves restructuring educational systems so that schools have responsibility for providing the facilities, resources and access to an appropriate curriculum suited to all students irrespective of their learning needs (Konza 2008). It is a social

Reflection 1.1: Defining inclusion

Ainscow, Booth and Dyson (2006) suggest that it is useful to distinguish between 'narrow' and 'broad' definitions of inclusion. Using their framework, narrow definitions of inclusion aim for the promotion of inclusion for a specific student group – mainly, students who have disabilities or learning difficulties – in regular educational settings. In contrast, broad definitions of inclusion focus not on specific student groups but on diversity itself and how schools respond to the differentness of all students and all members of the school community.

The use of the term 'inclusion' has already broadened from that of the 1990s, and this is likely to continue. Armstrong, Armstrong and Spandagou (2011, 32) note an important tension when they observe that both broad and narrow definitions of inclusion become 'fragmented' when they break down the groups that are to be included. For example, they cite a policy report from the United Kingdom that describes 'an educationally inclusive school as one in which the teaching and learning, achievements, attitudes and wellbeing of every young person matter' (Ofsted 2000, 4). In the same report, however, Ofsted (2000, 4) notes that the following main student groups are 'identified in relation to inclusion: "girls and boys; minority ethnic and faith groups; travellers, asylum seekers and refugees; pupils who need support to learn English as an additional language; students with special educational needs; gifted and talented students; children 'looked after' by the local authority; other children such as sick children; young carers; those children from families under stress; pregnant school girls and teenage mothers; and any other students who are at risk of disaffection and exclusion"'. This list divides the notion of 'every young person' into numerous groups. While such an approach may help identify commonalities and allocate resources, it also means that, as Armstrong, Armstrong and Spandagou (2010, 30) note, 'inclusion becomes a process of "managing" many different individuals and groups who are perceived as "problems"'. Inclusion, at its root, implies including people in settings where they were not previously; otherwise, they would have already belonged.

justice philosophy grounded in United Nations frameworks (for example, CSIE 2013; OHCHR 1989; United Nations Enable 1993).

As shown in the list of identifiers in reflection 1.1, many labels for disabilities, types of learning difficulties and social and cultural variations are currently used in education. These labels are derived from three main sources: medical science, psychological science and sociocultural contexts. (Some examples are shown in figure 1.2 grouped around a Māori representation of human growth and learning.) We are proposing a different way of thinking about learners, which will better support sustainable learning and reframe teaching. We see every learner in terms of capabilities rather than deficits or disabilities and in this way seek to avoid limitations that may be inherent in the interpretation of labels. The ATRiUM capabilities framework (introduced later in this chapter) provides a way to think about the learning needs of all learners. A focus on individual students' learning needs is obviously important to implementing inclusion and in this book means providing what is necessary for students to learn and to achieve: it requires removing all possible barriers to learning for

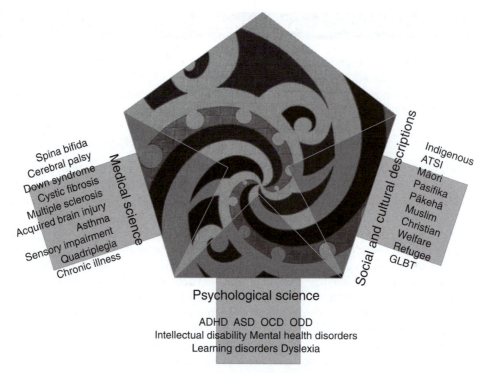

Medical science

Spina bifida
Cerebral palsy
Down syndrome
Cystic fibrosis
Multiple sclerosis
Acquired brain injury
Asthma
Sensory impairment
Quadriplegia
Chronic illness

Social and cultural descriptions

Indigenous
ATSI
Māori
Pasifika
Pākehā
Muslim
Christian
Welfare
Refugee
GLBT

Psychological science

ADHD ASD OCD ODD
Intellectual disability Mental health disorders
Learning disorders Dyslexia

Figure 1.2: *Examples of labels and their sources*

all. It is vital to remember that responding to individual student needs may require extra learning support or extending and enriching individuals' school experiences. Such education provisions may necessitate students moving around the school and community and in and out of class to access what they need.

In this book, therefore, we will be focusing on the capabilities of learners and teachers. However, we will refer to disabilities and learning difficulties when necessary, because these terms help us share meaning and are fundamental to accessing much of the available information. Students experiencing disabilities that are usually readily identifiable (physical, cognitive, visual, auditory, learning, behavioural, communicatory, social and emotional disabilities) generally require some kind of learning or behavioural support so they can access the curriculum and participate in educational settings. Similarly, 'learning difficulties' is a term used broadly in Australia and New Zealand to refer to those students who experience academic and school-related problems, and at least 20 per cent of school students are considered to have such problems at some time during their schooling (Ashman and Elkins 2009). There is no assumption that students experiencing learning difficulties have an underlying impairment, although some of them certainly may. Students with learning difficulties tend to be a diverse group. Difficulty with academic subjects can be experienced for myriad reasons.

In New Zealand, the term 'named learning difficulties' usually refers to the subset of students with learning difficulties who have attention deficit hyperactivity disorder, autism spectrum disorder or dyslexia. It is important to acknowledge both individuals who have a named learning difficulty and those who do not. There are many learners without labels who experience as much difficulty in learning as those with diagnosed learning difficulties. Responsive teaching is charged with exploring and addressing the learning needs of all learners.

Our concern is to not objectify people because of the disabilities and adverse conditions they may experience. Language use, in such instances, can frame the valuing of people and can shape understanding about teaching and learning and about the learning needs of students. We know, however, that language is representative of culture and attitudes and that it is highly significant in the context of inclusive education. Language has had to change from that used when learners who had disabilities or learning difficulties were not able to access education at all. It has altered in tandem with changes in society's view of difference and service provision for people who have needs that are in any way atypical.

Think and do 1.1: Describing people

In the past, disability was seen as being wholly within individuals: they 'had' the disability and were largely defined by it. Such an approach is in contrast to the social model of disability, which defines disability as a mismatch between the environment and the person and guides us to put people first in our language.

In August 2012, Radio New Zealand reporters interviewed people with disabilities about how they were described. The most disliked terms were 'handicapped' and 'special needs'. 'The disabled' was also a term many disliked, as it ignored the fact that they were people first. Interviewees suggested asking what terminology each person preferred, as it relates to their individual identity. In New Zealand, advocates have tended to use the term 'disabled people', as it reflects the social thinking model of the 2001 New Zealand Disability Strategy that people are disabled by society (Minister for Disability Issues 2001). In 'people first' language, that becomes 'people with disability'. Since the 2006 United Nations Convention of Persons with Disabilities, 'people with disabilities' has become a more commonly used term (Workbridge 2010). Stella Young (2012) from the ABC's *The Drum* makes two potent points on this issue:

> I am repeatedly asked in interviews exactly 'what's wrong' with me and I always give them the same answer; I don't identify the name of my condition in an interview unless it's relevant to the context of the story. The fact that I'm a wheelchair user is relevant to a story about access to public transport. The long-winded medical term for my impairment is not…

> Now, I find the concept of having to clarify my status as a person extraordinarily condescending. No one else is ever asked to qualify their status as a person. Gay men and women are not 'people with homosexuality'. Women are not 'people who are female'. Footballers are not 'people who play football'. I've met a lot of disabled people in my time, and not once have I ever met someone whose impairment is so profound that their status as a person is in doubt.

Think about how you use language to describe people, particularly people who have disabilities or learning difficulties. Check out media descriptions. Are they written with respect and consideration or with sensationalism? Share what you notice.

In Australia, the most important pieces of legislation that underpin the inclusive education of students in their local schools are the Commonwealth *Disability Discrimination Act 1992* and the Disability Standards for Education 2005. Under the Disability Discrimination Act, the definition of disability 'includes physical, intellectual, psychiatric, sensory, neurological, and learning disabilities, as well as physical disfigurements, and the presence of disease-causing organisms in the body. The definition includes past, present and future disabilities as well as imputed disabilities and covers behaviour that is a symptom or manifestation of the disability' (Department of Education 2010, 5).

The Disability Standards for Education aim to provide clarity about the rights of students by specifying how all educational and training services should be accessible to students with disabilities. The standards also define the meaning of the following important terms:

On the same basis: On the same basis means that a student with disability must have opportunities and choices, which are comparable with those offered to students without disability. This applies to: admission or enrolment in an institution; participation in courses or programs; and use of facilities and services.

> **Adjustments** are the changes, supports or modifications that can be made to enable all students to learn and demonstrate their learning.

Consultation: When deciding what to include in an educational course and how to teach it, an education provider should consult with each student with disability doing the course, or an associate of the student, about the effect of the disability on their ability to seek enrolment, and any reasonable **adjustments** necessary. Where possible the student, or their associate, and the education provider should work together to find adjustments and solutions to help the student access and participate in education and training.

Reasonable adjustment: Under the Standards, education providers have a positive obligation to make reasonable adjustments to accommodate the needs of a student with disability.

When assessing whether an adjustment is reasonable, the education provider is required to consider the interests of all parties affected, including the student with disability, the education provider, staff and other students. The education provider is required to consult with the student or their carer to identify and make an adjustment appropriate to the student's disability.

Unjustifiable hardship: The Standards do not require changes to be made if this would impose unjustifiable hardship on the education provider. All relevant circumstances are to be taken into account when assessing unjustifiable hardship including:
- benefit or detriment to any persons concerned
- disability of the person
- financial circumstances of the education provider (Department of Education 2010, 11)

All state and territory educational policies claim a philosophical acceptance of inclusion and support it where possible and when in the best interests of the child. The use of reasonable adjustments is fundamental to inclusive practice (Konza 2008).

In New Zealand, the *New Zealand Disability Strategy: making a world of difference, whakanui oranga* aims to create a more inclusive society that enhances full participation for all both in education and in post-school life (Minister for Disability Issues 2001). The strategy has educational aims to ensure that schools are responsive, accountable and inclusive and that teachers understand learning needs and have adequate resources and lifelong opportunities for learning. *Ka hikitia – managing for success: the Māori Education Strategy 2008–2012* sets the direction for Māori learners, including those with disabilities or learning difficulties, by advocating high-quality, culturally responsive education (Ministry of Education 2008). The New Zealand Ministry of Education is bound by legislation in the Education Act 1989, the Human Rights Act 1993 and the Building Act 2004 that supports education provision for students with special educational needs. All of this has implications for how schools need to act in the interests of students who have disabilities.

In 2013, educational priorities identified by the New Zealand Ministry of Education focused on improving learning for students who had not been doing as well as they could, including students with disabilities, learning difficulties or named learning difficulties. (For more on this, see Ministry of Education 2013.) These priorities build on the evaluation of the successful inclusion of students with high support needs, which concluded that 'approximately half of the 229 schools reviewed demonstrated mostly inclusive practice', with 30 per cent exhibiting some inclusive practices and 20 per cent few inclusive practices. This statistic underlines the reason for this book's emphasis on responsive teaching that will improve outcomes in learning for all students. The most successful inclusive settings employed three key principles:

- having ethical standards and leadership that built the culture of an inclusive school
- having well-organised systems, effective teamwork and constructive relationships that identified and supported the inclusion of students with high needs
- using innovative and flexible practices that managed the complex and unique challenges related to including students with high needs. (Education Review Office 2010, 1)

Teaching that matters

Learning that is mastered and maintained, fostered by good teaching and available to all *matters*. A message delivered throughout this text is that inclusion is facilitated by effective instruction, quality teachers with high expectations and the support of families; when learning is at the centre of everything that goes on in the classroom, teachers and students sustain each other's learning.

The teacher is the key to effecting sustainable learning in the school and classroom. Sustainable learning depends on effective teaching, which responds to individual learning needs in the best possible ways. By providing teaching that matters, responsive teachers help all learners develop the skills they need to meet their goals and to regulate their own learning. Responsive teaching practices ensure a match between students' learning needs and the learning opportunities provided and are characterised by the use of flexible, differentiated activities underpinned by carefully thought out assessment procedures. Responsive teaching sees learners in terms of their capabilities and works towards further developing and strengthening them. It builds on the prior learning and the cultural capital of each learner. It is teaching that is effective in motivating learning and in engaging with the worlds of the learners. Responsive teaching is characterised by a series of cycles of planning, activity and reflection, within which important teaching decisions are made. The responsive teaching framework (RTF), introduced in chapter 3 and revisited in subsequent chapters, is an important guide to teaching that matters. Responsive teachers are flexible and adaptable in order to meet the changing needs of all learners in their classes. The RTF meets the four descriptors set out by Sterling (2008, 65):

- *Sustaining*: it helps sustain people, communities and ecosystems;
- *Tenable*: it is ethically defensible, working with integrity, justice, respect and inclusiveness;
- *Healthy*: it is itself a viable system, embodying and nurturing healthy relationships and emergence at different system levels;
- *Durable*: it works well enough in practice to be able to keep doing it.

Specifically, in terms of learning that is sustainable and teaching that is effective, Van den Branden (2012) summarises the findings of research that has successfully improved the academic achievement of at-risk students with and without disabilities from disadvantaged and migrant backgrounds (for example, Finn and Rock 1997; Garcia and Kleifgen 2010; Hattie 2009; Marzano 2003; Muijs et al. 2004). He found that the following teacher behaviours and school and classroom factors make a difference that lasts:

(1) Students at risk should be presented challenging and interesting content, with teachers having high expectations of the students' learning potential and stimulating students' higher order thinking skills (from primary school onwards); crucially, the latter should not be put 'on hold'.
(2) Time available should be maximally devoted to academic content and the teaching of key competencies.
(3) The school should provide for a safe and secure environment for learning, characterized by a good disciplinary climate, warm and positive student–teacher relations, strong investment in students' well-being, self-confidence, and intrinsic learning motivation.
(4) New content should be related to individual students' prior knowledge and experiences; students' existing knowledge and skills (including the students' mother tongue skills) should be tapped as rich resources for new learning.
(5) Meaningful, situated, holistic learning in context should be complemented with explicit skills instruction. Overall, the teacher should display a wide array of methodologies and formats to cater

    to different learning styles, including formats that stimulate cooperative learning and independent learning.

(6) Language and literacy development should be stimulated across the curriculum and integrated with the teaching of interesting, challenging content teaching.

(7) Teachers should scaffold and actively guide the acquisition of complex skills and gradually increase student autonomy. Students should be provided with personalized feedback and support catered to their personal needs, with some students being granted more time to acquire key competences than others. (Van den Branden 2012, 296–7)

Additionally, educational contexts must be able to incorporate technological innovations and the increasing demand for flexible, creative inquiry. They require educators with adaptable professional skill sets and creative perspectives that equip them to explore how to develop every student's potential. Students who experience educational disadvantage as a result of poverty or disability have the most to gain from rich, powerful learning experiences and the most to lose if they encounter inappropriate learning environments and ineffective teachers.

Learning that lasts

Sustainable learning draws from concepts associated with education for sustainability (for example, ACARA, n.d.; UNESCO, 2012, n.d.). Specifically, such concepts include social justice, an emphasis on learning rather than teaching, the use of appropriate assessment approaches, acknowledgment of Indigenous peoples' perspectives on knowledge, ICT as a learning tool, problem-solving, lifelong learning and collaborative decision-making (Sterling 2001; Van den Branden 2012). Sustainable learning is based on the establishment, development and maintenance of the processes that humans use when learning. It aims to equip learners so that the processes of learning are capable of being activated whenever they are needed. In the dynamic, increasingly complex present, such a renewable resource is increasingly desirable. No longer do individuals train for one career and draw on a fixed bank of skills and knowledge for decades. Instead, they need to respond to the demands of new careers, new technologies, cultural shifts and rapid and unpredictable change. Because of the requirement for more sophisticated functioning throughout life, school curricula have the task of ensuring that learners can continue to be lifelong and 'life-wide' learners in all areas of endeavour. Thus, the focus of education has turned towards learning processes or capabilities rather than products, because such processes can be applied as needed across the curriculum to meet many different types of learning challenges.

    In sustainable learning, the focus is on the capabilities of individual learners as they engage and interact within their social worlds. Each learner is considered a holistic being for whom psychological, physical, spiritual and social wellbeing are integrated. The processes that are activated in learning grow out of five dimensions of functioning,

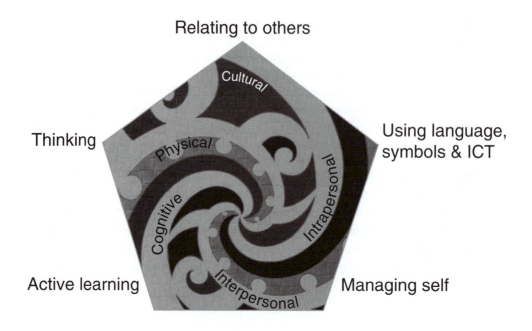

Figure 1.3: *The ATRiUM capabilities and five dimensions of human functioning*

Interpersonal
functioning
concerns a person's
communication and
action relating to
others.

Intrapersonal
functioning concerns
a person's own
emotions, wellbeing
and self-management.

which are cultural, physical, cognitive, **interpersonal** and **intrapersonal**. These are represented by the acronym ATRiUM: Active learning; Thinking; Relating to others; Using language, symbols and ICT; and Managing self. The relationship between the dimensions of human functioning and the ATRiUM capabilities for learning is shown in figure 1.3. This representation depicts an unfurling of the ATRiUM capabilities as the processes that support growth and learning develop.

An atrium is a meaningful metaphor for growth and learning. It is a large open space near the entry of a building. In ancient Roman times an atrium was a courtyard, but in modern architecture it has become more sophisticated and is typically several storeys high and glazed to let light flood the building. An atrium is connected to the environment and is therefore affected by the elements; it is associated with entries, openness, space and the environment. The atrium as a teaching metaphor suggests that learners have the space and light required to learn and can rise to higher levels of learning given the right conditions. Students' strengths are at the heart of their capacity to learn.

The photograph in figure 1.4 was taken looking up into an atrium, where there is light, including views of the world not available lower down. The feather sculptures

Figure 1.4: *The Atrium Building, Massey University, Auckland*
Source: Opus Architecture. Photograph J. Berman.

visible in this photograph are a reminder that individuals always remain connected to and affected by their wider environment. The atrium metaphor emphasises sustaining the strengths each learner brings as well as developing capabilities further. It opposes limiting students' potential by focusing on deficits, disabilities and what learners cannot do.

Sustainable learning, an approach that aligns a way of thinking about learning with classroom action for learning that lasts, is defined by an ethic of care and aims to equip learners and teachers with the capabilities to transform themselves and others, bearing in mind the wellbeing of the planet. For example, learners (both teachers and students can be thought of as such) in sustainable classrooms care about the following elements:

- resources and how they are used
- relationships with all the people in the classroom, school and community environment
- the classroom environment (ecology)
- energy and how it is used in the classroom (personal energy for students and teachers and the use and reuse of physical resources)
- cooperation and meeting shared goals that improve outcomes for everyone

As Redman (2013, 26) notes, 'Schools can lead the way towards sustainability by providing a supportive atmosphere for sustainable behaviours'. Actions and behaviours related to sustainable learning include those that are future oriented, cumulatively

Figure 1.5: *An ecological and holistic view of learning*

positive where 'every little bit counts', geared towards improvement, collaborative in a way that lifts all the individuals involved, encouraging of the participation of all, and valuing of everyone involved.

The challenge of sustainability in general is recognised as greater than ever, with government institutions, agencies and industry increasingly emphasising 'the importance of learning and capacity-building as solutions to sustainability challenges including climate change, disaster risk management, biodiversity loss and sustainable production and consumption'. The concept of sustainable learning is all the more timely because of the increasing recognition that sustainability challenges cannot be solved solely through technological advances, legislation or policies. Aligning learning with the sustainable management of classrooms responds to the need for 'synchronizing thinking and acting' identified in the UNESCO report on the UN Decade of Education for Sustainable Development (UNESCO 2012, 5).

Sustainable learning is related to notions of sustainable education and education for sustainable development. It differs from these because rather than focusing on ways that individuals can be prepared to actively support sustainable development by, for example, recognising interdependence, caring and conserving (WCED 1987; Sterling 2001), sustainable learning reorients the focus of sustainability to classroom learning processes and teaching practices. Sustainable learning seeks to ensure, as far as possible, that the needs of all students and educators are satisfied, while preparing for the future. For students this means they are guided to develop the

Reflection 1.2: Language is culture

This book is written for readers in both Australia and New Zealand and draws on the language used in schools and educational systems in both countries. In Te Reo Māori (the Māori language), the word *ako* reflects the weaving together of teaching and learning. The one word is used for both concepts. In this book, the blending of teaching and learning is reflected in the interaction of the holistic learner on a learning journey with teaching that is responsive to that learner's needs. Our definition of sustainable learning includes reference to teaching that matters, as this is what leads learning for all and learning that lasts.

The book also contains an expectation that teachers develop competence in different ways at different times and can support other teachers by acting as teachers for them. This idea is embedded in another Māori concept, *tuakana teina*, literally translated as 'older person, younger person'. The New Zealand Ministry of Education highlights two key issues that arise from this concept which are also inherent in this book. Firstly, it is vital for teachers and schools to know where students come from – what they bring to their learning. Secondly, teaching and learning must be carried out within partnership. Teaching today is a process of professionals engaging with learners and their families (*whānau*) in an interactive, mutually respectful partnership to ensure optimum learning outcomes for all learners.

Family (*whānau*) is a vitally important dimension within sustainable learning. Although we have written *whānau* paired with 'family' throughout, there is more to the concept of *whānau* than is generally understood by the English word 'family'. Its understanding is not limited to the nuclear family; it includes whatever constellation of people are core for individuals. It may be the mother and father and siblings, but it could also be extended family or other closely connected people who may or may not be genetically related. The term *whānau* is also used for more transient groupings of people, and it is sometimes used to refer to classes in schools.

competencies they will need in their future lives, while for teachers it means they are offered adequate support to develop and apply relevant teaching capabilities. All resources that both students and teachers bring to the classroom, such as talents, background knowledge, motivation and expertise, are respected so that they can be conserved and sustained. Concern about learning is at the centre of everything that teachers and students do.

Sustainable learning is ecological, because while they are at school learners are not separate from their cultures, communities and families (*whānau*). Learning is a result of interactions between the teachers, learners and educational settings, and all learning is demonstrated in those same relationships. An ecosystem for learning is shown in figure 1.5, in which learners are represented by the ATRiUM pentagon nested within educational, family (*whānau*) and community settings. As learners become part of formal educational settings, including school, the complexity of sociocultural influences at play increases. Social communities function within a larger social, structural, political, economic and cultural environment that provides resources, defines the curriculum and sets the cultural expectations of the educational setting and the teaching and learning interaction (Zubrick, Williams & Silburn 2000). These layers of context affect the engagement and functioning of the learners and teachers.

Think and do 1.2: Indigenous education

Explore the Māori Education Strategy: Ka Hikitia – Accelerating Success 2013–2017 (Ministry of Education, n.d.) and the Australian government's (n.d.) Indigenous educational initiatives.

1   What ideas in the documents about learning, teaching, diversity and schools are new to you?

2   How do they vary from your assumptions?

3   What impact might these documents have on your teaching?

Not only is learning ecological; it is also holistic. It affects all aspects (physical, cognitive, cultural, interpersonal and intrapersonal) of learners' lives. Indigenous models of human functioning from Australia and New Zealand describe ways of seeing learners and teachers as complex holistic learners (Bevan-Brown 2003; Durie 1998; Pere 1997; Yunkaporta 2009). Such models have been developed within both educational and professional psychological contexts and provide important ways to think about learners in every school. Teachers and schools need to be concerned not just with cognitive learning (the traditional scope of education) but also with the whole person: how each learner thinks, feels, acts, relates, imagines, believes and values – in fact, how each learner grows and applies the five ATRiUM capabilities of Active learning; Thinking; Relating to others; Using language, symbols and ICT; and Managing self.

Think and do 1.3: Van den Branden's list

How well do the sustainable-learning components – learning for all, teaching that matters and learning that lasts – encapsulate Van den Branden's (2012) list of teacher, school and classroom factors that improve academic achievement?

Organisation of this book

Each of the chapters shares a common structure, with 'Intended learning outcomes' presented first to highlight the main points and make clear the skills that the chapter will target, followed by 'Big ideas'. Articulating the key concepts of each chapter encourages integrated thinking across the entire book and relates directly in later chapters to the RTF and the ATRiUM capabilities for learning, which serve as organising frames for the discussion of inclusive practices. In addition to the text of each chapter, figures and tables illustrate key content, and important points are explained in more detail in 'Reflection' sections. *Sustainable Learning* also features 'Think and do' activities to guide reader involvement, discussion and learning; definition of terms throughout; and selected 'Further reading'.

The remaining chapters unpack the core organising definitions of sustainable learning as learning for all, teaching that matters and learning that lasts. Chapter 2, 'Learning processes', begins by contextualising an ecological view of learning and moves on to discuss principles and processes underpinning learning – specifically, information processing models. Chapter 3, 'Teaching processes', looks at the teaching profession and its most important procedures. It introduces the RTF as a keystone of sustainable learning. Teachers' professional skills at work, such as communication, organisation, collaboration and managing resources, are discussed before the text turns to instructional practices that support inclusion.

Chapter 4, 'Influences on learning', unpacks this subject in broad ecological terms. The ATRiUM capabilities are used to organise discussion of the physical, cognitive, cultural, interpersonal and intrapersonal foundations of diversity. Chapter 5, 'Assessment and feedback', considers the vital role of assessment in guiding and focusing relevant instruction, feedback and appropriate differentiation in order to meet students' needs. The chapter examines the why, what and how of assessment *for* learning, assessment *as* learning and assessment *of* learning.

Chapter 6, 'Learning for all', brings together a discussion of the vital evidence-based instructional practices that form the foundation of effective inclusive teaching. The first part of the chapter discusses 'learning not labels' for students with disabilities or learning difficulties. The subsequent sections use ATRiUM as an organising framework to identify students' capabilities and to link appropriate differentiation approaches to them. The chapter concludes with a review of important instructional approaches to enable learning for all.

Chapter 7, 'Teaching that matters', presents a model for appropriately differentiating instruction and content based on setting intended learning outcomes, organisation and action. Ten essential skills that guide differentiation and 11 example teacher responses for on-the-spot adjustments are identified. In addition, the text broadens the concept of teaching that matters in a wide-ranging discussion of risk-taking, help-seeking, the importance of learning strategies to lifelong learning, culturally responsive teaching, mind frames and evidence-based practice.

Chapter 8, 'Learning that lasts', provides further discussion of how learning can be fostered and maintained for all. It deals with transitions within and beyond schools and the lifelong learning journeys of students with disabilities or learning difficulties, suggesting that for teachers, learning that lasts is underpinned by reflection and an action research orientation in their practice.

Summary

Students with disabilities or learning difficulties, due to any combination of the myriad factors that can impact on an individual's ability to learn and participate, are present in all contemporary classrooms. All regular classroom teachers are required to cater for their students' learning needs in a meaningful way that personalises learning for each individual student. This chapter has described sustainable learning in terms of its three main ideas: learning for all, teaching that matters and learning that lasts. It has also introduced the use of a cohesive set of capabilities linked to the metaphor ATRiUM as a way of thinking about bringing light to learning through considering students' performance in terms of Active learning; Thinking; Relating to others; Using language, symbols and ICT; and Managing self. The chapter also introduced the importance of responsive teaching as a way of meeting students' learning needs and foreshadowed the RTF as an important guide to teaching that matters.

Further reading

8 Aboriginal Ways of Learning website: http://8ways.wikispaces.com.

Australian Curriculum, Assessment and Reporting Authority. n.d. 'Cross-curriculum priorities.' ACARA. www.acara.edu.au/verve/_resources/cross_curriculum.pdf.

Bevan-Brown, J. 2013. 'Including people with disabilities: an Indigenous perspective.' *International Journal of Inclusive Education* 17 (6): 571–83.

ComLaw. 2013. 'Disability Discrimination Act 1992.' Australian Government. www.comlaw.gov.au/details/c2013c00022.

Department of Education. n.d. 'Disability Standards for Education.' Australian Government. http://education.gov.au/disability-standards-education.

Durie, M. 1998. *Whaiora: Māori health development.* Auckland: Oxford University Press.

Education Counts. 2010. 'Te piko o te māhuri: the key attributes of successful Kura Kaupapa Māori.' New Zealand Government. www.educationcounts.govt.nz/publications/maori/105966/80403/2.-te-aho-matua.

Yunkaporta, T. 2009. 'Aboriginal pedagogies at the cultural interface.' PhD thesis, James Cook University. http://eprints.jcu.edu.au/10974.

References

ACARA (Australian Curriculum, Assessment and Reporting Authority). n.d. 'Cross-curriculum priorities.' ACARA. www.acara.edu.au/curriculum/cross_curriculum_priorities.html.

Ainscow, M. T., A. Booth and A. Dyson. 2006. *Improving schools, developing inclusion.* With P. Farrell, J. Frankham, F. Gallannaugh, A. Howes and R. Smith. London: Routledge.

AngloInfo. 2014. 'Special needs education in Australia.' AngloInfo. http://australia.angloinfo. com/family/schooling-education/special-needs.

Armstrong, A. C., D. Armstrong and I. Spandagou. 2011. 'Inclusion: by choice or by chance?' *International Journal of Inclusive Education* 15 (1): 29–39.

Armstrong, D., A. C. Armstrong and I. Spandagou. 2010. *Inclusive education: international policy & practice.* London: Sage.

Ashman, A. and J. Elkins. 2009. *Education for inclusion and diversity*, 3rd edn. Sydney: Pearson.

Asia Society. 2011. *Improving teacher quality around the world: the international summit on the teaching profession.* Hong Kong: Asia Society.

Australian Government. n.d. 'Indigenous education.' Australian Government. http://australia. gov.au/topics/education-and-training/indigenous-education.

Bank-Mikkelson, N. H. 1969. 'A metropolitan area in Denmark: Copenhagen.' In R. B. Kugel and W. Wolfensberger, eds. *Changing patterns in residential services for the mentally retarded: a President's Committee on Mental Retardation monograph*, 227–54. Washington, DC: President's Committee on Mental Retardation.

Bevan-Brown, J. 2003. *Cultural self-review: providing culturally effective, inclusive education for Māori learners.* Wellington: New Zealand Council for Educational Research.

Boserup, E., S. F. Tan and C. Toulmin. 2013. *Woman's role in economic development.* London: Routledge.

CSIE (Centre for Studies on Inclusive Education). 2013. 'The UNESCO Salamanca Statement.' CSIE. www.csie.org.uk/inclusion/unesco-salamanca.shtml.

Department of Education. 2010. 'Review of Disability Standards for Education 2005.' Discussion paper. Australian Government. December. http://docs.education.gov.au/system/files/doc/ other/review_of_disability_standards_for_education_2005.pdf.

Durie, M. H.1998. *Te mana, te kāwanatanga: the politics of self determination.* Auckland: Oxford University Press.

Education Review Office. 2010. 'Including students with high needs.' New Zealand Government. www.ero.govt.nz/National-Reports/Including-Students-with-High-Needs-June-2010.

Finn, J. D. and D. A. Rock. 1997. 'Academic success among students at risk for school failure.' *Journal of Applied Psychology* 82 (2): 221.

Garcia, O. and J. A. Kleifgen. 2010. *Educating emergent bilinguals: policies, programs, and practices for English language learners.* New York: Teachers' College Press.

Hattie, J. 2009. *Visible learning: a synthesis of over 800 meta-analyses relating to achievement.* London and New York: Routledge.

Konza, D. 2008. 'Inclusion of students with disabilities in new times: responding to the challenge.' In P. Kell, W. Vialle, D. Konza and G. Vogl, eds. *Learning and the learner: exploring learning for new times*, 38–65. Wollongong: University of Wollongong.

Marzano, R. J. 2003. *What works in schools: translating research into action.* Alexandria, VA: Association for Supervision and Curriculum Development.

Minister for Disability Issues. 2001. *The New Zealand Disability Strategy: making a world of difference, whakanui oranga.* Wellington: New Zealand Government.

Ministry of Education. 2008. *Ka Hikitia – managing for success: the Māori Education Strategy 2008–2012.* Wellington: New Zealand Government.

——. 2013. 'Operating priorities.' New Zealand Government. www.minedu.govt.nz/the Ministry/PublicationsAndResources/StatementOfIntent/SOI2013/OperatingIntentions/ OperatingPriorities.aspx.

——. n.d. 'The Māori education strategy: Ka Hikitia – Accelerating Success 2013–2017.' New Zealand Government. www.minedu.govt.nz/theMinistry/PolicyandStrategy/KaHikitia.aspx.

Muijs, D., A. Harris, C. Chapman, L. Stoll and J. Russ. 2004. 'Improving schools in socioeconomically disadvantaged areas: a review of research evidence.' *School Effectiveness and School Improvement* 15 (2): 149–75.

Nirje, B. 1970. 'Symposium on "normalization". I. The normalization principle: implications and comments.' *Journal of Mental Subnormality* 16 (31): 62–70.

Ofsted (Office for Standards in Education). 2000. *Evaluating educational inclusion: guidance for inspectors and schools.* London: Ofsted.

OHCHR (Office of the High Commissioner for Human Rights). 1989. 'Convention on the rights of the child.' United Nations. www.ohchr.org/en/professionalinterest/pages/crc.aspx.

Pere, R. T. R. 1997. *Te wheke: a celebration of infinite wisdom*, 2nd edn. Gisborne, New Zealand: Ao Ako Global Learning.

Redman, E. 2013. 'Advancing educational pedagogy for sustainability: developing and implementing programs to transform behaviors.' *International Journal of Environmental & Science Education* 8 (1): 1–34.

Sterling, S. 2001. *Sustainable education.* Dartington, United Kingdom: Green Books.

——. 2008. 'Sustainable education: towards a deep learning response to unsustainability.' *Policy & Practice: A Development Education Review* 6 (spring): 63–8.

UNESCO (United Nations Educational, Scientific and Cultural Organization). 2012. 'Shaping the education of tomorrow: 2012 full-length report on the UN Decade of Education for Sustainable Development.' UNESCO. http://unesdoc.unesco.org/images/0021/002164/ 216472e.pdf.

——. n.d. 'Education for sustainable development: mission.' UNESCO. www.unesco.org/ new/en/education/themes/leading-the-international-agenda/education-for-sustainable -development/mission/.

United Nations Enable. 1993. 'Standard rules on the equalization of opportunities for persons with disabilities.' United Nations. www.un.org/disabilities/default.asp?id=26.

Van den Branden, K. 2012. 'Sustainable education: basic principles and strategic recommendations.' *School Effectiveness and School Improvement* 23 (3): 285–304.

WCED (World Commission on Environment and Development). 1987. 'Report of the World Commission on Environment and Development: our common future.' United Nations. www.un-documents.net/our-common-future.pdf.

Wolfensberger, W. 1970. 'The principle of normalization and its implications to psychiatric services.' *American Journal of Psychiatry* 127 (3): 291–7.

Workbridge. 2010. 'Review of Special Education 2010 discussion document.' Workbridge. Available at www.workbridge.co.nz/?page=215.

Young, S. 2012. 'Reporting it right: how the government got it wrong.' *The Drum*. ABC. 15 November. www.abc.net.au/news/2012–11–15/young-reporting-it-right/4371912.

Yunkaporta, T. 2009. 'Aboriginal pedagogies at the cultural interface.' PhD thesis, James Cook University.

Zubrick, S. R., A. A. Williams and S. R. Silburn. 2000. *Indicators of social and family functioning*. Canberra: Department of Family and Community Services.

Chapter 2

Learning processes

Intended learning outcomes

Engagement with the text in this chapter will enable readers to do the following:

- articulate an understanding of what learning is in the context of school

- describe how the ATRiUM capabilities relate to the cultural, interpersonal, intrapersonal, physical and cognitive dimensions of learning

- explain some key learning theories and principles and identify how they are evident in effective teaching practice

- develop an understanding of learning as a developmental process that results in individual differences

- describe cognitive processes of learning from an information processing perspective

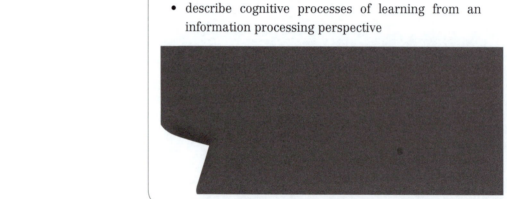

Big ideas

- Learning is a thinking process. It is developmental and cumulative. Understandings of what learning is are often culturally determined.

- Despite diverse perceptions of what constitutes knowledge and learning and the myriad factors that impact on how individuals and societies value and transmit knowledge, there are common cognitive processes that constitute the mechanisms of learning. Inclusive, effective pedagogy addresses these cognitive processes of learning.

- Teaching and learning are enhanced when teachers have evolving understandings of the cognitive processes of learning and when they develop knowledge about their students' strengths and needs in terms of these.

Introduction

Learning processes vary with each student, teacher and learning environment. Factors such as values and attitudes, prior experiences and skills and the context and content of the intended learning task determine how individual students engage in learning activities and what they learn. Also, social, emotional and cultural factors impact on student learning and the learning environment. The cultural, interpersonal, intrapersonal, physical and cognitive dimensions of human functioning work together to underpin development and learning. Consequently, learning is complex and diverse, and unique to each individual student.

While it is essential that teachers develop an awareness of the various factors that impact on learning and reflect upon them as they develop and refine programs for their students, they must also know about how students learn. Effective teachers develop and apply understandings of how thinking and learning actually take place – the cognitive processes of learning and how these play out in everyday classroom contexts. Such knowledge is particularly relevant for teachers seeking to understand how best to teach and support students who are low achieving, disengaged or have a disability, because this leads to deeper understanding of strategies and approaches for **scaffolding** and supporting learning. For example, a teacher who has informed knowledge about the processes and functions of **working memory** will be well positioned to understand why breaking a task down into smaller steps will make it much more achievable for some students, and that teacher will have insights into which students would particularly benefit from such an approach.

This chapter is about learning for all and learning that lasts. In this book we interpret the phrase 'learning for all' as an allegory of inclusion. To provide learning for all students, educational systems and individual teachers need to ensure they facilitate learning for students who are low achieving, disengaged, have a disability or are educationally

> **Scaffolding** is support given during the learning process and gradually withdrawn as it is no longer needed.

> **Working memory** is the part of memory that temporarily holds information for thinking or processing.

disadvantaged, as well as for students who are attaining expected educational standards. Fullan (2011, 2) describes this obligation as 'the moral imperative of raising the bar (for all students) and closing the gap (for lower performing groups) relative to higher order skills and competencies required to be successful world citizens'. Implicit in this stance is the necessity of ensuring that all students, to the extent of their potential, access teaching and learning that guarantee they not only attain mastery of basic academic skills but also learn how to think critically and solve problems.

Learning for all requires that teachers have high expectations for all their students and that they do not accept low achievement and competency with mundane tasks as adequate for any student who has the potential to accomplish more. Accordingly, sustainable learning is about knowledge transformation, not just knowledge transmission. It relates to the purpose and value of the learning process – it provides students with the ability to maintain, connect and use learning to enable further development, to think creatively, to innovate and to apply knowledge of problem-solving in many different contexts. To facilitate learning that lasts for students, teachers need to teach not only content but also how to apply and develop knowledge and skills. Teachers have a professional mandate to ensure they prepare students to become successful for life, not just successful in meeting minimum curriculum standards.

Learning is multifaceted; it is not a unitary concept but a diverse and nuanced topic that draws on knowledge from a wide range of disciplines. Learning can be described, among many other ways, as a behavioural process, a psychosocial concept or a function of reward and motivation. If a range of people were asked, 'What is learning?' there would be many different answers: gaining knowledge in the '3Rs', problem-solving, developing self-knowledge, knowing about human endeavours or developing moral values. Clearly, in this chapter we cannot discuss the many different facets of learning. Instead, we review selected aspects of learning processes based on what we perceive to be most relevant to the sustainable-learning metaphor and to what pre-service and beginning-career teachers need to know about learning in a contemporary school context. Underpinning this is our commitment to the ideas that inclusive education is best served, in the first instance, by effective teaching in everyday classroom contexts and that to be effective, teachers need to know about how students think and learn and how to promote ways of thinking and learning that will support them to be successful at school and throughout their lives.

Accordingly, this chapter begins with an examination of learning in relation to each capability identified by ATRiUM (introduced in chapter 1). Learning processes are then discussed in relation to traditional western psychology's learning and development theories and to established learning principles. Next, learning is considered as a developmental process and as a function of self-regulation. The remainder of the chapter focuses more specifically on learning as cognition, identifying and discussing cognitive processes of learning common to all humans. Since the early 1990s, technological advances in neuroscience and its associated fields have enabled the development of new and refined knowledge about human brain functions in relation to thinking and learning, and some of the key findings are discussed below. The information and the perspectives on learning presented in this chapter frame discussions in later chapters about teaching and assessment.

ATRiUM capabilities

In formal learning environments, different kinds of learning are required, including learning academic skills and other curriculum content, social learning, learning skills to perform or to make products, and developing a sense of inquiry by learning to question, solve problems and reflect. Understanding learning processes by viewing learning as a set of capabilities is an inclusive approach. It recognises the individuality of each learner yet acknowledges the commonalities in the learning processes of all humans.

> **ATRiUM** Active learning; Thinking; Relating to others; Using language, symbols and ICT; and Managing self.

ATRiUM is used within the notion of sustainable learning to describe a holistic perspective on the broad capabilities of all learners. It is based on the key competencies and general capabilities that are described in the Australian and the New Zealand curricula (see ACARA, n.d.; Ministry of Education 2009). The ATRiUM capabilities encompass the physical, cognitive, interpersonal, intrapersonal and cultural dimensions of learning, as represented in figure 1.3. Teachers need to be acutely aware of the interplay of these capabilities for each learner in the classroom. Although it is not possible to visibly observe what is going on inside any of the learners' heads, it is vital to focus on the learning processes that underlie all teaching and learning activities.

Active learning

Learning is a transformative process. It is not the passive receipt of knowledge. Knowledge is socially and culturally defined as well as personally constructed, so learners need to be actively engaged in the construction of their own knowledge bases. Learning begins outside learners; it exists within the sociocultural domain before it becomes individual learning that is internalised and personal. As learners transform knowledge, they also become transformed – they develop.

> **Self-regulated learning** is learning guided by metacognition, strategic action and motivation to learn.

Teachers can struggle with the concept of active learners, since passive learners are so much easier to organise and manage as a group! This tension has grown as knowledge has become increasingly fluid and dynamic and not so easily captured in a curriculum and printed texts. Ideally, active learning begins with acts of curiosity and evolves into sophisticated **self-regulated learning**. Teachers also need to be prepared to act as partners in learning and not founts of knowledge; they should continue to be active learners themselves.

Thinking

Learning uses thinking as the primary tool of transformation. Humans think and share that thinking, and that sharing can also alter thinking. Individuals have the cognitive capacity to perceive and make sense of what they experience through their senses. Capacity for thinking is developmental, with young children thinking about things quite differently from adults. Schools take developmental thinking into account through curriculum expectations and in the organisation and management of educational settings. For learning to be sustainable, thinking about everyday matters and experiences needs to be integrated with thinking about intellectual ideas and scientific concepts. When there are gaps between these focus points of thinking, there will be incoherence in learners' attempts to make meaning and to understand more abstract notions.

Cognitive processes, including perceiving, reasoning, comprehending, analysing, linking with prior knowledge, memorising and recalling, are integral to making sense of culture and developing understandings about society and the wider world. Prior knowledge, for instance, 'acts as a lens through which we view and absorb new information. It is a composite of who we are, based on what we have learnt from both our academic and our everyday experiences' (Kujawa and Huske 1995, 3). Further, humans seek input about learning from other humans in ways that influence their attention to learning and provide motivation and opportunities to learn more. Within each classroom there will always be variability in the range of student thinking capabilities. Some students will come into the classroom with ways of processing very different from typical development. Such learners can find classroom engagement and learning challenging unless teachers are able to create learning opportunities that match their learning needs.

Relating to others

Active learning depends on interpersonal engagement. Classrooms and schools are complex social systems within which learners need to relate to each other and to those charged with facilitating their learning. Establishing a classroom climate that supports appropriate social interactions and relationships is an important task for teachers. This process depends on teachers' understandings of what they bring to the classroom, what their students bring and how these perspectives match or mismatch. Students bring their world, their lived experiences and their families' and communities' values to their learning and interactions. This means they bring their cultures, which will play out through observable interpersonal interactions in relation to the classroom environment, their teachers and other students.

Using language, symbols and ICT

Social engagement and information communication are carried out through elaborate and complex systems of symbols – that is, language. Sustainable learning is dependent on facility with the key communication systems, as well as on processes that support adaptation to new forms of communication. In any educational setting, literacy and numeracy are the tools of active learning, often enabling participation, thinking, relating to others and managing the self. Language, in itself a tool, is supported by cultural nuances that may or may not resonate for learners. Language is used in many forms, from the essential face-to-face spoken language to written language and to electronic forms of language and communication.

We are increasingly dependent on ICT for engagement in learning, pursuit of careers and everyday living. The rapidly changing demands of technology are influencing both learners and languages; not only do sustainable learners need to be able to adapt as technology changes, but language is being altered by the use of technology. The most obvious language change is seen in text talk, in which words are altered in order to increase fluency, thereby cre8ing new symbol systems ☺.

Written language, encompassing both literacy and numeracy, is of course foundational to academic learning. Proficiency with written language is the focus of early learning in schools, and it is used as a tool for all subsequent learning. 'Learn to read in order to read to learn' is an adage that highlights the power of written language as a tool for literacy and learning. Literacy is embedded in all school learning as well as in activities used for demonstrating learning – that is, assessment activities; likewise, numeracy has broad applications well beyond the subject of mathematics.

Managing self

An aim of the school journey is for students to become self-managing, self-sustaining lifelong learners. As students grow and develop, they learn how to regulate their physical body, becoming more adept with self-care, ensuring their physical needs are met or managed and adjusting their physical actions and interactions with regard to their effects on other people and the environment. School, family (*whānau*) and societal expectations about managing the physical self are often quite explicitly expressed, and they generally increase with the age of the child.

Managing thinking and learning is also developmental, but expectations and attributes around this important dimension are more often implicit, with less attention given to articulating and demonstrating how and what students can do to manage their thinking. Managing thinking involves a wide range of mental processes, including organising and evaluating ideas, connecting new knowledge to past learning and experiences, sustaining attention, curbing impulses and persisting with a task or train of thought. Managing thinking is influenced by 'self factors' such as self-esteem, self-concept and self-efficacy.

Managing self also relates to interpersonal and intrapersonal functioning and can become a substitute term for 'behaviour'. Students bring to the classroom their intrapersonal development, including self-awareness, which cannot be separated from their culture or their previous school experience because these factors continue to shape them. As they develop, students become increasingly capable of self-managing their emotions and how they think about them. However, this is never a linear development pathway, and it is affected profoundly by experience and by the values expressed in families, communities and society.

Think and do 2.1: ATRiUM capabilities

1   Using ATRiUM as a framework for classroom practice, consider what each capability looks like, feels like and sounds like for learners of different ages.

2   Using ATRiUM as a framework for reflection, describe what learning looks like, feels like and sounds like for you as a learner.

Learning theories

As thinking is largely a mental process that cannot be readily observed, much investigation and theorising, particularly within the behavioural sciences and especially in the field of psychology, have been devoted to the quest to understand what learning is and how it takes place. Within the paradigm of traditional western psychology, a range of learning theories, or models, have been developed over the last century. Teachers benefit from understanding these theoretical perspectives, because such knowledge provides a framework for making informed, consistent decisions about approaches to teaching and learning. Figure 2.1 provides a brief overview of some key learning theories.

The theories involve contrasting ideas about the purpose and process of learning and education (Rice 2006), but there are also commonalities between them, and sometimes the work of one theorist contributes to several different theories. Learning theories give teachers ways of thinking about learning so that they can make more-informed, well-considered decisions about teaching practice. For example, some of the long-established principles of behaviourist learning theories are still relied on in contemporary classrooms and schools, but they are now often used within a much more inclusive framework that recognises the complexity of human learning – which the original behaviourist theories did not. Most recent theories acknowledge not only the dynamic nature of learning and development but also the ecological context of learning. When reviewing the traditional western learning theories, it is important for teachers to be aware that they carry assumptions and perspectives that may not reflect or include values from other, less dominant cultures. Accordingly, teachers will need to inquire about and consider in their practice local cultural values related to learning.

Principles of learning

Educators and psychologists working to develop knowledge about effective pedagogy have identified key principles of learning said to underpin successful teaching

Behaviourism

Key theorists include Watson, Pavlov, Skinner and Thorndike
- Learning results from a change in behaviour.
- The environment can be changed or arranged to elicit desired responses.
- Learning is competency based, requiring skill, development and training.
- Learning proceeds according to rules, with rewards and consequences.
- Direct instruction provides stimulus for learning; task analysis determines components of the content to be learned.

Instructivism

Key theorists include Bruner, Gagné, Briggs and Wagner
- Learning involves making associations with stimuli.
- The external environment is reality; students need to learn about it, and their learning can be measured and compared.
- Teachers are the agents of learning; education is about improving students' knowledge and learning.
- Learning is an active process directed by the content and the teacher.
- The scope of learning is determined by goals and objectives.
- Effective pedagogy includes explicit instruction, drill, practice, precision teaching, mastery learning and standardised assessment.

Cognitivism

Key theorists include Tolman, Piaget, Ausubel and Sweller
- Learning requires internal (cognitive) structuring using processes of perception, information processing, memory and insight.
- The learner, as an active participant, is an 'information processor', and their cognitive processes develop sequentially.
- Learners need support to develop prior knowledge and to use knowledge of patterns to develop new knowledge.
- Effective teachers focus on what learners know and how they acquire knowledge.
- The context for learning needs to be authentic to students' lived experiences, and students require structures and models to lead their learning towards standard knowledge.

Humanism

Key theorists include Rogers, Maslow and Steiner
- Learning is an individual process, based on curiosity, that enables a person to fulfil their potential.
- Learning should be student centred, with content determined by the learner and outcomes measured by self-evaluation.
- Motivation to learn is innate, fuelled by conscious aspiration for higher-order learning and self-actualisation.
- The teacher's role is as facilitator, to encourage and enable the learner as they grow and develop throughout their life.
- Discovery learning is achieved by providing access to appropriate resources without obtrusive interference.

Constructivism

Key theorists include Piaget, Vygotsky, Dewey and Bruner
- Knowledge is subjective and unique to the individual.
- Learners interact with their environment and construct new knowledge based on prior experiences.
- Meaningful learning requires inquiry, reflection and refinement. It cannot be rushed or imposed.
- Education is student centred, active and contextual, and assessment of learning is based on authentic student work.
- Teachers act as facilitators, negotiating goals for student learning and providing feedback about strategies used to solve real-world problems.

Figure 2.1: *Learning theories and perspectives on learning*

and to be present when students learn best. These principles are generic and not specifically related to one learning theory or another but instead provide information about what supports effective learning. It is important for teachers to develop awareness of these principles of learning so as to better support all students to learn more effectively. Some of the principles are listed below:

Prior knowledge: Students' prior knowledge and experiences, including their cultural contexts, can support or challenge new ideas. What students learn is influenced by their existing ideas, knowledge and lived experiences. New learning needs to be linked to prior knowledge.

Conceptual knowledge is understanding of an abstract idea, what it is and how it works.

*Organisation of **conceptual knowledge**:* How teachers present information and how students organise ideas influence learning. Development in learning typically moves from concrete (materials and senses) to abstract (application of concepts). The organisation of conceptual knowledge can be scaffolded by modelling and by using aids such as graphic organisers.

Developmental progression: A student's current development level interacts with new learning. There are situations in which readiness to learn cannot be contrived, whereas in other contexts of learning the teaching can actively lead development. Skills improve in an orderly and sequential fashion from simple to complex.

Component skills are the capabilities that must be combined and integrated to accomplish a task.

Mastery: To develop mastery, students need to acquire **component skills**, practise them singularly and then practise integrating them. Mastery is demonstrated not just when students can perform a task or skill but when they recognise the need to apply their knowledge automatically in a novel context.

Motivation and engagement: Students' motivation is a key determinant of what they will learn and how they will participate in learning experiences. Students who perceive positive value in the content and context of learning and anticipate the likelihood of success are more likely to be motivated to engage and persist with learning activities.

Feedback: Feedback about learning is essential. Effective feedback provides students with meaningful information about achievement and the effectiveness of strategies and learning behaviours. To improve performance and learning efficiency, feedback should also correct misunderstandings and provide information about how students can improve.

Think and do 2.2: Reflecting on learning

Discuss the ways in which you access, acquire, retain, make sense of and use knowledge in your learning and everyday living. What supports learning most effectively for you?

Learning as development and self-regulation

The foundations for learning begin while a child is in utero. The first few years of life are flooded with learning as the developing brain and nervous system process sensory information, begin to recognise and manage emotions and develop language and motor skills. The years prior to school are critical for learning, with much of this occurring in informal learning environments.

The ongoing development of neurological systems in the early years of life supports sensory, motor and perceptual development in domains such as gross motor skills, manipulation skills, body awareness and posture, which in turn provide the foundations for higher-level and more complex learning development. The developmental systems that need to be in place for learning academic skills and the formal curriculum include language, visual and auditory perception, memory, self-regulation and many other interrelated affective, motor, sensory and perceptual factors.

Learning is a developmental process, and the rate and profile of development, the trajectory for learning, is unique to each individual. Just as a child cannot walk before appropriate balance, motor coordination and muscle-tone are in place, students need to have developed underlying systems and skills in order to access academic learning and the formal curriculum. An individual's readiness to learn is mediated by a range of internal and external factors. Internal factors include heritable traits such as intelligence, physical characteristics and personality. External factors are related to the environment in which a child is immersed and include family (*whānau*) and community, culture and education. A complex interaction between internal and external factors determines each individual student's developmental profile. The relative impact of these factors, commonly referred to as 'nature versus nurture', is the subject of much research and debate in psychology and other related fields.

Importantly, readiness to learn cannot be standardised and, in an individual context, should not be expected based on criteria like age or grade. A young student who can read some words but has relatively underdeveloped conceptual knowledge and vocabulary may struggle even to see the need to extract meaning from text and will thus not yet be able to do a simple comprehension task such as retell a story. In contrast, classmates of the same age may have relatively well developed language, sequencing and memory skills, leading to comprehension of the text to a high level, yet if they experience slower development in the domain of auditory perception, this will lead to less facility in reading words. Throughout the years of formal education, each individual's developmental profile is different, and each student requires tailored support and experiences in order to progress.

This notion has wide-ranging implications for learning. Many learners progress through developmental stages in sequence, yet many others do not follow a typical trajectory. The acquisition of a new skill or concept depends on whether prerequisite competencies are in place. Development in learning improves with maturation and experience. It can be supported by experiences that consolidate existing knowledge or skills and by exposure to the kinds of novel stimuli and targeted feedback that lead to new applications or understandings. Clearly, the learning environment, including learning experiences and instructional input provided by teachers (and peers), has a significant role to play in determining growth and development in learning.

Another key condition of development in learning is self-regulation. Broadly defined, self-regulation is our awareness of the ways in which we think and learn and the gradual development of internalised systems that assist us to manage our cognitive processes. The development of self-regulated learning is a major schooling goal. As will be explored later in this text, facilitating self-regulation does not consist simply of teaching students a series of cognitive strategies; affective and metacognitive learning dimensions must also be considered. The main functions which combine to result in self-regulated learning are **metacognition**, motivation and self-efficacy (Graham and Berman 2012):

> **Metacognition** is the ability to 'step back' from thinking and become aware of one's own processes of thinking.

Metacognition is the awareness of one's own thinking processes, including knowledge about how to best perform a task or develop understanding of a concept. It frequently involves activating prior knowledge, setting goals and implementing selected strategies. Metacognition can be thought of as 'thinking about thinking about the task'. It has two components: thinking about thinking, and regulating this thinking and, with it, learning behaviours.

Motivation is the desire to learn and to achieve; it can be extrinsic, based on rewards, or, more sustainably, intrinsic, based on enjoyment, interest and self-satisfaction. Importantly, motivation can increase based on a student's perceived likelihood of success and can decrease in the face of failure and poor achievement.

Self-efficacy is the range of self-beliefs students hold about their capacity and effective participation as learners. A key determinant of self-efficacy is the learner's perception of control over learning and achievement, referred to as **attributions** for success or failure. Attribution theory posits that learners can, rightly or wrongly, attribute their success or otherwise to ability, effort, task difficulty or luck, with the veracity of their attributions connected to their motivation, participation level and achievement in learning (Weiner 1972).

> **Attribution** is the process of inferring the causes of events or behaviours.

Learning processes are unique to individuals, shaped by their genetics, culture and experiences in formal and informal learning environments. Students learn at a level determined by their maturational readiness, prior knowledge and experiences. Teachers can support the developmental processes underlying learning by knowing the usual sequences and providing an environment for learning that 'meets learners where they are at', facilitates the growth of student thinking and provides direction for learning activities towards new knowledge, skills and understandings. Teachers also need to be aware of the 'self' factors that impact on learning and participation and to take steps to empower students to manage themselves and their learning behaviours to attain positive outcomes that they, their families and their communities will value.

Cognitive processes of learning

Teachers with knowledge about cognitive processes of learning better understand the learning needs of their students and make more-informed instructional decisions, including effective differentiation and provision of appropriate adjustments, to maximise the engagement, motivation and achievement of all their students. Such knowledge is of particular importance in contemporary educational contexts; a vast amount of information about learning is available, and teachers need to draw on a solid knowledge base in order to discern reliable and evidence-based information from that which is skewed or misrepresented to promote a particular agenda or commercial product.

Information processing

The information processing model has been developed, since its inception in the 1960s, to explain the cognitive processes of learning. It focuses on the structure and function of mental processing within specific contexts, environments or ecologies (Huitt 1997). The model often uses the 'mind as a computer' metaphor to aid descriptions of cognitive development and learning.

The information processing model of cognition identifies stages, or component parts, within complex thought processes. Swanson (1987) described three general components of the model as structural, within which information can be processed at a particular stage; strategic, which controls the operations at various stages; and executive, by which learners' cognitive activities are overseen and monitored (Swanson and Stomel 2012). The information processing model recognises that the flow of information inherent to these components occurs in a sequence of stages, and information is transformed in each stage. The output information from one stage or subsequent stages informs the input into the next stage.

Limited central capacity theory

An important premise for understanding the information processing model is the idea that cognitive resources are limited. Kahneman's (1973) limited central capacity theory implies that there are constraints on how much information humans can think about at one time, for how long they can hold information and how quickly they can process information. When a system operates with limited resources, the distribution and efficient use of those resources are key performance determinants. When considering effective learning, the focus is very much on the efficient use of resources in cognitive processing rather than on the amount of cognitive resources used.

Memory

In seeking to describe what happens when learners encounter new information, the information processing model commonly refers to memory. If learning is to be sustained, memory is required to retain information 'in mind' for future use, to recall information previously experienced, to recognise previously encountered stimuli and to draw together retained information. Memory is not a unitary cognitive process; rather, it is the result of complex cognitive operations and is impacted upon by the experiences of the individual within the context of family (*whānau*), community and culture.

The stage, or multi-store, memory theory (Atkinson and Shiffrin 1968) defines three stages of information storage. These are sensory memory, short-term memory and long-term memory. Information processing begins with sensory perception (for example, sound, sight and smell), which may be influenced by prior knowledge or expectations. The sensory impulses are registered in sensory, or immediate, memory. When attention resources are devoted to sensory perceptions, memory codes are created in short-term memory, which holds about seven pieces of unrehearsed information for about 20 to 30 seconds (Miller 1956). Information then needs to be rehearsed or acted upon to pass into long-term memory; otherwise it is lost. Attention has a significant role in the selection of perceptions that will enter memory stores. Information is stored in long-term memory in a range of forms – for example, as visual, semantic or verbal data – and can be held there for a lengthy period of time but is subject to distortion and decay (Payne and Blackwell 1998). Long-term memory has been classified into different types of memories, most commonly declarative (knowledge of concepts, meaning and events) and procedural ('how to' knowledge).

Although the multi-store theory has been criticised as being too simplistic, particularly in relation to short-term memory, it remains an informative and useful framework for developing understanding about the different stages of memory. Baddeley and colleagues (for example, Baddeley 1996; Baddeley and Hitch 1974; Baddeley and Logie 1999) proposed a more complex construct called 'working memory', which has become increasingly influential. Some cognitive psychologists consider working memory to be a reconceptualised version of short-term memory, while others view it as a separate model. Still others think short-term memory is an activated portion of long-term memory (Cantor and Engle 1993). The debate about whether there are actually separate memory stores is yet to be resolved (Weiten 2004).

Working memory

Working memory is modelled as a temporary, simultaneous storage mechanism for incoming information required in the performance of a complex task (Baddeley 1992; Swanson and Keogh 1990). Simply stated, working memory is memory at work, using and making sense of incoming information. Everyday activities that involve working memory include holding an address in mind while listening to directions about how to get there or remembering an item's price while calculating the correct amount of change due (Swanson 2009).

An essential characteristic of working memory is that it functions by simultaneously storing and processing information (Ashbaker and Swanson 1996). In this way, it acts as a mental workspace where information can be held 'in mind' while performing another relevant task. Working memory is limited to a 10- to 20-second duration and to a capacity of between seven and nine units of information (Hulme and McKenzie 1992). This means that only a defined amount of information can be held temporarily in working memory before it must be attended to, through rehearsal or connection to prior knowledge, or else it is lost and not transferred to long-term memory.

Baddeley and Hitch's (1974) model presented working memory as consisting of a central executive with two subsystems, the phonological loop and the visuo-spatial sketchpad. Later, the model was modified to include a third subsystem, the episodic buffer (Baddeley 2000). Each subsystem is responsible for different cognitive activities (Baddeley and Logie 1999; Swanson and Sachse-Lee 2001). The phonological loop and visuo-spatial sketchpad process and maintain either verbal or visual information, while the episodic buffer integrates information from a range of sources into a single episode which is time sequenced.

The central executive, which has a limited capacity, is regarded as the most important component of working memory with regard to its general effect on cognition (Baddeley 1996). Its function is to coordinate the manipulation and flow of information between parts of the cognitive system, including the subsystems and long-term memory. It is essentially responsible for attention and the control of behaviour. Executive functions include selecting what stimulus or task to attend to, switching attention, ignoring distractions, sequencing activities and evaluating performance.

Working memory improves throughout childhood, adolescence and early adulthood and then declines in older adults (Wilson and Swanson 2001). Many classroom activities require students to use working-memory processes to perform learning tasks or solve problems that have demands more complex than simply recalling knowledge. Working memory requires attention control and mental effort. Its capacity varies between people, with each individual having a relatively fixed capacity (Gathercole and Alloway 2007). However, it is not so much the working memory's capacity that affects learning but the use and coordination of resources between working memory components, short-term memory and long-term memory.

Think and do 2.3: Working memory

Work with a partner. Say aloud a sequence of randomly selected numbers and ask your partner to repeat the numbers aloud in reverse order. Start with two numbers (for example, 17 and 56, repeated as 56 and 17), then increase to numbers you say aloud by one at a time. How many numbers in sequence can your partner correctly say in reverse order? Swap roles so that your partner gives you a sequence to repeat.

Levels and types of thinking

The ways in which the brain processes information differ according to each learner's developmental profile, the purpose of the task and the kind of information encountered. Reproducing a rhyme or a formula may be a simple recall task for an experienced learner or a difficult problem to be solved for a novice. Reading a text to acquire information requires different thinking processes from those used to analyse a data set. Studies of the cognitive processes of learning have resulted in models that describe thinking processes, and categorisations that help to order and relate the various cognition processes. These frameworks are the focus of this section.

Controlled and automatic processing

An influential and informative model developed by Shiffrin and Schneider (1977; see also Schneider and Shiffrin 1977) argues that information processing can be divided into two fundamental modes, controlled and automatic, each entailing different kinds of processing. Controlled processing, as the name implies, is exercised by the individual. It is relatively slow, requires active attention and is serial, permitting only one sequence to be performed at a time. In contrast, automatic processing is fast; and as it is triggered by appropriate inputs, it does not require active attention (although it can temporarily utilise cognitive capacity). Automatic processing is parallel in nature, with potential to process a series of stimuli simultaneously, and it is generally impervious to other inputs.

All learning begins as the by-product of controlled processes, with some of these becoming automatic. For example, learning to move in different ways initially involves mental and physical effort for a toddler who will later automatically run at speed as required for a game. Similarly, recognising marks on a page or screen will be a problem-solving activity for a preschool student who will later automatically read and comprehend complex text, never again needing to think about what letters the marks make. Importantly, automatic processing 'uses up' very little of our limited cognitive capacity, while controlled processing often requires all available cognitive resources to engage in the task at hand.

Controlled processing involves thinking and reasoning in an intentional manner and is inherently attention demanding – it is thinking that takes effort. Processes commonly considered as higher-order thinking, including comprehension, analysis, application and evaluation of newly encountered knowledge or experiences, require controlled processing and do not become automatic with practice. Self-regulation activities related to executive functioning, such as switching attention and resisting distractions to maintain focus, delaying gratification and applying persistence, are also controlled processes. So too are metacognitive thinking skills such as setting goals, making plans and selecting effective strategies. Controlled processing takes time. As it is performed it consumes almost all available cognitive resources, with the consequence that we cannot perform more than one higher-order task at a time.

Automatic processes are characteristically mandatory, or unstoppable, with **automaticity** related to increased accuracy. It should not reduce the capacity for doing another simultaneous task (Shiffrin and Dumais 1981). Thus, automaticity enables us to do several things at once. Despite the apparently instantaneous and effort-free process of automaticity, it actually requires a complex, fast and efficient interaction of cognitive processes (Perfetti 1985; Samuels 1987). Automaticity develops after learning, repetition and effective practice.

In reality, performing almost any task requires both automatic and controlled processing, although components of word identification during reading can be considered a purely automatic process, as can effortlessly recalling basic mathematics facts. Anderson (1990) proposes that it may be more correct to think of automaticity as a matter of degree rather than a well-defined category.

> **Automaticity,** usually the result of learning, repetition and practice, is the ability to respond automatically without occupying the mind with low-level details.

Think and do 2.4: Control and automaticity

Think about the different tasks and activities you did yesterday. Identify five tasks or activities that required controlled processing and 10 or more tasks or activities that you performed automatically. Would some of the automatic tasks you identified be controlled tasks for a younger person or child? Do you foresee that eventually you will become automatic in any of the controlled tasks?

Bloom's revised taxonomy

An approach to distinguishing types of thinking is to describe and categorise the cognitive processes required to participate in learning. A widely referenced framework for this approach is **Bloom's taxonomy**, which describes the cognitive learning behaviours in a hierarchical sequence: knowledge, comprehension, application, analysis, synthesis and evaluation (Bloom 1956). The taxonomy was revised in 2001, with reordering of the two highest categories and revision of the words used to describe the categories, with all categories now expressed as verbs: remembering, understanding, applying, analysing, evaluating and creating (Anderson and Krathwohl 2001). Despite the popularity of this framework and its widespread use in teacher education courses, limitations have been identified, including the simplicity of categorising thinking in a hierarchical manner when cognition is known to be a complex process involving variable and interactive progressions, and the fact that the taxonomy has not been subject to research or evaluation (Hattie 2011).

> **Bloom's taxonomy** is a framework for categorising educational goals. It was revised in 2001 to become a taxonomy for teaching, learning and assessment.

The Structure of the Observed Learning Outcome taxonomy

Another taxonomy of learning, the **Structure of the Observed Learning Outcome (SOLO) taxonomy**, focuses on the quality of a student's learning and how learning grows in complexity as the student engages in a task or series of tasks (Biggs and Collis 1982). The SOLO taxonomy suggests that learning proceeds through five stages:

The **Structure of the Observed Learning Outcome (SOLO) taxonomy** describes students' learning development using levels of increasing complexity through five stages.

Pre-structural: The student doesn't understand the task and attempts to use strategies that are ineffective.

Uni-structural: One aspect of the task is attended to in a relatively naive and isolated manner.

Multi-structural: Several aspects of the task are attended to but with no connections between them.

Relational: The learner connects together several aspects of the task in an integrated whole.

Summative assessment is the assessment *of* learning usually performed at the end of a teaching period.

Extended abstract: The previous integrated whole is conceptualised at a higher level, and this knowledge is generalised to contexts beyond the task.

The SOLO taxonomy is potentially more useful for teachers than Bloom's taxonomy, because it goes beyond simply categorising knowledge and focuses on student learning. It can also be used as a diagnostic assessment tool, providing feedback to teachers and learners about students' understandings and the effectiveness of instruction. The SOLO taxonomy may be utilised as a **summative assessment** tool for comparing understandings of complex concepts and as a planning tool for teachers in determining objectives and success criteria. (SOLO is further discussed in chapter 4.)

Cognitive processes of learning in the classroom

While teachers and schools are often prolific in their descriptions of appropriate behaviours and the learning outcomes that students are required to demonstrate for successful participation in school life, much less attention has been devoted to describing how students can think and learn at school or to instilling such cognitive behaviours in students for lifelong learning. Costa and Kallick (2000) developed a curriculum called 'Habits of mind', which represents – in language accessible to students – ways to think about how people learn. Explicitly teaching students about how to think and what to do when they are 'stuck' can provide them with skills and strategies, and tools to use for problem-solving that they can intentionally select and use in academic and real-life learning contexts. Many of the habits of mind relate to the cognitive processes of learning already mentioned. The 16 habits of mind are listed below:

- Persisting
- Thinking and communicating with clarity and precision
- Managing impulsivity
- Gathering data through all senses
- Listening with understanding and empathy
- Creating, imagining, innovating
- Thinking flexibly
- Responding with wonderment and awe
- Thinking about thinking (metacognition)
- Taking responsible risks
- Striving for accuracy
- Finding humor
- Questioning and posing problems
- Thinking interdependently
- Applying past knowledge to new situations
- Remaining open to continuous learning (Costa and Kallick 2000)

Cognitive neuroscience

While information from psychology and its associated fields has provided foundational insights into learning processes, more recent advances in technology and cross-disciplinary collaboration are set to significantly advance knowledge about how humans learn and how teachers can more effectively support and facilitate learning. Since the 1990s, **cognitive neuroscience** has emerged as a field of inquiry with great potential to further develop knowledge about learning processes, shape technologically sophisticated research agendas and inform practice in education. Hence, findings from cognitive neuroscience are very relevant for teachers, adding to and sometimes questioning established knowledge in the field of education. Despite some considered scepticism and criticism of the links that can validly be made between neuroscience and classroom practice (Bruer 1997), there are indications that neuroscience may deliver findings relevant to how students learn and how teachers teach (OECD 2007; PMSEIC 2009).

> **Cognitive neuroscience** explores the interactions between biological processes and mental phenomena, with a particular focus on learning.

The relatively recent convergence of neuroscience, psychology and education into a cohesive field of inquiry has been largely enabled by the development of non-invasive brain scanning and functional neuroimaging technologies capable of identifying which parts of the brain are implicated during which types of cognitive tasks (Müller 2011). A common element in descriptions of cognitive neuroscience is that research in this field requires collaboration between scientists from different disciplines, including neuroscience, psychology and education, and other associated fields, such as biology, physiology, behavioural science and computational modelling (OECD 2007). Further, descriptions positioning cognitive neuroscience in education imply that the aim is to gain improved understanding of how learning takes place using a more 'scientific' approach, with a view to examining how such information can underpin more effective teaching methods, curricula and educational policy (Cadle 2013), and can ultimately contribute to a more skilled workforce.

Examples of work in cognitive neuroscience relevant to education include its growing understanding of the neural bases of reading, writing and arithmetic, along with knowledge about how to optimise learning in these domains (Goswami 2006). Further, the exploration and increasing understanding of developmental disorders such as dyslexia, dyscalculia, attention deficit hyperactivity disorder (ADHD) and autism are providing insights into possible causes and effective educational responses (Price, Mazzocco and Ansari 2013; Howard-Jones 2007; Baron-Cohen, Golan and Ashwin 2012). Other factors relevant to learning and educational practice, such as the importance of sleep, motivation, memory and self-regulation, are also being investigated by cognitive neuroscientists. Such applications are likely to provide further impetus for evidence-based approaches to education (Geake 2009) and to offer new knowledge, as well as important confirmation or questioning of existing knowledge, about learning and teaching processes.

There is a need for caution in assessing claims about learning and teaching and in applying findings from cognitive neuroscience directly to educational practice. Coltheart (2013, 9) has warned against the 'hijacking' of cognitive neuroscience by some advocates of brain-based approaches to education. These approaches, which advocate, for example, coloured overlays, learning styles, educational kinaesthetics, neurolinguistic programming and multiple intelligences, commonly involve a profit-seeking marketing component. Some brain-based ideas seem to have an inherent appeal to educators despite the fact that they lack an evidence base from either neuroscience or educational research (Dekker et al. 2012; Geake 2008). The unsubstantiated yet widespread influence of such educational approaches forms the basis for the argument that educators need to develop greater knowledge about secure ways to interact with research findings emerging from cognitive neuroscience. Otherwise, the profession is vulnerable to 'the allure of everything neuro' (Anderson and Della Sala 2012, 6), at the cost of implementing effective, evidence-based instructional approaches to enhance learning in the key educational domains of literacy and numeracy. However, reliable neuroscientific information is becoming increasingly available in accessible formats for educators (see, for example, Geake 2009; Howard-Jones 2007; Howard-Jones et al. 2010; OECD 2007).

Neuroplasticity is change that occurs in neural pathways and synapses due to changes in behaviour, environment and neural processes, as well as changes resulting from injury.

Useful information for teachers from recent findings in cognitive neuroscience includes the notion of **neuroplasticity** (also referred to as synaptic plasticity or neural plasticity). Until relatively recently it was thought that cognitive functions were determined by processes in a particular location in the brain, that critical periods for brain development and function occurred mainly in childhood and that damage in such specific locations would be permanent. A corollary assumption was that students' intelligence and potential to learn were capped by an immutable intelligence quotient level determined by genetics. However, findings in the field of neuroscience have led to new knowledge that the brain has the capacity to change by creating and strengthening some neuronal connections and weakening or eliminating others in response to environmental demands. New learning occurs at a neuronal level as complex neural networks are created through connections that form between neurons. This process of neuroplasticity is available throughout each person's life. Neuroplasticity underpins the brain's capability to acquire, store and retrieve information (PMSEIC 2009).

Other information discovered through research into neuroplasticity is that although there are sensitive periods when specific types of learning are most effective, learning is a lifelong activity, and the more it continues, the more effective it is – 'use it or lose it'. The repetition and interconnectedness of background knowledge have key roles in supporting the long-term development of new knowledge, as described by another neuroscience aphorism: 'neurons that fire together, wire together' (Hebb 1949).

The discovery of mirror neurons is perhaps one of the most significant recent findings in neuroscience (Geake 2009), with great potential to create further nuances in our understanding of how learning occurs through imitation and interpretation of the actions and intentions of other people. Mirror neurons are brain cells that respond similarly when a person performs an action or when the person witnesses someone else performing the action (Winerman 2005). It is thought that a variation in this system may underlie autism spectrum disorders (ASD) and, importantly, may be a central mechanism that facilitates information transfer in educational and non-educational settings (PMSEIC 2009). Further research from cognitive neuroscience about mirror neuron systems may enhance understandings of how learning occurs through imaginative play and social imitation. It may also illuminate the role of demonstration and explicit instruction in skill acquisition.

Opportunities for cognitive neuroscience findings to impact on educational practice are just beginning to emerge. The advent of new understandings about learning and teaching is an exciting prospect for educational practitioners seeking to provide relevant contemporary educational experiences for young people. Fresh scientific understanding of the complex interactions between social, cognitive and neural processes that can facilitate learning needs to be considered alongside other established educational perspectives in order to develop **evidence-based practices** that improve educational outcomes (Howard-Jones 2011; Oliver 2011). Importantly, findings from cognitive neuroscience have the potential to enrich rather than diminish curricula, as research supports the view that creative arts such as music, drama and visual arts can act as meaningful contexts for problem-solving, motivation and collaboration and can improve listening and concentration (Carew and Magsamen 2010).

> **Evidence-based practices** are used because they 'work'; their selection is informed by research, professional experience and individual examples of effectiveness.

Neuroscientific research into the cognitive reorganisation that takes place in adolescence (see Blakemore and Choudhury 2006), a key phase in an individual's educational career, may also influence the design of curricula and learning environments for young people, with approaches tailored to meet adolescents' social and emotional needs more specifically. Educational practices need to be informed by perspectives on teenage behaviour and to address motivation and engagement issues so that greater proportions of young people participate in secondary and tertiary education during this important period of cognitive development.

In its role as a more scientific approach to understanding learning mechanisms, cognitive neuroscience is set to make a significant contribution to future teaching and learning. Multiple bridges need to be built, however, connecting the science to educational practices (Ansari and Coch 2006). To begin breaking ground for such bridges from an educational perspective, teacher professional learning about the brain, the cognitive processes of learning and basic facts from neuroscience need to be available at pre-service, in-service and postgraduate levels. The education community can perhaps look forward to the time when educators work in partnership with cognitive neuroscientists in directing joint scientific investigations into essential questions, leading to more effective teaching and improved educational experiences for all students.

Summary

To truly understand the physiological complexity of cognitive processing, of thinking itself, is beyond many of us. However, it is possible to understand the range and nature of the capabilities that facilitate classroom learning. The ATRiUM capabilities described in this chapter provide a concise and memorable approach for thinking about students' learning functions and making sense of what is going on for each learner in the classroom. Using frameworks that support the development of higher-order thinking, both to direct teaching and to assess learning quality, is a sign of a clever practitioner. (Further strategies for using these tools are discussed in chapter 6.)

Research into the process of how learning takes place is ongoing. This development of knowledge about learning is currently fuelled by the explosion in technology that has allowed monitoring of brain function as the brain is in use, and this has led to many theories that represent different ways of understanding learning. With such a rich base of understanding at their disposal, teachers must develop robust conceptualisation of what happens for students as they learn, so that instruction can support optimal levels of student engagement and learning. Teachers, as learners themselves, can draw from traditional ways of understanding, as well as from more recent theories and relevant cultural perspectives, in order to make sense of learning and teaching. Well-grounded teacher conceptualisations about learning processes can increase the likelihood of successful learning for all students.

Further reading

Australian Curriculum, Assessment and Reporting Authority. n.d. 'General capabilities in the Australian Curriculum'. ACARA. www.australiancurriculum.edu.au/GeneralCapabilities/Over view/general-capabilities-in-the-australian-curriculum.

Australian Science of Learning Research Centre website: http://slrc.org.au/.

Centre for Educational Neuroscience website: www.educationalneuroscience.org.uk/.

Cunningham, T., J. Gannon, M. Kavanagh, J. Greene, L. Reddy and L. Whitson. 2007. 'Theories of learning and curriculum design: key positionalities and their relationships'. Level 3. http://level3.dit.ie/html/issue5/tony_cunningham/cunningham.pdf.

Educator Network website: http://theeducatornetwork.ning.com/.

Gathercole, S. E. and T. P. Alloway. 2007. 'Understanding working memory: a classroom guide'. University of York. www.york.ac.uk/res/wml/Classroom%20guide.pdf.

The Institute for Habits of Mind website: www.habitsofmindinstitute.org.

Minister for Education. 2008. 'Official version of Te aho matua o ngā kura kaupapa Māori and an explanation in English: pursuant to Section 155A of the Education Act 1989'. Supplement to *New Zealand Gazette*, no. 32. 22 February. http://nzccs.wikispaces.com/file/view/Supplement_TeAho32Feb08.pdf.

Ministry of Education. 2009. 'What are key competencies?' New Zealand Government. http://keycompetencies.tki.org.nz/What-are-key-competencies.

Westwell, M. n.d. 'Creating capacity (to escape from the moment).' Australian Youth Mentoring Network. www.youthmentoring.org.au/assets/pages/westwell_webinar%20slides.pdf.

'What are habits of mind?' 2007. Green River Regional Educational Cooperative. www.grrec.ky.gov/Thoughtfuled_files/Cadre2/Habits_of_Mind1.pdf.

References

ACARA (Australian Curriculum, Assessment and Reporting Authority). n.d. 'General capabilities in the Australian Curriculum'. ACARA. www.australiancurriculum.edu.au/General Capabilities/Overview/general-capabilities-in-the-australian-curriculum.

Anderson, J. R. 1990. *Cognitive psychology and its implications*. New York: Freeman.

Anderson, L. W. and D. R. Krathwohl, eds. 2001. *A taxonomy for learning, teaching, and assessing: a revision of Bloom's taxonomy of educational objectives*, complete edn. With P. W. Airasian, K. A. Cruikshank, R. E. Mayer, P. R. Pintrich, J. Raths and M. C. Wittrock. New York: Longman.

Anderson, M. and S. Della Sala. 2012. 'Neuroscience in education: an (opinionated) introduction.' In S. Della Sala and M. Anderson, eds. *Neuroscience in education: the good, the bad and the ugly*, 4–12. Oxford: Oxford University Press.

Ansari, D. and D. Coch. 2006. 'Bridges over troubled waters: education and cognitive neuroscience.' *Trends in Cognitive Sciences* 10 (4): 146–51.

Ashbaker, M. H. and H. L. Swanson. 1996. 'Short-term memory and working memory operations and their contribution to reading in adolescents with and without learning disabilities.' *Learning Disabilities Research and Practice* 11 (4): 206–13.

Atkinson, R. C. and R. M. Shiffrin. 1968. 'Human memory: a proposed system and its control processes.' In K. W. Spence and J. T. Spence. *The psychology of learning and motivation*, vol. 2, 89–195. New York: Academic Press.

Baddeley, A. D. 1992. 'Working memory.' *Science* 255 (5044): 556–9.

——. 1996. 'The fractionation of working memory.' *Proceedings of the National Academy of Sciences* 93 (24): 13468–72.

——. 2000. 'The episodic buffer: a new component of working memory?' *Trends in Cognitive Sciences* 4 (11): 417–23.

Baddeley, A. D. and G. J. Hitch. 1974. 'Working memory.' In G. H. Bower, ed. *The psychology of learning and motivation*, vol. 8: 47–89. New York: Academic Press.

Baddeley, A. D. and R. H. Logie. 1999. 'Working memory: the multiple-component model.' In A. Miyake and P. Shah. *Models of working memory: mechanisms of active maintenance and executive control*, 28–61. New York: Cambridge University Press.

Baron-Cohen, S., O. Golan and E. Ashwin. 2012. 'Educational cognitive neuroscience: designing autism-friendly methods to teach emotion recognition.' In S. Della Sala and M. Anderson, eds. *Neuroscience in education: the good, the bad and the ugly*, 299–311. Oxford: Oxford University Press.

Biggs, J. B. and K. F. Collis. 1982. *Evaluating the quality of learning*. New York: Academic Press.

Blakemore, S. J. and S. Choudhury. 2006. 'Development of the adolescent brain: implications for executive function and social cognition.' *Journal of Child Psychology and Psychiatry* 47 (3–4): 296–312.

Bloom, B. S. 1956. *Taxonomy of educational objectives, handbook I: the cognitive domain*. New York: David McKay.

Bruer, J. 1997. 'Education and the brain: a bridge too far.' *Educational Researcher* 26 (8): 4–16.

Cadle, C. R. 2013. 'Effects of using a neuroeducational intervention to enhance perseverance for online EDD and EDS students.' EdD thesis, Liberty University.

Cantor, J. and R. W. Engle. 1993. 'Working-memory capacity as long-term memory activation: an individual-differences approach.' *Journal of Experimental Psychology: Learning, Memory, and Cognition* 19 (5): 1101.

Carew, T. and S. Magsamen. 2010. 'Neuroscience and education: an ideal partnership for producing evidence-based solutions to guide 21st century learning.' *Neuron* 67 (September): 685–8.

Coltheart, M. 2013. 'Weird neuroscience: how education hijacked brain research.' *Learning Difficulties Australia Bulletin* 45 (1): 9.

Costa, A. and B. Kallick, eds. 2000. *Habits of mind: a developmental series*. Alexandria, VA: Association for Supervision and Curriculum Development.

Dekker, S., N. Lee, P. Howard-Jones and J. Jolles. 2012. 'Neuromyths in education: prevalence and predictors of misconceptions among teachers.' *Frontiers in Psychology* 3 (October): 1–8.

Fullan, M. 2011. 'Learning is the work.' Michael Fullan. www.michaelfullan.ca/media/13396087260.pdf.

Gathercole, S. E. and T. P. Alloway. 2007. 'Understanding working memory: a classroom guide.' University of York. www.york.ac.uk/res/wml/Classroom%20guide.pdf.

Geake, J. 2008. 'Neuromythologies in education.' *Educational Research* 50 (2): 123–33.

——. 2009. *The brain at school: educational neuroscience in the classroom*. Maidenhead: McGraw-Hill International.

Goswami, U. 2006. 'Neuroscience and education: from research to practice?' *Nature Reviews Neuroscience* 7 (5): 406–13.

Graham, L. and J. Berman. 2012. 'Self-regulation and learning disabilities.' *Special Education Perspectives* 21 (2): 41–52.

Hattie, J. 2011. 'National education standards for New Zealand: a research agenda.' In M. Hodis and S. Kaiser, *Proceedings of the Symposium on Assessment and Learner Outcomes*, 285–96. Wellington: Victoria University.

Hebb, D. O. 1949. *The organization of behavior*. New York: Wiley.

Howard-Jones, P. 2007. 'Neuroscience and education: issues and opportunities; a commentary by the Teacher and Learning Research Programme.' Teacher and Learning Research Programme. www.tlrp.org/pub/documents/Neuroscience%20Commentary%20FINAL.pdf.

——. 2011. 'From brain scan to lesson plan.' *The Psychologist* 24 (2): 110–13.

Howard-Jones, P., M. Ott, T. Van Leeuwen and B. De Smedt. 2010. 'Neuroscience and technology enhanced learning.' Futurelab. www.futurelab.org.uk/sites/default/files/NTEL_online_AW.pdf.

Huitt, W. 1997. 'The SCANS report revisited.' Paper presented at the Fifth Annual Gulf South Business and Vocational Education Conference. Valdosta, GA. 18 April. Text available at Educational Psychology Interactive. www.edpsycinteractive.org/papers/scanspap.html.

Hulme, C. and S. McKenzie. 1992. *Working memory and severe learning difficulties*. Hove: Lawrence Erlbaum.

Kahneman, D. 1973. *Attention and effort*. Englewood Cliffs, NJ: Prentice Hall.

Kujawa, S. and L. Huske. 1995. *The strategic teaching and reading project guide book*. Oak Brook, IL: North Central Regional Educational Laboratory.

Miller, G. A. 1956. 'The magical number seven, plus or minus two: some limits on our capacity for processing information.' *Psychological Review* 63 (2): 81.

Ministry of Education. 2009. 'What are key competencies?' New Zealand Government. http://keycompetencies.tki.org.nz/What-are-key-competencies.

Müller, E. 2011. 'Neuroscience and special education.' inForum. July. www.nasdse.org/LinkClick.aspx?fileticket=MIeZ4KBTInU%3d&tabid=36.

OECD (Organisation for Economic Co-operation and Development). 2007. 'Understanding the brain: the birth of a learning science; new insights on learning through cognitive and brain science.' OECD. www.oecd.org/site/educeri21st/40554190.pdf.

Oliver, M. 2011. 'Towards an understanding of neuroscience for science educators.' *Studies in Science Education* 47 (2): 211–35.

Payne, D. G. and J. M. Blackwell. 1998. 'Truth in memory: caveat emptor.' In S. J. Lynn and K. M. McConkey, eds. *Truth in memory*, 32–61. New York: Guilford.

Perfetti, C. A. 1985. *Reading ability*. Oxford: Oxford University Press.

PMSEIC (Prime Minister's Science, Engineering and Innovation Council). 2009. 'Transforming learning and the transmission of knowledge: preparing a learning society for the future.' Australian Government. www.chiefscientist.gov.au/wp-content/uploads/Transforming-Learning-EWG-report-FINAL.pdf.

Price, G. R., M. M. Mazzocco and D. Ansari. 2013. 'Why mental arithmetic counts: brain activation during single digit arithmetic predicts high school math scores.' *The Journal of Neuroscience* 33 (1): 156–63.

Rice, R. 2006. 'The theory and practice of mentoring in initial teacher training: is there a dichotomy in the role of learning theories?' Paper presented at the British Educational Research Association Annual Conference. Warwick. 6–9 September.

Samuels, R. J. 1987. 'Information processing abilities and reading.' *Journal of Learning Disabilities* 20 (1): 18–22.

Schneider, W. and R. M. Shiffrin. 1977. 'Controlled and automatic human information processing: I. Detection, search and attention.' *Psychological Review* 84 (1): 1–66.

Shiffrin, R. and S. Dumais. 1981. 'The development of automatism.' In J. R. Anderson, ed. *Cognitive skills and their acquisition*, 111–40. Hillsdale, NJ: Lawrence Erlbaum.

Shiffrin, R. M. and W. Schneider. 1977. 'Controlled and automatic human information processing: II. Perceptual learning, automatic attending and a general theory.' *Psychological Review* 84 (2): 127.

Swanson, H. L. 1987. 'Information processing theory and learning disabilities: an overview.' *Journal of Learning Disabilities* 20 (1): 3–7.

——. 2009. 'Working memory, short-term memory, and reading disabilities: a selective meta-analysis of the literature.' *Journal of Learning Disabilities* 42 (3): 260–87.

Swanson, H. L. and B. K. Keogh, eds. 1990. *Learning disabilities: theoretical and research issues*. Malwah, NJ: Lawrence Erlbaum.

Swanson, H. L. and C. Sachse-Lee. 2001. 'Mathematical problem solving and working memory in children with learning disabilities: both executive and phonological processes are important.' *Journal of Experimental Child Psychology* 79 (3): 294–321.

Swanson, H. L. and D. Stomel. 2012. 'Learning disabilities and memory.' In B. Y. L. Wong, ed. *Learning about learning disabilities*, 4th edn., 27–58. San Diego, CA: Academic Press.

Weiner, B. 1972. *Theories of motivation: from mechanism to cognition*. Chicago: Markham.

Weiten, W. 2004. *Psychology: themes and variations*, 7th edn. Belmont, CA: Wadsworth.

Wilson, K. M. and H. L. Swanson. 2001. 'Are mathematics disabilities due to a domain-general or a domain-specific working memory deficit?' *Journal of Learning Disabilities* 34 (3): 237–48.

Winerman, L. 2005. 'The mind's mirror.' *Monitor on Psychology* 36 (9): 48–9.

Chapter 3

Teaching processes

Intended learning outcomes

Engagement with the text in this chapter will enable readers to do the following:

- explain why teaching is considered a profession and describe the fundamental professional responsibilities of inclusive teachers

- understand that effective, responsive teaching results from a reiterative teaching–learning cycle of evaluating teaching, planning for learning and assessment, teaching, and reflection, as described in the RTF, introduced in this chapter

- recognise that workplace skills such as organisation, communication and fostering good interpersonal relationships have specific applications in teaching, and that collaboration and data literacy are increasingly important for teachers' professional learning

- describe pedagogy, effective pedagogy and pedagogical content knowledge and articulate how they relate to inclusive teaching practice

Big ideas

- Teaching is a profession that provides service for the benefit of others. As professionals, teachers engage in continuing professional learning and open their activities and decision-making processes to constructive evaluation by other members of the profession.

- Teachers design instruction and facilitate student learning. Effective teaching occurs within a continuous, responsive cycle of understanding context, planning, implementing teaching and learning activities, assessment procedures, providing feedback, reflection and evaluation.

- There are particular ways of organising information and resources and of interacting with others that are specific to the teaching profession. Collaborating with colleagues about student learning is a powerful way to improve teacher knowledge and practice.

- Teaching *matters*: it impacts on student outcomes throughout their lives and affects national productivity. Effective, responsive teaching for all students is a key approach for achieving equity of educational outcomes.

Introduction

This chapter introduces one of the book's main topics – the work of being an effective, inclusive teacher capable of using a range of skills and instructional strategies to respond to the learning needs of all students. It is our first discussion of teaching that matters – teaching for sustainable learning in the 21st century. Just as it is vital for effective teachers to know how students think and learn, they also need to develop clear understandings and skills that enable them to teach – that is, to facilitate learning, sometimes explicitly – for all their students. Learning and teaching are inextricably linked. In fact, when learning and teaching are observed in a classroom, there is interplay, with student learning influencing teaching, the teaching influencing learning, teachers learning and students teaching. However, for teaching to be effective it must be intentionally planned, implemented with expertise and reflectively reviewed. These teaching processes are at the core of teacher work.

Definitions of effective teaching vary, and the terminology used to describe effective teaching is not always consistent. Westwood (1993) defines effective teaching as the clear teaching of important skills, information and appropriate strategies. Effective teaching may differ in its delivery in each subject area, in relation to the material to be learnt or in response to students' differing capabilities. However, general features of effective teachers, which are evident despite differences in circumstances, include the following elements:

- maximising students' **time on task**

- facilitating students' active participation in lessons

> **Time on task** is the time spent engaged in learning activities.

- ensuring students understand learning tasks
- getting the task difficulty and challenge level right, to ensure high rates of success
- creating a supportive classroom environment
- responding to student behaviour appropriately
- motivating students to learn (Westwood 2004, 79)

Far more than the 'stand and deliver' of classrooms of the past, many contemporary teaching processes happen through planning and organising and through thinking about teaching, the students, the content, the context and how they all fit together.

A **mindset** is a default assumption or perspective held by a person that is often unquestioned.

These processes happen before, during and after each teaching episode and often in collaboration with other teachers. Indeed, the thinking and planning, collaboration and communication, instruction and responses, and management, organisational and relational skills that are required to underpin almost any successful lesson at school render it no small feat. To deliver effective, responsive teaching for all students, lesson after lesson, day after day, over a sustained period of time is an ongoing challenge. Teachers require extensive professional knowledge and skills, as well as a positive **mindset**, to be able to operate effectively in classrooms and within schools and communities. The teaching processes so essential to being an effective teacher need to be learnt but, in a continual paradox, are never fully known, because of variability across students, content and contexts.

The teaching profession

Teaching is considered a profession because it requires prolonged pre-service education and ongoing in-service and postgraduate professional learning opportunities. Common definitions of profession also refer to the provision of a service in the interests of others, a commitment to behaving ethically and membership of a professional body that defines and monitors professional practice. In Australia, the Australian Institute of Teaching and School Leadership and some state and territory bodies provide this professional oversight, while in New Zealand, teachers must be registered with the New Zealand Teachers Council.

A teacher's ethical obligations are considerable. They include ensuring students acquire knowledge and skills, a duty of care to protect students from risk and enacting equitable treatment of all students. A key ethical obligation emphasised in this text is that teachers ensure that their service offers learning for all: the opportunity for all students to learn the knowledge and skills they need to prosper throughout their lives. Hence, teachers need to offer appropriate learning experiences and utilise a wide range of skills and strategies to engage all students – students who learn readily, students who are disengaged or reluctant, students with disabilities or learning difficulties, students from a range of cultural and ethnic backgrounds and students experiencing emotional or social difficulties. All students have a right to learn content, skills and self-regulated learning approaches that will be useful to them and enrich their lives. This places a heavy professional responsibility on teachers. Teaching matters, and it matters for *all* students.

In earlier times, there was a societal perception that teachers were among the 'gatekeepers' of knowledge – they possessed knowledge and controlled access to that knowledge. In contemporary society, this notion is no longer valid, as access to knowledge is open to all those who are literate and have proximity to libraries and the internet. Also, knowledge is now considered more broadly – it is widely recognised that learners bring the knowledge gained through their own experiences to almost any learning context, so that teachers can learn from students and students are able to learn from each other and from sources outside the formal learning environment. Contemporary society still has expectations, however, of those in the teaching profession with regard to imparting knowledge, ensuring the information students learn is valid and relevant and anticipating that teachers will evaluate evidence and apply scrutiny to information, will show intellectual curiosity, will not be vulnerable to spin (whether it relates to a commercial product or a fad) and will ensure students learn valid and relevant information. Teachers as professionals are expected to apply intellectual rigour to both the content they present and the methods they use to facilitate learning. They frame and filter an overwhelming body of available knowledge by being cognisant of the frameworks within which they teach and to which they are accountable.

Teaching is about student outcomes. Effective teaching results in maximally improved student outcomes within a sustainable context. The notion of improving student outcomes is not necessarily synonymous with high levels of student achievement, although this may well be an outcome of effective teaching for some students. Improving student outcomes involves developing students' knowledge, skills and learning processes; it implies growth in learning that is meaningful, relevant and useful for living, working and lifelong learning.

Teaching for sustainable learning incorporates, in action, learning for all, teaching that matters and learning that lasts. From this perspective, the contemporary teaching profession is delineated by notions of providing service that benefits others, equity, active participation, the sustainable use of resources, and collaboration. Teaching for sustainable learning has a futurist perspective, with its emphasis on teaching learning processes – that is, how to learn, problem solve and collaborate. Teaching for sustainable learning as described by the **ATRiUM** model, introduced in chapter 1, requires that students acquire the capabilities necessary for successful future lives. It involves teachers using, but not depleting, current resources and creating and collaborating to meet challenges and solve problems – some of which have perhaps not even been imagined as yet. Our perspective can be challenged when we consider that young people entering school in the next few years will likely be active and influential in the 2070s, perhaps developing as part of their work educational policy and its

> **ATRiUM** Active learning; Thinking; Relating to others; Using language, symbols and ICT; and Managing self.

direction for the 22nd century! The teaching profession faces the challenge of preparing learners to meet future needs that cannot, as yet, be fully articulated.

This book's focus on inclusive practices rests on the premise that good teaching – that is, providing quality instruction and learning experiences in the regular learning environment to a heterogeneous mix of students – is the bedrock of inclusive education. From this perspective, classroom teachers who enact effective teaching that facilitates learning for all their students are practising inclusion. While some students with disabilities require access to specialist teaching and different settings in order to master the knowledge and skills they need, the great majority of students benefit most from all teachers doing their jobs well – presenting pre-planned, differentiated lessons, utilising a range of well-organised resources, providing appropriate adjustments tailored to students' learning needs and giving feedback that enhances their future learning. In terms of sustainable learning, effective teaching, crafted in response to the learning needs of students, is the definitive inclusive practice: inclusion in action.

The impact of teaching matters in the immediate and future lives of all students. Regardless of individual, family and environmental factors, teacher proficiency and other teacher-controlled factors and classroom instructional processes are vital in influencing students' attainment levels at school and beyond. In other words, educational effectiveness for all students is crucially dependent on the provision of quality teaching by competent teachers (Darling-Hammond and Bransford 2005; Hattie 2003, 2005; Hill and Crévola 2003). Students who experience disabilities or learning difficulties are particularly vulnerable to poor pedagogy and are more likely to benefit from effective teachers' skills and professional knowledge (Strain and Hoyson 2000; Sanders and Rivers 1996).

It is quite feasible that experiencing effective, responsive teaching may also influence student decisions about remaining in school until the end of Year 12. Higher levels of school completion enhance opportunities for personal fulfilment, meaningful work and increased earnings, all of which are key factors for workforce participation and productivity and lifelong wellbeing. Having a good education is an important prerequisite for finding a job. Students who complete Year 12 are more likely to be employed and to earn a higher salary compared to early school leavers, with every additional year of education adding to the earnings of an Australian worker by between 5.5 and 11.0 per cent, and similar rates for New Zealand workers (Education Counts 2014).

Unsurprisingly, educational attainment rates are lower for students who experience disability or restrictive long-term health conditions. In Australia, of these, 62 per cent attained a Year 12 qualification in 2011 compared with 78 per cent of those who did not have a disability or a health condition (ABS 2011). In New Zealand, 'learners with special [educational] needs or disabilities have low levels of educational achievement' compared with their peers and 'are much less likely to go on to further education and employment when they leave school' (Ministry of Education

2012). Effective and responsive teaching has a key role to play in meeting the educational needs of all students and in shaping their futures.

Despite public perceptions of short working days and long holidays, most school teachers work long hours in complex, changeable and demanding environments. Most feel their work is never done – that there is always more to do and better ways to do it. Increased societal expectations about the scope and depth of issues schools and teachers should address add to the pressure. Becoming an effective, responsive teacher in a contemporary, inclusive school setting is a worthy goal and not a challenge for the faint hearted.

However, despite the demands on individual teachers to meet the professional challenges of inclusive education, teaching must be seen as a shared responsibility. Teachers need to share information and collaborate with colleagues; local school and systemic executives must consult with teachers, offer appropriate professional learning opportunities and monitor effectiveness; and families and communities should support and contribute to the work of schools and teachers. Teachers function best as part of a community, as part of the ecosystem of influences that impact on the lifelong opportunities and choices available to students.

The responsive teaching framework

Teaching that matters requires commitment from teachers to follow a broad plan for the delivery of effective, responsive instruction – a cycle of planning, teaching and evaluating. In this section, the RTF is introduced as a structure that organises the important components of a teaching–learning cycle. The RTF poses a series of eight questions, which are referred to throughout this book. The questions, if asked by teachers of themselves, can guide teaching practice. The first five are sequential steps that usually take place when preparing to teach, with the final three occurring iteratively during and after teaching. The framework, depicted in figure 3.1, is built on the core practices of planning, teaching and learning, assessment and feedback, and evaluation and reflection. Sometimes teachers will complete the teaching and learning cycle multiple times in a lesson. At other times, teachers will consider work units or a whole year of teaching with their classes from this perspective. Each step of the framework is considered in detail below.

1 What frameworks do I need to consider?

This is the most stable of the questions. Although curricula, communities and schools do change, they are less dynamic than the other factors that affect teaching and learning. Teachers respond to this question early in the planning, as the answers can act as foundations for the more dynamic processes to follow.

To begin with, teachers must have a thorough understanding of legislative frameworks that have specific relevance to schools and teaching, such as child protection, anti-discrimination and privacy laws. Other overarching frameworks that need to

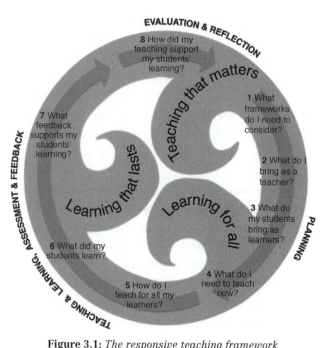

Figure 3.1: *The responsive teaching framework*

be considered include the Australian Institute of Teaching and School Leadership's professional standards for teachers or the New Zealand Teachers Council's code of ethics, the Australian curriculum or the New Zealand curriculum, and syllabus documents adopted by the relevant educational jurisdictions. School, or state or territory documents reflecting mission statements, charters, core values and codes of conduct also require close consideration by teachers, because they commonly describe the parameters of professional responsibilities and the values and behavioural standards that teachers are expected to uphold. Local, state or territory or national priorities and strategic plans, which by their very nature change quite regularly, should be included in the initial appraisal of the landscape within which teaching occurs.

Think and do 3.1: The hidden curriculum

In addition to the formal curriculum, schools and school systems are also said to propagate a 'hidden' curriculum, a set of values and norms not overtly articulated but nonetheless pervasive and influential. Schools' hidden curricula often contain values, attitudes and principles believed by many to be valid and justifiable, such as reward for achievement, respect for rules, obedience and punctuality. However, the hidden curriculum is also seen as a powerful means of social control, predisposed to advantage those who currently have most power and influence.

Research and discuss the hidden curriculum, then consider this statement: 'The purpose of the hidden curriculum is to coerce conformity and obedience to the belief that social inequities are just and correct'. In relation to your own experiences of schooling, do you think this statement is valid?

2 What do I bring as a teacher?

Although all teachers work within stipulated frameworks, individuals bring unique perspectives, strengths and needs, their own values and experiences, to their roles. Personal and professional influences have a powerful impact on the way teachers do their work and consequently on how students experience school and learning. Therefore, it is important for teachers to recognise and acknowledge the pervasive influence of their personal attitudes and beliefs on their professional lives.

A vitally important aspect of teachers' self-knowledge is awareness of the cultural influences that have shaped them as people and community members. Reflecting on their own cultural identities provides teachers with the opportunity to recognise how these are similar to and different from those of their students and the community in which they teach. This can then be taken into account in developing relationships and refining teaching approaches. Further, recognising the 'fit' (or lack of it) between the culture of the educational setting and the culture of the students' families and communities can provide valuable insights into students – how they learn and how their teachers can best facilitate their learning in a culturally responsive and respectful way.

It is also important for teachers to know themselves as professionals, to recognise their professional preferences and, particularly, to develop self-awareness about significant influences on their professional practice. For example, teachers must understand their own educational history: whether there is a teacher they want to emulate or a kind of teacher they never want to be. They may particularly value a specific theory or approach or hold strong opinions about the teacher's role. Further, for teachers to know themselves and their capabilities as professionals, they need to be aware of their personalities and how they impact on their work and interactions. Teachers can use their strengths to support themselves professionally (for example, learning how to use a sense of humour to build relationships with students) and to manage personal foibles (for example, curbing a propensity to sarcasm or better handling feelings of frustration).

For Australian teachers, the graduate student attributes identified by the Australian Institute of Teaching and School Leadership define beginning professional knowledge using a standards framework. In terms of professional knowledge, skills and attributes, it is important for teachers to recognise, however, that there is not a fixed body of skills and knowledge that will serve them throughout their whole career; rather, professional knowledge needs to be continually developed, updated and refined.

3 What do my students bring as learners?

Developing and refining understandings about the learning needs of students enables teachers to better tailor effective learning experiences. This part of the RTF prompts teachers to observe and inquire about what students already know and have experienced, how they learn best and what strategies facilitate individual and group learning. It is also important for teachers to learn about the personalities and characteristics of individual students in their classes and give attention to how each student participates in the social dynamic of the classroom. More broadly, developing knowledge about the communities students come from is essential for understanding learners' backgrounds and how best to meet their educational needs. These learning needs may just as easily stem from individual students' gifts and talents as from any disabilities or learning difficulties.

To understand the nature of students as learners, teachers should consider, as far as practicable, their diversity of experiences and understandings, different interests, motivations and capabilities and varying abilities. Learning behaviours such as a motivated approach to tasks, persistence, attention and focus, as well as students' attitudes to themselves as learners must be considered as part of the teacher's inquiry in this step.

At this point, it is also informative to review existing assessment information about each student and individual plans for students with disabilities (educational plans, behavioural plans, health plans and so on) and to consider what extra information will be needed in order to plan for inclusive teaching and learning that meet the particular needs of these students.

Another important consideration is what the students already know and can do in relation to intended outcomes and to any prerequisite knowledge, skills or learning processes. This implies gathering knowledge of students' developmental levels and evaluating their readiness to learn. Teachers can know the curriculum content and what the expectations are for each stage or grade, but this knowledge will need to be tempered in response to the reality of where learners are in their development at the beginning of an instructional cycle. There is no point in teaching something that is well outside the initial grasp of a group of learners. There is also no point in teaching the same thing at the same time and in the same way to all students in a class. It is likely students will be at different points in any given learning domain, with different prior learning experiences to draw from and different capabilities or constraints to bring to any new topic.

4 What do I need to teach now?

In this step, teachers' knowledge of their students and of the curriculum combines to help them define the most important learning needs of the class and of individual students. Curriculum documents and school or state or territory scope and sequence plans will broadly define the content to be taught and the learning processes that most students need to experience and develop. Planning for content delivery and learning activities means teachers will need to devise, as part of initial preparation, differentiated learning experiences to further develop all students' abilities. In addition, some students in the class may not yet be ready to learn the expected content and will need to have learning opportunities provided which enable them to develop knowledge, skills and processes that bring them closer to being able to achieve the same specified outcomes as their peers or to work towards related outcomes from an individual instructional plan.

5 How do I teach for all my learners?

The final step in the planning part of the teaching–learning cycle is to consider, in the context of the predetermined content and understanding of student-learning needs, which strategies and approaches are most likely to facilitate learning for all students and how these can be delivered in the classroom. Almost invariably, each lesson will involve a variety of strategies, including revision, modelling and demonstration, practice, collaboration, performance and extension. Some lesson parts will follow a familiar routine, while others will require students to learn new processes and procedures. The learning experience may contain some direct instruction provided by the teacher followed by opportunities for students to be self-directed in their work. During planning, consideration should be given to student groupings, the duration and sequence of the tasks that make up a lesson flow, transitions between learning activities and what resources will be needed and how they will be distributed and used.

Other important considerations that influence planning prior to teaching relate to procedures for engaging students' attention, monitoring their performance, assessing learning and recording information about attainment and effort. Importantly, teachers need to think about how they will make clear to students the purpose of the learning and the criteria used to signal success. Related concerns include how to monitor students' progress and participation during each lesson and across a series of lessons and exactly how students will be asked to demonstrate their skills and understandings (for example, orally, in a written report, individually or as part of a group).

6 What did my students learn?

Knowing and understanding what the students learnt, and having insights into how and why they learnt it, is very important information for teachers as they begin to evaluate the effectiveness of the lesson or series of lessons they are teaching. This focus on the students' learning, when effective, is referenced against intended learning outcomes, considers unintended outcomes and measures, in some way, development, improvement, gain or growth. When reflecting on this question teachers need to ensure they think about learning specifically, quantitatively and broadly, and look to qualitative dimensions of learning, such as student participation, motivation and the communication and interactions that took place during the learning process.

Information from assessment provides key evidence for the answer to this question. In contemporary classroom contexts, assessment is much more than just tests. It has different purposes and processes. It is often an in-built part of learning activities – almost all tasks and activities students perform can yield assessment information. It is always important to consider the assessment's validity: whether it really measures what it purports to be measuring and, importantly, whether it allows *all* students to demonstrate their learning.

7 What feedback supports my students' learning?

Feedback is information about the processes and the success (or lack of it) achieved in tasks, activities and participation for learning. It is gathered through observation and assessment and is then provided to learners. Feedback gives students information about what they have learnt and what they need to learn next. It is provided in many ways, either deliberately or implied. Effectively utilised, it works to assist students reduce the gap between their current performance and the teacher's intended learning outcomes. Importantly for teachers, feedback is very influential in the cycle of learning and effective teaching. As some feedback types are more effective than others, it requires extensive consideration and reflection as part of effective teaching practice. (Chapter 5 discusses feedback in depth.)

8 How did my teaching support my students' learning?

This important question requires teachers to reflect on their own teaching, and to consider why and how their planning, actions and use of resources supported or perhaps hindered student participation, learning and development. Key considerations include whether the teaching was effective and efficient in terms of time and effort expended, whether it had the desired effect and whether associated and unanticipated outcomes occurred. As it is somewhat difficult for teachers to make these considerations objectively, information from classroom observation and feedback provided by peer coaches or teacher mentors can be informative for teachers seeking to evaluate their own practice and how it interacts with student learning.

Professional skills at work

In addition to the big-picture cycle of planning, implementation and reflection described in the RTF, teaching requires a wide-ranging set of professional skills in organisation and relationships that are implemented variably and flexibly. It is helpful in understanding teachers' work to consider such domains of practice separately and apart from pedagogy, though in reality these areas are interconnected.

Communication, organisation and relationships

A closer examination of the 'doing' part of teaching from the perspective that inclusive teaching practice begins with effective teaching in regular classrooms indicates that inclusive practices permeate all aspects of teachers' work. Inclusion requires teachers to organise lessons from the outset by considering the needs of all learners and to persevere in modelling and building respectful relationships with all students, even those who seem the most disengaged.

When they enter a classroom at the beginning of a day or lesson, teachers need to be ready to teach, equipped with coherent lesson sequences, stimulating strategies and approaches and appropriate resources. They must also practise what might be termed 'professional standards in interpersonal skills' – that is, the ability to get on with, listen to and share relevant information with others and, to varying extents, to put aside personal biases or opinions so they can proceed with their work. Organisational and interpersonal skills are key criteria for effective teachers. Some teachers may be caring about their students and passionate about their subject; yet if they do not prepare well and organise stimulating learning experiences, many students will find lessons boring and become disengaged or, quite possibly, disruptive. Similarly, students, colleagues, parents and carers may soon conclude teachers are not effective if, despite the use of the most recent technologies, lessons are disorganised and learning sequences lack cohesion. Such a lack of structure can lead to challenges to teachers' authority or professionalism. Good teaching matters to students, colleagues, parents, carers, the community and the teaching profession. Key organisational and interpersonal skills that teachers need in their daily work are listed below. While not exhaustive, the information provided does indicate the breadth of detail teachers need to attend to as part of their daily work. Other important professional competencies required by effective, responsive teachers that are more specifically related to inclusion are discussed in the subsequent sections.

Communication

Teachers have to communicate orally, both effectively and appropriately, with students, colleagues, other professionals, parents and carers and community members. Specific oral communication skills needed for teaching include offering precise and concise explanations, using language accessible to students, questioning for understanding, creating motivation, facilitating discussions, and providing effective modelling and demonstrating skills and strategies. Appropriate body language is important in all spoken communication and includes facial expressions, posture, gestures, voice, movement and appearance. Effective written communication skills are also required, for tasks such as providing feedback to students and writing notes, student reports and reports for other professionals.

Organisation

Adhering to timetables and duty rosters is vitally important, especially when duty of care is considered. There are serious professional implications for a teacher should an adverse event occur when they are absent from a scheduled class or supervision duty. Organisation skills are needed for curriculum, assessment and lesson planning, as well as time management. Teachers must also carry out administrative support tasks, such as record keeping, organising materials and resources, photocopying, ensuring accessibility of electronic resources, maintaining assets, dealing with correspondence and collecting money.

Respectful, professional relationships

Teachers' relationships with students benefit from strategies such as providing opportunities for students to express ideas and opinions, listening effectively and responding appropriately, identifying common interests, recognising student strengths, knowing when students are likely to need additional support and, critically, managing student behaviour that disrupts learning. Relationships with colleagues vary in function and intensity, from social staffroom relationships to intense professional partnerships. Most schools have a hierarchy in the staffing structure, and this influences the nature of relationships between colleagues.

Building relationships and communicating with parents and carers, families and community members is essential for supporting shared responsibility for education. Such relationships can be illuminating and enriching but also challenging and even confrontational. At all times, teachers are expected to interact within professional boundaries.

Human and material resource management

In the context of sustainable learning, all resources present in the school, including the knowledge, experiences and expertise of staff and students, as well as material resources, need to be used sustainably to ensure future availability rather than depletion. In addition, teachers should ensure that teacher assistant time is used for maximum benefit. At times, this requires additional planning and collaboration, but failing to plan these sessions may result in the waste of what is, in most contexts, a scarce and valuable resource.

Organisation of classroom furniture, displays and resources is vital, so they are accessible and functional and effectively support learning and participation. This extends to pre-booking other rooms and loan materials, organising library resource collections, managing school equipment and checking for risks.

Collaboration for professional learning

Collaboration is working with others to achieve a goal, using shared knowledge. The idea of teachers working together to support one another is not new, and in many schools there is a tradition of teachers sharing ideas and resources, planning curricula and talking about students, learning and teaching. This kind of collegiality is highly valued by teachers and a key factor in staff morale. Informal collaboration between teachers involves sharing tasks and resources, discussing students and engaging in activities that build camaraderie and trust. More formal teacher collaboration traditionally involves work on programming and planning documents or operational tasks, participating in meetings and professional learning events and being on school committees with a specific purpose (for example, student wellbeing, technology or implementation of a new initiative).

Until relatively recently it was not uncommon for teacher collaboration to stop at the classroom door, due to the perception that what happened in each classroom was the business of the individual teacher and that questioning or seeking to discuss colleagues' professional practice encroached on their professionalism. This attitude couched teaching practice within classrooms as a private endeavour, somewhat isolated from other influences and cut off from possibilities for innovation and improvement. Now, 'de-privatising' teaching is seen as an important step towards encouraging collaboration and professional learning. This notion is built upon the premise that effective professional learning and growth are achieved when teachers work together to teach and learn from each other.

Increasingly, teacher collaboration focused on teaching and learning is linked with school improvement, increased teacher effectiveness and job satisfaction and, most importantly, improved student outcomes (ACER 2012; AITSL 2014; Goddard, Goddard and Tschannen-Moran 2007). The link between collaborative practice and improved student outcomes is formed by ongoing collaborative teaching practices that develop teachers' instructional practices and professional capacity, as Fullan (2011, 2) writes: 'The research has been clear and consistent for over 30 years – collaborative cultures in which teachers focus on improving their teaching practice, learn from each other, and are well led and supported by school principals result in better learning for students'. In contemporary schools, effective collaboration between teachers requires far more than willingness to share resources and sit on committees. Teaching is a shared responsibility, and teacher collaboration requires a shared vision, clarity of intention and mutual trust built on appropriate structural supports. A crucial role for school leaders and educational jurisdictions is to facilitate the mindsets, time and organisational mechanisms that enable the conditions for effective collaboration to occur in an authentic and purposeful manner.

South-East Asian areas that demonstrate high rates of student achievement, including South Korea, Hong Kong, Singapore and Shanghai, support teachers to engage in 'active collaboration' by providing more non-teaching time than is provided to teachers in Australia and New Zealand, albeit with the trade-off of larger class sizes. During non-teaching time, teachers engage in practices such as mentoring, cooperative lesson and assessment planning, classroom observation and discussion of feedback about teaching practice (Grattan Institute 2012). For such an approach to be successful, colleagues need to have an open, not private, mindset about teaching. They need to trust and respect each other and share responsibility for developing and refining technical teaching skills.

Professional environments can undermine authentic collaboration if, for example, teachers have to compete for higher salaries or fear repercussions for trialling innovative evidence-based approaches. At times, relationship factors and personal and communication issues can also prevent effective teacher collaboration. It is 'risky business' and requires careful consideration, planning and reflection at system, strategic and personal levels in order to be effective. Also, the ongoing development of social media and web 2.0 technologies, such as wikis, blogs, online communities and Twitter, require new conceptualisations of teacher collaboration that go beyond the idea of teachers sitting in a room together. The work of contemporary teacher collaboration includes the following tasks:

> **Formative assessment** provides information to help teachers understand what students bring as learners and what needs to be taught now; it informs teaching.

- identifying key outcomes wanted for all students
- developing common assessment tasks
- discussing ways to monitor student learning using **formative assessment**
- planning appropriate and timely **interventions**
- putting in place strategies for collecting and analysing data
- evaluating the effectiveness of teaching approaches and strategies

> **Interventions** are planned procedures aimed at teaching a specific set of academic or social skills.

An influential contemporary approach for encouraging teacher collaboration and improving school effectiveness is to develop schools as strategically supported professional learning communities that include flexible and variable professional learning teams. This approach transforms teacher professional learning, which was more traditionally delivered by 'outside experts', into a collaborative on-the-job pursuit initiated by teacher groups and focused on their own teaching practices and their own students' learning needs. Significantly, such approaches are underpinned by the ideas that effective teaching is driven by the 'moral purpose' of serving all students to a high standard and that student learning depends on continuous teacher learning (Fullan, Hill and Crévola 2006).

DuFour and colleagues have developed a practice-based model and a range of support resources to guide the implementation of professional learning communities (for example, DuFour 2004; DuFour, DuFour and Eaker 2003; DuFour et al. 2009). Key ideas underlying their model for implementing these are presented below:

> *Ensuring that all students learn:* Teachers should teach 'not simply to ensure that students are taught but to ensure that they learn'. Engagement with colleagues centres on three crucial questions: 'What do we want each student to learn?', 'How will we know when each student has learnt it?' and 'How will we respond when a student experiences difficulty in learning?' (DuFour 2004, 8)

> *A culture of collaboration:* The collective purpose of ensuring that all students learn requires flexible and supportive structures to promote a collaborative culture. Collaborating for school improvement involves common agreement on critical outcomes, developing common assessment formats and consistently analysing student results. Professional learning communities should identify and remove barriers to learning. (DuFour 2004, 9–10)

> *A focus on learning:* Professional learning communities work together towards improving student achievement. Each teacher functions within the ongoing cycle of identifying the current student achievement level, setting a goal to develop the current level, working together to achieve that goal and seeking evidence of progress (DuFour 2004, 10).

From an inclusion perspective, what is appealing about DuFour and colleagues' (2009) approach to teacher collaboration and professional learning is their specific focus on whether *all* students are actually learning the concepts taught, based on an inherent valuing of equality of opportunity – that all students have the chance to learn. The authors challenge contemporary educators to 'move beyond pious mission statements pledging learning for all and to begin the systematic effort to create procedures, policies and programs that are aligned with that purpose' (DuFour et al. 2009, 26).

Behaviour for learning

For many teachers, striving to provide an environment that is conducive to learning while managing behaviour for learning is a complex, ongoing challenge (Calderhead and Shorrock 2004; Hobson et al. 2009). Before a teacher can effectively respond to student disruptions of learning activities, they need to know how to regulate their own emotional responses and develop and utilise personal attributes such as patience, flexibility, stoicism, resilience and compassion.

Although challenging student behaviours that disrupt learning and affect safety and wellbeing do occur, in many school settings low-level, persistent student behaviours are experienced more often – a student who continually calls out despite repeated reminders, an anxious student who leaves the room and won't come back in, students being derogatory to other students or students who passively refuse to participate in learning. The norm of automatic respect for authority, often based on fear of repercussions, no longer pervades schools or wider society (Richmond 2007). Instead of having might on their side, teachers now need to rely on developing fair boundaries and facilitating respectful relationships in order to ensure the safety and security of their students, minimise disruptions to learning and maximise student participation.

All student and teacher behaviours in the classroom impact on learning, but student behaviour that is actually or potentially dangerous or considerably disruptive to learning necessitates actions by the teacher. To be effective, teacher actions to manage student behaviour need to be considered professional responses drawn from a 'toolbox' of classroom management strategies and discrete skills that the teacher has intentionally cultivated and can implement according to context and need. There is rarely a single approach that works best in managing learning, and understandably it is not uncommon for teachers to make mistakes when interacting with students about behaviour for learning.

When student behaviour disrupts learning, teachers should consider what student needs may be motivating the behaviour and to responsively and, as feasible, proactively plan organisational changes or teaching strategies and adjustments to more effectively meet those needs. A key consideration is the difficulty level of classroom tasks and students' perceptions of their ability to engage with them. For example, students who find set academic work too hard may act out due to frustration or in an attempt to mask their lack of understanding. A responsive, proactive approach by teachers in planning future learning activities would be to ensure that the content level is adjusted or appropriate scaffolds are provided to improve the likelihood of students succeeding in the activity. Further information about specific strategies for classroom management are contained in chapter 6, but when planning to minimise disruptive student behaviours, teachers should consider the following organisational factors:

- initiating and maintaining effective routines for transitions within the classroom (moving from one activity to another), between classrooms and as students go to and return from breaks
- minimising lining up and waiting times
- ensuring the classroom environment is well organised and has clear access in high-traffic areas
- carefully considering student groupings
- giving clear instructions, broken down into step-by-step procedures as appropriate
- having routines in place for late student entry or early student exit during lessons and for managing external disruptions

Data literacy skills

Teachers are decision-makers. They continuously make innumerable nuanced decisions about what and how to teach, how best to respond to student learning and behaviour, how to interact with colleagues and how to effectively manage time and resources. Increasingly, teachers need to be accountable for these decisions, and working with data is key to being able to rationalise, justify and explain professional practice. This can perhaps be considered a new professional skill for teachers. As Matters (2007, 8) points out, 'Today, owing to advances in computing and communications technology, the widespread use of data for decision making is possible and practicable at every level of the education system – from students and teachers to parents and school administrators to stakeholders and policymakers'.

Data literacy is the capability to gather, read, interpret and meaningfully share many types of data.

The use of data in teaching was once limited to tasks such as monitoring student progress and assigning marks and grades. It is now inescapably prevalent, especially in relation to school improvement, and requires that teachers are competent and confident in collecting, collating, analysing and making appropriate use of many types of data from a wide range of sources. In their daily practice, teachers use this variety of data – quantitative, qualitative and demographic, about individuals and student groups, and from formal sources like standardised assessments and informal sources such as observation. Broadly, they use this data to monitor student outcomes and progress towards learning goals.

In Australia, the National Assessment Program – Literacy and Numeracy (NAPLAN) is an annual assessment for students in Years 3, 5, 7 and 9, which is undertaken across all states and territories. NAPLAN results are reported using the national School Measurement, Assessment and Reporting Toolkit, an online reporting resource that provides school leaders and teachers with detailed data and analysis of student and cohort achievement, gains, comparisons and response patterns.

In New Zealand, teachers can access data about student achievement and support for instructional decision-making from the Assessment Tools for Teaching and Learning program. This provides teachers, students, parents and carers with information about students' achievement levels relative to the curriculum achievement outcomes and national student performance norms.

Although the protocols used in Australia and New Zealand are different in intent, design and delivery, their existence indicates the vital importance of data for the teaching profession – both programs represent systematic attempts by governments to provide reliable data to schools for identifying learning needs and informing priorities for improvement.

Data from national assessments or achievement standards is important for benchmarking and measuring learning, but it does not follow that this is the most important kind of data or that it yields the most relevant information. Teachers collect data in many forms and use it for many purposes as a continuous process throughout the teaching cycle. This everyday data is vitally useful to teachers when they engage in responsive, effective teaching as outlined by the RTF.

Summative assessment data (the achievement data and assessments against outcomes and standards that are normally available at the end of a unit, term or semester) is useful for determining, in part, what students need to learn. However, formative assessment data, which is available throughout the teaching cycle, remains more fine-tuned to learning components and skills and can provide teachers with information useful in making instructional decisions which align teaching more closely with the learning needs of particular student groups. Such data may include information collected from the observation of work in progress, work samples, portfolio entries, quiz results, performance or demonstration evaluation, and from peer and self-assessment grades.

Once data has been collected, teachers need to collate, analyse and interpret it. Invariably, this involves teachers' analytic skills and professional judgment. Love (2009, 7) advocates a collaborative inquiry model for analysing and interpreting data whereby teachers 'construct their understanding of student-learning problems and embrace and test out solutions together through rigorous use of data and reflective dialogue'.

Data is not only analysed and interpreted with regard to student results and individual and group patterns but is also related to teacher effectiveness through judging how instructional practices can be fine-tuned or reviewed to enhance student learning and participation. Collaborative inquiry approaches to data analysis and interpretation ensure that teachers learn with and from each other and then combine their knowledge to focus on issues most relevant to their particular students.

To handle data effectively, teachers use ICT tools such as programs or applications for producing illustrative graphs and common data metrics (for example, averages and percentiles) as well as spreadsheets and statistical programs to generate reports. They are also able to interpret data analyses and make sense of reports generated by others. The challenge in all this work with data is to keep in mind the human context: the students and their circumstances, and how data can be used to improve learning for all.

Ethical practice

It is very important for teachers to show respect for ethical requirements of privacy and confidentiality. In the context of school education, confidentiality is a professional ethics issue, while privacy requirements relate more to legislative obligations. Confidentiality is necessary when information is given in trust to a teacher or teacher group with the expectation that this trust will not be betrayed by disclosure. In such a situation, there is an obligation to protect and hold in strict confidence information concerning the person, with few circumstances permitting its ethical disclosure. (One such circumstance would be a child protection matter relating to neglect or abuse.)

There are many situations and contexts in which confidentiality is expected of teachers. These include reviews of student files and records, some conversations with parents, carers or students, meetings involving planning for individual student needs and conversations with school counsellors or other teachers about individual student wellbeing issues.

In both Australia and New Zealand there are specific policy and legislative frameworks regarding privacy that are relevant to teachers' daily work. In Australia, the *Privacy Act 1988* and the *Privacy Amendment (Enhancing Privacy Protection) Act 2012* are the key federal privacy legislations (see OAIC 2014). In New Zealand, the legislation is set out in the Privacy Act 1993 (see also Dalziel 2009). Privacy legislation relates to the collection, storage, use and disclosure of students' personal information. As with many other aspects of teaching, further development and review of privacy legislation have been necessary because of technological advances that have resulted in schools having the capacity to collect, use and store more personal information data in more accessible formats than ever before.

Working with a diverse student population, teachers are likely to discover, particularly on enrolment, sensitive, detailed personal information about students with disabilities or learning difficulties, serious illness or adverse family circumstances. Although this information may be interesting, unusual or illustrative, teachers need to be aware of both their ethical and their legislative obligations with regard to how they handle it. Schools usually have specific policies about privacy and confidentiality, and state or territory or regional government departments have overarching legislation or policies. Teachers need to know and adhere to the relevant privacy policies and procedures in their broad and local contexts.

Think and do 3.2: Ethics for teachers

Access and read the article about ethics for teachers by Bourke and O'Neill (2009). What pointers does it give for your practice?

Professional skills in the classroom

This section begins a closer examination of how responsive teachers actually do their work in the classroom environment with their students. (The doing part of being a teacher will be the subject of much discussion throughout the remainder of this book, especially in chapters 6 and 7.) In practice, the domains of learners, learning, reflection and planning, and classroom teaching are intricately linked and overlapping. Effective, responsive teachers work in cycles that are both sequential and iterative. Their work involves adjusting, developing and supporting routines, programming at different levels, delivering interesting explanations and demonstrations and selecting from a wide range of interactive strategies and approaches. Teachers who teach well are likely to have experience to draw upon and to have undertaken much reflection, planning and evaluation practice. Good lessons do not happen by chance. Perhaps nowhere is the adage 'a failure to plan is a plan for failure' more relevant than it is in reference to teaching!

There are some problems with the language commonly used to describe teaching that need to be acknowledged and discussed. Firstly, the term 'classroom' holds assumptions of an enclosed, static space, and while there are certainly still many such classrooms in schools, it is perhaps more freeing to think of 'learning environments' instead. Contemporary learning environments include learning pods, stations and multi-age classrooms and encompass more frequent student transitions between learning spaces, multiple teachers in large open spaces and, of course, the thoughtful use of virtual learning environments and grouping strategies. Secondly, the word 'lesson' suggests teacher-led learning delivered in discrete units, when actually, in order to engage with content, students often experience a range of learning experiences that might relate to a number of different outcomes, sometimes extended over days or weeks. Finally, even the terms 'teachers' and 'learners' are open to interpretation. In an important sense, teachers are also learners, because they need to continually learn about how to refine and develop their practice. Also, at times students are teachers, as they can lead learning for their peers and even their teachers. So, while it is likely such terms will remain in everyday language, it is important to be mindful that they are increasingly used in a variety of ways and convey multiple meanings.

Pedagogy

'Pedagogy' is a Greek word which translates as 'to lead the child'. Across the world it is used somewhat differently, but in English it is generally seen in the context of school education and describes the 'art and science' of teaching and learning. It concerns the ways in which teachers provide instruction for their students – the design and structure of a lesson or series of lessons, the type of instructional input provided and the strategies and approaches used to facilitate student learning and participation. As an art, effective pedagogy reflects the needs of all learners and responds to those needs in ways that fit the context and develop the learner. As a science, effective pedagogy improves student-learning outcomes. Effective pedagogy under-pins responsive teaching.

Acknowledging that students are different and that their differences matter in terms of how they engage with content and learning activities is an important start-ing point for delivering effective pedagogy. It follows, then, that differentiation – of content, learning activities, assessment and feedback – is an essential foundational approach for effective pedagogy. (Differentiation as a core process of inclusive teach-ing for sustainable learning is explored in detail in chapter 7.)

Effective pedagogy is demonstrated when teachers know which method to use with which particular content in a specific context with an individual or group of students (Mizell 1999, cited in Beutel 2003), all situated within a basic instructional approach that encompasses flexibility and innovation. The notion of effective peda-gogy is holistic, subjective and variable with context; it is not something that teachers can just do but requires planning, practice and constant refinements. Reflecting on the questions of the RTF can support teachers as they develop practices for effective pedagogy.

Shulman (1986, 1987) introduced and later developed the model of pedagogi-cal content knowledge to describe expert teachers' knowledge and practice. This is a kind of practical knowledge implemented in classrooms that promotes teacher understanding and consequent comprehension among students. Schulman (1986, 8) described pedagogical content knowledge as representing 'the blending of content and pedagogy into an understanding of how particular topics, problems, or issues are organised, represented, and adapted to the diverse interests and abilities of learn-ers, and presented for instruction'. Pedagogical content knowledge is said to have three interacting and overlapping elements: content knowledge (subject, topic, cur-riculum), pedagogical knowledge (methods, approaches, strategies) and knowledge of the learners and their contexts. The key contribution of Shulman's model is that it promotes the idea that 'expert' teachers, whose work is clearly understood by their students, rely on far more than knowledge about content; they also need to know about their students and the context for learning. In fact, teacher intellectual and ver-bal ability and skills in building interpersonal relationships are more strongly linked to teacher effectiveness than knowledge of content (Hattie 2009).

Instructional approaches

The methods teachers use for teaching can, for the purposes of discussion, be broad-ly described as either teacher directed or student centred, each of which is briefly described below. However, in the classroom context, the instructional approaches actually used by teachers are often a combination of both methods (Westwood 2013), with various strategies being used at different stages of the lesson and with different student groups. When thinking about which teaching methods to use, it is important for teachers to ensure that their rationale for selecting a particular method is ground-ed in pedagogy and student-learning needs rather than because of a commitment to a particular method or a lack of knowledge of other methods that might be more suitable.

This is mentioned because the issue of which approach is 'best' remains a source of passionate debate and strongly held opinions in academic, school, community and political agendas. Ideology at times seems to overshadow considerations of what really matters with regard to teaching methods – that they are selected according to their propensity to meet the learning needs of a particular student group at a certain point in time or learning stage. Teachers and others in the educational profession need to advocate to keep this perspective at the forefront of discussions.

Student-centred learning approaches, as the name suggests, have the learners as the focus; their interests, motivations, interactions and capacity to develop knowledge and understanding are used to determine the curriculum and pedagogy. The teacher's role is that of learning facilitator, managing the environment and resources to support opportunities for students to engage in activities that stimulate learning. Student-centred learning is frequently exploratory and experiential, with hands-on and interactive activities used to initiate and stimulate learning. Constructivism is a key theoretical framework for this style of learning. Discovery learning, active learning based on student-generated questions and self-directed learning are examples of student-centred learning approaches. Cooperative learning and inquiry learning also pertain to student-centred learning, but they contain elements of teacher-directed instruction.

Teacher-directed methods have instruction as a core component, and the curriculum and pedagogy are largely focused on what the students need to learn as determined by the teacher (with reference to assessment data and syllabus frameworks). The teacher is central in instruction, using strategy instruction, modelling (including peer modelling), demonstrations, lectures and structured learning activities to show the students what to do and how to do it. Experiential learning and hands-on activities can be valuable components of a teacher-directed instructional cycle, but these are used in a confirmatory way after the concept or property to be explored has been explained.

Teacher-directed methods, lacking some definitional clarity but variously referred to as explicit instruction, direct instruction, systematic instruction, content enhancement and strategy instruction, do not imply that students are not active in the learning process. Instead, their activity is guided, directed and supplemented by instructional input from the teacher or another influential person. Direct instruction methods were traditionally linked to behaviourist learning theories, but in a contemporary context these methods, more broadly referred to as direct and explicit instruction, are closely aligned with cognitivist theories, which take into consideration how students learn and how teachers can scaffold the learning process. Direct and explicit instruction and interactive whole-class teaching are effective teacher-directed approaches to learning (Westwood 2013). Many different instructional approaches can be accommodated within the construct of sustainable learning, but it would be remiss not to acknowledge strong evidence in the literature to support direct and explicit instruction as an effective approach for improving learning outcomes of all students, with perhaps particular suitability for students with disabilities or learning difficulties (see Arief, Liem and Martin 2013; Purdie and Ellis 2005). Some content, including learning basic academic skills, is particularly amenable to direct and explicit instructional approaches.

Direct and explicit instruction can take many forms, including highly scripted lessons focusing on mastery of content, lessons with demonstration and practice routines and lessons that use supports such as graphic organisers or specific strategies to help students do a task or procedure. Task analysis – knowing how a task is accomplished in a step-by-step process – is essential teacher prerequisite knowledge for this important instructional approach. Direct and explicit instruction approaches commonly feature fast-paced lessons and require iterative interaction between students and the teacher. Although direct instruction is not a singular procedure, lessons often contain some key sequential components, as described below.

Despite its effectiveness for improving student-learning outcomes, it is neither desirable nor feasible for teachers to use direct, explicit instruction all the time; rather, it is an approach for specific purposes and at particular times in the teaching and learning cycle, one in a range of methods. Nonetheless, the strength of the evidence base supporting direct instruction suggests it should have a prominent, regular place in contemporary classroom practice.

Direct and explicit instruction sequence

Scaffolding learning

Before teaching, plan how you will support student learning:

- Know your learners: what do they know now and what do they need to learn next? A pre-test can provide useful information.
- Instructional clarity is key: what do the students need to do before, during and after the task?
- Anticipate errors and develop a procedure for error correction.
- Develop routine procedures to acknowledge progress and effort.
- How will you tap into prior learning and make connections with students' lived experiences?
- How will you communicate to students that they can learn this task, procedure or concept?

Target learning intentions

At the beginning of the teaching and learning sequence, clearly communicate to students what they are going to learn and how they will know when they have learnt it:

- Discuss and display the learning outcome in language that is accessible to the learners.
- Use common acronyms for this component: WALT (we are learning to), WALHT (we are learning how to) and WILF (what I'm looking for).

- Show students what the task looks like when satisfactorily completed – for example, an annotated work sample clearly indicating the target new knowledge, skill or concept.
- Use predetermined learning goals related to the learning outcome to help students understand what is required to be successful with the task – for example, 'I will write an interesting sentence with two describing words in it' or 'I will measure, record and compare four objects using square centimetres'.
- Encourage students to use personal bests when appropriate to monitor the development of their learning or performance.

Delivering information

Explaining and teaching critical content most commonly relies on teacher talk and demonstration (at times augmented by peer contributions):

- Consider scripting this instructional input part of the lesson prior to teaching it, so you know exactly what needs to be said to facilitate student learning.
- Focus exclusively on aspects of content directly related to the outcome.
- Break down tasks and provide step-by-step demonstrations or explanations; sequence conceptual knowledge in stages from easy (known) to hard (new).
- Use instructional talk that is clear and succinct, as too much teacher talk can confuse rather than clarify.
- Provide examples and non-examples.
- Include metacognitive strategies – that is, not just what to do but how to think about and approach the task, and what to do if students get 'stuck'.
- Ensure the duration of instructional input is brief and the pace is brisk.

Questioning to check understanding

When delivering information, use questioning to promote student interaction and to gauge student learning:

- Require students to respond frequently, using a variety of response modes.
- Ask questions that you reasonably anticipate students will be able to answer. Avoid trick questions or trying to 'catch out' students.
- Consider using a strategy, with some discretion, that randomly selects students to answer a question rather than having them raise their hand to be selected to answer.
- Encourage students to engage in reasonable risk-taking and 'having a go' when answering questions and in doing so acknowledge effort, even if the answer is incorrect.
- Use response cards, such as mini whiteboards, true–false or yes–no cards, so that the whole group can respond and display their responses simultaneously. This promotes participation by all students and provides the teacher with instant feedback about student learning.

Provide opportunity for practice

During and after the delivering-information stage of the lesson, provide opportunities for guided and then independent practice of the target knowledge or skill:

- Practise both previously encountered (known) and new knowledge and skills to support increased knowledge, fluency and accuracy.
- Use a variety of modes – individual, small-group and whole-class practice.
- Use a variety of approaches – oral, written and demonstrations.
- Consider how technology applications can be incorporated into practice routines – for example, recording oral responses on a device and then playing back to check for accuracy and using appropriate apps or online games.
- Monitor progress in practice and ensure this information is available to students – for example, by checking for accuracy (number or per cent correct) and fluency (response time). Reference such information to past individual performance rather than group average performance.

Seek proof of learning

After instruction and practice, ensure students can generalise the new knowledge or skill:

- Situate the new knowledge or skill in a different context within the subject and check for understanding; for example, have students use newly acquired number knowledge to solve a money problem.
- Make links between the new knowledge and everyday living situations or apply the new knowledge to another subject.
- Turn it around by having students set a problem for the group or class to answer or providing students with 'the answer' and asking them to create a relevant problem.
- Have students complete an assessment task – for example, the pre-test administered again as a post-test, a summative assessment task and a performance or demonstration.

Lesson structure

Regardless of which instructional approach a lesson or series of lessons uses, an effective lesson almost invariably involves following a coherent structure, with a beginning, middle and end. The lesson structure is reflected in the lesson plan and the discrete sequence of events that comprise the lesson. It should be broadly consistent with recognised learning principles (as discussed in chapter 2). An effective lesson structure supports the achievement of learning outcomes, with connections to long-term instructional goals. While there can be no single lesson structure that is the 'best' in all contexts, it is important for teachers to consider the optimal sequence of lesson segments for learning to occur, with particular attention paid to time on task, lesson pacing and gradual release of responsibility.

Time on task: Time on task is the 'amount of time actually spent learning' and is distinct from allocated time – the total amount of time available for learning (Slavin 2003). There are clear links between the time students spend engaged with learning and their achievement (Doyle 1983; Slavin 2003). Time on task is about both quantity and quality of learning. It comprises interactive presentations and activities as well as more focused academic work involving instruction of a new concept or skill, working on tasks of an appropriate difficulty and independent practice to develop knowledge or expertise. Time on task is often contingent on good classroom management processes and engaging, interactive teaching. Time on task and time off task can be measured by observing, recording and analysing the frequency and duration of certain pre-determined student behaviours.

Pacing: Lesson pacing is the duration, timing, pace and overall flow of a lesson. Appropriate pacing reduces unengaged time and keeps students involved and on task. An appropriately paced lesson balances maximal time on task with considerations about student needs and learning capabilities and provides opportunities for students who progress at different rates. Teachers can effectively mediate a lesson's pace by checking how well students are receiving and understanding instruction and by responsively slowing down or speeding up the lesson segments or making changes to the task demands.

Gradual release of responsibility: This model provides a framework for lessons and learning activities and has been shown to be effective across different content areas and for a variety of student groups (Pearson and Gallagher 1983; Kong and Pearson 2003; Fisher and Frey 2007). It is especially relevant to teaching new concepts or information. The model, which uses the catchphrase 'I do, we do, you do', describes an instructional sequence moving from explicit demonstration or modelling to teacher-guided and collaborative student practice and independent student practice that promotes incremental learning.

Summary

Teaching processes that are effective in engaging students in meaningful learning and supporting improved student learning outcomes do not happen by chance or just because the teacher has a comprehensive knowledge of the relevant content. Effective teaching requires teachers to be constantly involved in key professional processes – planning, implementing teaching and learning that incorporates assessment and feedback, and evaluation and reflection. This cycle needs to happen iteratively, within a context in which teachers have insights into their own values, preferences and biases, as well as knowledge about their students' cultures and communities. The profession of teaching requires teachers to be lifelong learners and committed to inquiry and collaboration in order to improve their practice in response to evolving needs and new circumstances.

In a fast-changing society that has increasing quantities and qualities of knowledge and is constantly evolving modes of accessing information and demonstrating learning, the challenge for teachers to deliver effective, responsive teaching has never been greater. 'Future levels of educational attainment in Australia will be key determinants of individual, social and economic prosperity. For individual Australians, higher levels of education and training offer the possibility of escaping disadvantage, realising potential, securing meaningful work and achieving increased earnings' (BCA 2007, 8).

It could also be argued that the stakes are now higher – students who do not succeed at school, students who are failed by the educational system, have more limited options for future social and workforce participation. Accordingly, teaching that matters is an issue of equity: if we do not teach to engage and include all learners, if poor teaching fails to deliver for some, the excluded students become vulnerable and at risk of an uncertain future. Effective, responsive teaching delivered by professionals who are valued and supported holds promise for a more just and inclusive society: an exciting challenge indeed!

Further reading

Australian Education Union. 2006. 'AEU beginning teacher national survey results 2006.' Media release. AEU. 2 February. www.aeufederal.org.au/Publications/2006/Btsurvey06.html.

Australian Institute of Teaching and School Leadership. n.d. 'Australian professional standards for teachers.' AITSL. www.aitsl.edu.au/australian-professional-standards-for-teachers.

Bourke, R. and J. O'Neill. 2009. 'Professional development for ethical teaching.' *New Zealand Annual Review of Education*, no. 18: 107–22. Available at Victoria University. www. victoria. ac.nz/education/research/nzaroe/issues-index/2008/pdf/06text-bourke.pdf.

e-asTTle (Assessment Tools for Teaching and Learning) website: http://e-asttle.tki.org.nz/.

New Zealand Teachers Council website: www.teacherscouncil.govt.nz/.

Office of the Australian Information Commissioner. n.d. 'The Privacy Act.' Australian Government. www.oaic.gov.au/privacy/privacy-act/the-privacy-act.

Parliament of Australia. n.d. 'Privacy Amendment (Enhancing Privacy Protection) Bill 2012.' Parliament of Australia. www.aph.gov.au/Parliamentary_Business/Bills_Legislation/Bills _Search_Results/Result?bId=r4813.

Parliamentary Council Office. n.d. 'Privacy Act 1993.' New Zealand Government. www. legislation.govt.nz/act/public/1993/0028/latest/DLM296639.html.

Rosenshine, B. 2012. 'Principles of instruction: research-based strategies that all teachers should know.' *American Educator*, spring: 12–39. Available at Education Resources Information Center. http://files.eric.ed.gov/fulltext/EJ971753.pdf.

Tomlinson, C. 2011. 'Carol Tomlinson on differentiation: responsive teaching.' Workshop for teachers held at University of Virginia. QEP. Video published on YouTube, 5 October. www.youtube.com/watch?v=01798frimeQ.

References

ABS (Australian Bureau of Statistics). 2011. 'Australian social trends, March 2011: Year 12 attainment.' Catalogue no. 4102.0. ABS. www.abs.gov.au/AUSSTATS/abs@.nsf/Lookup/ 4102.0Main+Features40Mar+2011.

ACER (Australian Council for Educational Research). 2012. *National school improvement tool.* Melbourne: ACER.

AITSL (Australian Institute for Teaching and School Leadership). 2014. 'Disciplined collaboration in professional learning.' AITSIL. www.aitsl.edu.au/professional-growth/research/disciplined -collaboration-in-professional-learning.

Arief, G., D. Liem and A. Martin. 2013. 'Direct instruction.' In J. Hattie and E. M. Anderman, eds. *International guide to student achievement*, 366–8, Hoboken, NJ: Taylor & Francis.

BCA (Business Council of Australia). 2007. 'Restoring our edge in education: making Australia's education system its next competitive advantage.' Paper prepared by G. Masters, 7–24. BCA. August. Details and link to document. www.bca.com.au/publications/restoring-our -edge-in-education.

Beutel, D. 2003. 'Pedagogical concerns in the middle years of schooling.' *Australian Journal of Middle Schooling* 3 (1): 29–33.

Bourke, R. and J. O'Neill. 2009. 'Professional development for ethical teaching.' *New Zealand Annual Review of Education*, no. 18: 107–22. Available at Victoria University. www.victoria. ac.nz/education/research/nzaroe/issues-index/2008/pdf/06text-bourke.pdf.

Calderhead, J. and S. B. Shorrock. 2004. *Understanding teacher education: case studies in the professional development of beginning teachers.* London: Routledge.

Dalziel, K. 2009. 'Privacy in schools: a guide to the Privacy Act for principals, teachers and boards of trustees.' Privacy Commissioner. www.privacy.org.nz/assets/Files/Brochures -and-pamphlets-and-pubs/Privacy-in-Schools-September-2009.pdf.

Darling-Hammond, L. and J. Bransford. 2005. *Preparing teachers for a changing world: what teachers should learn and be able to do.* San Francisco, CA: Jossey-Bass.

Doyle, W. 1983. 'Academic work.' *Review of Educational Research* 53 (2): 159–99.

DuFour, R. 2004. 'What is a professional learning community?' *Educational Leadership* 61 (8): 6–11.

DuFour, R., R. DuFour and R. Eaker, eds. 2003. *On common ground: the power of professional learning communities.* Bloomington, IN: Solution Tree.

DuFour, R., R. DuFour, R. Eaker and G. Karhanek. 2009. *Whatever it takes: how professional learning communities respond when kids don't learn.* Moorabbin: Hawker Brownlow.

Education Counts. 2014. 'Filters.' New Zealand Government. www.educationcounts.govt.nz/ indicators.

Fisher, D. and N. Frey. 2007. 'Implementing a schoolwide literacy framework: improving achievement in an urban elementary school.' *The Reading Teacher* 61: 32–45.

Fullan, M. 2011. 'Learning is the work.' Unpublished paper.

Fullan, M., P. Hill and C. Crévola. 2006. *Breakthrough.* Thousand Oaks, CA: Corwin Press.

Goddard, Y., M. Goddard and M. Tschannen-Moran. 2007. 'A theoretical and empirical investigation of teacher collaboration for school improvement and student achievement in public elementary schools.' *Teachers' College Record* 109 (4): 877–96.

Grattan Institute. 2012. *Catching up: learning from the best school systems in East Asia*. Melbourne: Grattan Institute.

Hattie, J. 2003. *Teachers make a difference: what is the research evidence?* Melbourne: ACER.

——. 2005. 'The paradox of reducing class size and improving learning outcomes.' *International Journal of Educational Research* 43 (6): 387–425.

——. 2009. *Visible learning: a synthesis of 800+ meta-analyses on achievement*. London and New York: Routledge.

Hill, P. and C. Crévola. 2003. 'From a school based to a system based approach to balanced literacy.' Paper presented at Quest Conference. Toronto. 20–21 November.

Hobson, A. J., P. Ashby, A. Malderez and P. D. Tomlinson. 2009. 'Mentoring beginning teachers: what we know and what we don't.' *Teaching and Teacher Education* 25 (1): 207–16.

Kong, A. and P. D. Pearson. 2003. 'The road to participation: the construction of a literacy practice in a learning community of linguistically diverse learners.' *Research in the Teaching of English* 38 (1): 85–124.

Love, N. 2009. *Using data to improve learning for all: a collaborative inquiry approach*. Thousand Oaks, CA: Corwin Press.

Matters, G. 2007. 'Towards a national core curriculum for Year 12.' *Research Developments* 17 (17): 5.

Ministry of Education. 2012. 'Ministry of Education funded supports and services for learners with special education needs/disabilities.' New Zealand Government. April. http:// shapingeducation.govt.nz/wp-content/uploads/2012/09/SpecialEducationOverview.pdf.

Mizell, H. 1999. 'Thirty and counting.' Paper presented at the Middle Grades Education Conference. Atlanta, GA.

OAIC (Office of the Australian Information Commissioner). 2014. 'Australian privacy principles.' Privacy Fact Sheet 17. Australian Government. January. www.oaic.gov.au/images/ documents/privacy/privacy-resources/privacy-fact-sheets/privacy-fact-sheet-17-australian -privacy-principles_2.pdf.

Pearson, P. D. and Gallagher, M. C. 1983. 'The instruction of reading comprehension.' *Contemporary Educational Psychology* 8 (3): 317–44.

Purdie, N. and L. Ellis. 2005. 'Literature review: a review of the empirical evidence identifying effective interventions and teaching practices for students with learning difficulties in Year 4, 5 and 6.' ACER. February. http://research.acer.edu.au/cgi/viewcontent.cgi?article =1006&context=tll_misc.

Richmond, C. 2007. *Teach more, manage less: a minimalist approach to behaviour management*. Gosford: Scholastic.

Sanders, W. L. and J. C. Rivers. 1996. *Cumulative and residual effects of teachers on future student academic achievement*. Knoxville, TN: University of Tennessee Value-Added Research and Assessment Center.

Shulman, L. S. 1986. 'Those who understand: knowledge growth in teaching.' *Educational Researcher* 15 (2): 4–14.

——. 1987. 'Knowledge and teaching: foundations of the new reform.' *Harvard Educational Review* 57 (1): 1–23.

Slavin, R. 2003. *Educational psychology: theory and practice*. Boston, MA: Pearson Education.

Strain, P. S. and M. Hoyson. 2000. 'The need for longitudinal, intensive social skill intervention LEAP follow-up outcomes for children with autism.' *Topics in Early Childhood Special Education* 20 (2): 116–22.

Westwood, P. 1993. 'Striving for positive outcomes for students with learning difficulties.' *Special Education Perspectives* 2 (2): 87–94.

——. 2004. 'Effective teaching to reduce educational failure.' *Australian Journal of Learning Disabilities* 3 (3): 4–12.

——. 2013. *Inclusive and adaptive teaching*. Oxford: Routledge.

Chapter 4

Influences on learning

Intended learning outcomes

Engagement with the text in this chapter will enable readers to do the following:

- understand the kinds of ecological factors (social, structural, political, economic, cultural, community, family and school) that influence learning and provide specific examples of these

- reflect on the nature of physical, cognitive, intrapersonal, interpersonal and cultural diversity and compare the types of developmental differences that can occur between learners

- analyse how specific aspects of development support and hinder learning

Big ideas

- Each learner brings a complex combination of abilities, strengths and potential to the school setting, embedded within particular cultural, linguistic, emotional, spiritual and familial contexts. Many factors can support or hinder learning. Influences on student learning can be found both within and outside the individual learner.

- Each educational setting and classroom creates its own context and operates using a set of embedded expectations. Effective teachers understand and manage classroom diversity to create equitable learning opportunities for all students.

- All learners can experience periods of learning difficulty due to different developmental rates, health, home resources, family (*whānau*) stressors and relationships as well as mismatches between teaching and learning needs. These influence the key learning processes, which can be summed up in the acronym **ATRiUM**.

> **ATRiUM** Active learning; Thinking; Relating to others; Using language, symbols and ICT; and Managing self.

- Students experiencing significant difficulties in learning and behaviour in the classroom may have complex disabilities or learning difficulties. Specific impairments (for example, auditory, visual, physical or intellectual, or those brought about through chronic illness or brain injury) generate the need for particular long-term adaptations to allow equity of access to learning opportunities.

- Teachers and families (*whānau*) need to develop a shared understanding of each learner's strengths and learning needs without creating limitations or barriers to learning based on labels, language or assumptions. Teachers must make sense of what supports and what hinders learning for individual learners in order to effectively personalise teaching and differentiate instruction for their students.

Introduction

There are many factors that support learning and others that hinder learning. In the past, teachers mostly looked 'inside' the learner and attributed teaching and learning success or otherwise to the learner's inherent nature – their intelligence, character, motivation and ability. In general, teachers now hold more sophisticated views of what is required for successful learning and not only take into account what is inherent in individual learners but give due consideration to the relationship between learners and their learning environments and to how such environments provide appropriate learning opportunities. Learning can be conceptualised as the outcome of the match between learners, teachers and the environments in which learning occurs.

Each educational setting and individual classroom creates a cultural, linguistic, emotional and spiritual context with its own embedded expectations. A classroom of learners contains inherent diversity in which relative ability levels, learning skills and emotional, behavioural and social capabilities exist. There will be levels that are considered 'giftedness' – ability to use higher-level thinking, superior sporting proficiency, musical skills and leadership talent. There will also be levels that are considered 'disabling' with respect to learning in the classroom. Effective teachers understand and manage their classrooms' diversity to create equitable learning opportunities for all students.

Holistic and ecological views of learning

Explicit acknowledgment of human wholeness is a feature of Māori wellbeing models such as 'Te whare tapa wha' (Durie 1998) and 'Te wheke' (Pere 1997), and of the Aboriginal model 'The dance of life' (RANZCP, n.d.; see figure 4.1). Durie (1998) depicts wellbeing as a meeting house (*whare*) and stresses the need for all four of its walls to be in good order for it to remain standing. The walls represent physical health (*te taha tinana*), spiritual health (*te taha wairua*), psychological health (*te taha hinengaro*) and family health (*te taha whānau*).

Pere's (1997) model is presented as the image of an octopus (*wheke*). The head represents the child and family (*whānau*), and each tentacle symbolises a dimension that is needed to support the whole. The tentacles cross over and merge, blurring the distinctions between themselves at times. They need to be understood in relation to each other and to the whole. They stand for the physical body (*taha tinana*), emotions (*whatu manawa*), mind or intellect (*hinengaro*), extended family relationships (*whanaungatanga*), spirituality (*wairuatanga*), one's uniqueness (*mana ake*), the life principle (*mauri*) and the breath of life from ancestors (*ha a kore mā a kui mā*).

'The dance of life', the third model presented, also stresses the need for the health of multiple dimensions and for a balance between physical, social, spiritual, psychological and cultural aspects of living. 'The dance of life' is an Aboriginal metaphor for mental health. It acknowledges the many dimensions of human functioning as well as the delicate balance of these as they work together throughout the journey of life. (For a full explanation of 'The dance of life', see RANZCP, n.d.)

The indigenous models emphasise the complexity that students bring to their learning. Each student in a classroom is a physical being, a family (*whānau*) and wider community member and part of a culture that has a history, as well as being an emotional, spiritual and intellectual being. Each learner brings life experiences to school that have affected the development of their engagement with learning.

It is interesting that 'Te whare tapa wha' and 'The dance of life' have both been generated as part of attempts to understand mental wellbeing. They demonstrate that psychological health depends on all aspects of a person's life. Any assessment of wellbeing and intervention must take a broad view of the individual, including their family (*whānau*).

Figure 4.1: *Holistic models of human wellbeing: 'Te whare tapa wha', 'Te wheke' and 'The dance of life'*

Source: Developed from Durie 1998; Pere 1997; RANZCP, n.d. (See the final source cited for Helen Milroy's original 'The dance of life' artwork.)

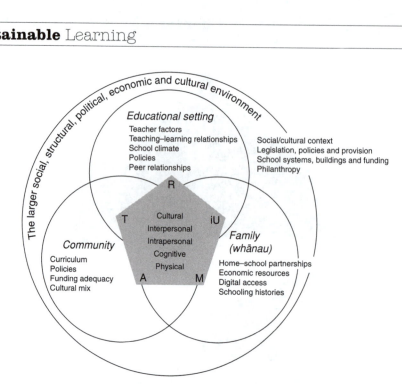

Figure 4.2: *An ecological and holistic view of learning, extended*

This **holistic perspective** is important for understanding what supports and hinders learning. It is not enough to look at academic performance alone or to assume that achievement levels are simply the direct result of the learner's abilities and motivations. Instead, it is necessary to consider all the holistic – and the ecological – factors. Figure 4.2, first introduced in a simplified form in chapter 1, shows how learning as characterised as the development of ATRiUM capabilities is influenced by elements of the many layers of students' lives, within family (*whānau*) and community. As they mature, children become part of formal educational settings, including schools, which function within the broader social, political, economic, structural and cultural environments that provide resources, define the curriculum and the cultural expectations of the educational setting and set up conditions for teaching and learning interactions. Context affects the engagement and functioning of both learners and teachers. For example, 'Te aho matua' (a set of principles used in Kura Kaupapa Māori, schools for Māori children who are taught in the people's language, Māori Te Reo) guides teachers to acknowledge that being part of humankind is fundamental to establishing the nature of teacher–student interactions that nurture and develop children's total wellbeing (*wairua*).

The holistic and ecological human functioning models derived from thousands of years of culture in Australia and New Zealand that are shown in figure 4.1 are also reflected in the work of more recent western sociocultural learning theorists like Vygotsky, writing in Russia in the early 20th century, and proponents of the more recent **dynamic systems theory** of development (Smith and Thelen 2003). These theories purport that humans function holistically and must be considered within their historical, cultural and social contexts in order to gain an understanding of the factors that may support and hinder learning. Although teachers and other professionals (physicians, psychologists, occupational therapists, speech pathologists and physiotherapists) separate and focus on distinct aspects of learning at times, teachers need constantly to consider students and their learning profiles holistically within historical, cultural contexts.

The term **complex constructionist ecology**, coined by Claiborne and Drewery (2010), emphasises key influences that teachers need to keep in mind when trying to understand learning from the perspective of each student. Claiborne and Drewery suggest that every classroom is a complex constructed context within which students function across time within relationships that can be continuing (as in family, or *whānau*), somewhat less permanent or transient. In turn, classrooms are embedded within the broader systems of the school, community (*marae*), educational jurisdiction and political system.

> **Complex constructionist ecology** involves combined interacting influences shaping the quality of learning outcomes.

Think and do 4.1: Understanding learning

1   Research two or more of the theoretical frameworks mentioned in this section and compare and contrast their explanations of learning.

2   Draw up the ecological framework as in figure 4.2 and note your thoughts about what factors affected your own learning at school. Then do the same for someone else you know or for a child in your class.

Sustainable learning means that both students and teachers are active learners who develop and apply processes of thinking, relating to others and using language, symbols and ICT and who manage themselves in order to participate in and contribute to their environments. Factors that affect these processes can be found within learners, but as figure 4.1 depicts, this is only part of the picture. Factors that support and hinder learning can also be found within teachers, teaching–learning relationships, the curriculum, physical environments, relationships in the classroom, school policies and procedures, home–school partnerships, families, wider communities and educational systems.

Influences outside learners

All educational settings are affected by the politics, legislation, policies and provisions of the wider context. For example, economics affects schools profoundly, and debate around financial provisions for schools seems perpetual. While some schools proudly display well-maintained, functionally updated heritage buildings along with modern sporting and cultural facilities, less well off schools function in minimally appropriate buildings with few resources. A proportion of this difference is dependent on the philanthropy of past students and their wealth and commitment to their schools. Inevitably, those who enjoy and benefit from school will contribute in the future, while less successful and less wealthy people will not be able to give and often do not want to have anything to do with school once they have left. Educational inequity is expanded through this type of contribution to schools over generations.

Structural factors related to schools include the school buildings and grounds and the community connections within which the school functions. Contemporary education at some levels is becoming less bound by structural constraints, particularly as online education is taken up in force by many learners. In addition, distance learning has a long history in Australia, with correspondence schooling and Schools of the Air part of the educational landscape since the 1950s.

As curricula (that is, everything that is taught in schools) are written under the auspices of the government of the time, they reflect a mainstream perspective that can be controversial, because they are selected in terms of what the government in power considers important in the world and what it sees as essential for developing young people to engage with and learn. For example, in January 2014, the federal Australian government, led by Tony Abbott, ordered a review of the development of the Australian curriculum before it would continue with its implementation. Australia has a history of different curricula across the states and territories and in 2014 was in the process of negotiating a homogeneous national curriculum. New Zealand, as a bicultural country, follows a national curriculum as well as 'Te aho matua'.

The matching of the curriculum to the learner can affect learning, and a number of unintended and negative outcomes for young people can be related to a mismatch between culture and curriculum. School attendance, suspension and exclusion rates among Aboriginal and Māori students, for example, are well out of proportion compared to those of the rest of the school population (Education Counts 2013a, 2013b; Department of Education and Communities 2013; CESE 2012).

It is impossible to meaningfully consider children's development outside the context of their families (*whānau*); the two are totally interrelated. This is why family–school partnerships are so vital. Teachers often do not get to see inside the family but may make assumptions and judgments about factors that affect engagement and learning. All such assumptions need to be checked carefully and negotiated respectfully. Some families choose not to send their children to schools, instead providing education at home, within the family. In these cases, the family context becomes the schooling context.

Much has been written about the impact of a mismatch between the culture of an educational setting and the learners' cultural contexts. Related to this, the correlation between social wellbeing and background and educational achievement is well established. Belonging to particular cultural groups is strongly connected with students' achievement levels; this is illustrated most significantly in involuntary minority groups such as Indigenous peoples (see, for example, ABS 2011). As measured by the 2012 Programme for International Student Assessment, the impact of social background on the academic performance of 15 year olds in both New Zealand and Australia, except for immigrant students, is greater than the average across 41 countries (OECD 2012). This means that social background makes a bigger difference in Australia and New Zealand than in many other countries around the world.

Where there is conflict or tension between the learner's cultural context and that espoused by the school, there is likely to be less than optimum learning. One way of understanding this situation is through considering that perhaps some disaffected and discouraged learners have encountered a **forced-choice dilemma** (Gross 1989) that required them to choose between success in school or belonging to their cultural group. The effect of this contextual dilemma was first recognised by researchers in the gifted education field who found that gifted children from minority groups tended to choose to belong culturally rather than to achieve academically. Chaffey (2008, 2009) highlights such 'invisible underachievement' by Aboriginal children.

> A **forced-choice dilemma** is the feeling that many gifted children have that they must choose between social acceptance and academic achievement.

Learning can also be influenced by what the teacher brings to the classroom. Each teacher is a unique individual with an identity, particular cultural competence, life experiences, beliefs about teaching and learning, interpersonal skills and relationships, different degrees of self-awareness, levels of flexibility and developing professional skills and knowledge. All of these contribute to the success (or not) of classroom teaching and learning. For example, cultural competence has been highlighted as significant in situations in which the school and classroom have learners who are from minority cultural groups, in particular from involuntary minority groups such as Indigenous peoples (Gay 2010; McAllister and Irvine 2000). Many of the reasons that students have particular learning needs are not in any way under their teachers' control: they are complex issues related to society, families, homes and communities which can significantly affect learning. Teachers, however, need to work closely with families and with their professional colleagues to do whatever they can to compensate for difficulties and accommodate all learners, so that their classroom teaching has the greatest possible impact.

Each educational setting creates a unique cultural, linguistic, emotional and spiritual context with embedded expectations. Some of these are explicit, while others are implicit and known only to those who have a shared cultural knowledge. The social organisation of many learners into classrooms results in inherent diversity. Effective teachers understand and manage this diversity to create equitable learning opportunities for all students. Effective teachers know their strengths and weaknesses and what they bring to classroom interactions before trying to make sense of what their students bring and how these personal and professional factors match. (See chapters 6 and 7 for more on factors related to effective teaching.)

Reflection 4.1 shows how the first documented experience in special education looked at both the student's inherent capabilities and the teaching that might make a difference for them. Although much work in developmental and educational psychology is based on medical models that consider differences to be situated

Reflection 4.1: Education for students with disabilities

The first documented attempt to make up for a student's significant missed learning opportunities was Itard's work with Victor of Aveyron, an abandoned child who lived alone in the French countryside until 11 or 12 years of age. Itard, a medical doctor, wanted to 'experiment' with instructional practices to see what Victor could be taught. Itard's (1802, 18) comments on society's perception of his pupil resonate poignantly with us today in terms of inclusive education: 'They saw him, without properly observing him; they passed their judgment on him, without knowing him'. Instead of assuming that Victor had no potential to learn, Itard began teaching him with the aim to 'attach him to social life' (35), acknowledging that the basis of much learning is social and takes place within the broad context of 'society'.

within individuals and emphasise what behaviours differ from the 'norm', the contemporary perspective on disability is much more sociocultural in nature. It gives due emphasis to the vital cultural and social dimensions of students' contexts and how these affect learning. In line with this view, people with a disability are not 'objects' requiring 'charity, medical treatment and social protection' but '"subjects" with rights', who are able to make decisions for themselves based on free and informed consent and are actively engaged members of society (UN 2007; Chopra 2013).

> An **impairment** is any loss or abnormality of physical, cognitive, sensory or emotional function.

Impairment is a medical condition that leads to disability, while disability is the result of the interaction between the experience of what it is like to live with impairment and barriers in the physical, attitudinal, communication and social environments. For example, it may not be the inability to walk that keeps a person from entering a building but the barrier presented by a set of inaccessible stairs. In the same way, it may not be difficulty with writing, spelling or remembering that prevents some learners from achieving educationally but insufficient practice, tasks that are too difficult, fear of negative comparison with peers or unclear instruction.

Although it is often attempted, it is not possible to simply classify learners and place them in discrete categories for which particular types of teaching are appropriate. Learners are far more complex than that, displaying a combination of competencies which change in response to situations over time. Some of the largest changes in humans occur during their school years and need to be taken into account by educational systems and teachers.

Developmental differences imply changes in both ATRiUM capabilities and their underlying bases, in physical and cognitive development, interpersonal and intrapersonal skills and cultural understanding (see figure 4.3). These differences in development and functioning, and how they affect ATRiUM capabilities, need to be well understood by teachers. Learners also need to understand their own capabilities and to learn how to manage them.

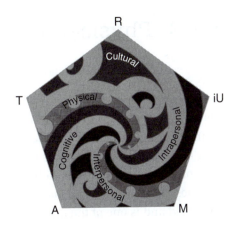

Figure 4.3: *Foundations of sustainable learning*

Physical dimensions

Physical growth and development can affect learning in many ways. Curriculum documents expect children to develop their physical skills and coordination in a particular pattern. On entry to school in Australia and New Zealand, students are anticipated to be physically capable of writing letters (usually to form their name), sitting in a chair of the typical size, carrying a bag, unwrapping their lunch, speaking nearly all sounds clearly, running, jumping, hopping, climbing and managing personal space. Patterns of physical difference between children, however, can flag the possibility of conditions related to differences in learning success. For example, 'failure to thrive' in a baby is an early indicator of developmental difference. If students' bodies are not growing as expected, it may be that their brains are also not developing as expected, which can hinder cognitive as well as social and emotional development.

The development of motor skills is related to learning success and opportunities. In young children, the skills of walking, running, hopping, skipping, climbing, hitting, kicking, grasping, holding and drawing are readily observable indicators of their development rate. These skills have been plotted against age levels to develop reputable trajectories with which individuals' performance can be compared. The roles of experience and opportunity to learn are important in the development of physical skills. Many of the tasks used to describe developmental milestones are bound by the culture within which they are assessed. Being able to ride a pushbike, for example, is a skill that depends on the opportunity to learn to do so.

Many generations of children have had their physical development compared to typical growth patterns. The measurements gathered by health professionals show that children's typical development rate and pattern have altered. It is well known, for example, that children today are larger than children of previous generations, and considered judgment is required about whether a developmental deviation is significant.

Think and do 4.2: Physical development

Research typical and atypical physical growth and development ranges online. What implications might there be at school for students who have differences in physical growth or development from other children of the same age?

Sensory development is an aspect of physical functioning that is closely related to learning success. Students smell, taste, touch, hear and see as they actively participate in school learning. Not being able to see or hear what is happening in the classroom can have a profound impact on learning and needs to be taken into account when planning learning opportunities. Whether a child has hearing and vision within normal limits is easily determined and is one of the first things to check when a child begins to show learning difficulties.

The need for physical activity during the school day to support cognitive activity in the classroom is advocated by many educators (for example, Sibley and Etnier 2003). Physical exercise has also been demonstrated to be important for the management and prevention of depressive conditions (Sallis, Prochaska and Taylor 2000). Once children enter a formal educational setting, aspects of physical development can become artificially separated from learning in the classroom, as students are required to sit and learn, individually and in groups, in an ordered way. Physical skills become more sophisticated as students mature and are interrelated with the development of skills for learning, such as being able to write letters of an increasingly small size and with growing fluency. Visual motor integration is the process through which vision, perception and motor skills combine to allow students to achieve the sophisticated tasks of drawing and writing. Slower rates of visual motor skills development are often early indicators of later learning difficulties, with some children needing more structured teaching and practice to develop proficiency.

Physical health is also a key factor that affects both students and teachers at school. A short bout of acute illness may mean missing a few days of school, but longer bouts of illness or chronic conditions mean school life is significantly interrupted. Indigenous peoples' health issues need to be considered, as some Indigenous children have an increased likelihood of contracting rheumatic fever or glue ear (Gracey and King 2009). In fact, a healthy childhood can become a major support for future learning. Poverty, with concomitant issues of not enough food, unhealthy housing and inadequate health care, impacts on how well students flourish at school.

Physical safety can affect children's learning. Risks to physical development from accident and assault are present across all socioeconomic strata before children are born, when they are growing as babies and young children and later in life.

Cognitive dimensions

Cognition is thinking or intellectual functioning. It is both developmental and responsive to teaching. Cognitive capacity, or 'intelligence', is not a fixed capacity for life; instead, educational researchers and neuroscientists have established that the brain continues developing until early adulthood and undergoes changes throughout life as individuals learn, experience and mature (Blakemore and Choudhury 2006; Geake 2009).

Cognitive development has been an area of significant controversy, largely due to the misuse of 'intelligence' tests. What was really being measured by early tests such as the Binet-Simon scale, developed by Alfred Binet and Theodore Simon in 1905, was the likelihood of success at school. Such tests have been erroneously used to support views that some people are superior to others. Many early intelligence tests were heavily laden with the assessment of learning products that were dependent on previous access to opportunities to learn. More recent tests focus on intelligence processes rather than learning products. It is important, however, to recognise that the social, emotional and spiritual aspects of individual functioning affect cognition, and although we can focus on cognition processes these can never be separated entirely from other aspects of human functioning. Cognitive psychology – that is, the work of those interested in cognition and intellectual functioning – helps us to make sense of learning. A useful way to think about learning and the factors that support or hinder it is to look through the lens of the information processing learning theory, introduced in chapter 2. The discussion below builds on that chapter's content.

Metaphorically speaking, our brains are information processors like computers. First, and very importantly, we must pay attention to particular input. After that, we take in information, we process it, and we produce output (a description that simplifies a very complex process). The first phase of taking in information concerns the operation and direction of the senses through the focusing of attention. Our brains' attention to sensory information and translation of that information into perceptions – and into meaning – are the beginnings of cognition. Cognition then involves different types of processing, which are supported by different forms of memory. Evidence of thinking is produced through different output products, or mechanisms, which may be verbal or non-verbal.

Other cognition and learning theories can be considered alongside this simple way of thinking about how humans function, but the idea of information processing is a useful view of the mechanisms underlying learning. In short, efficient sensory organs (particularly hearing and vision), attention skills, perceptual processes, **receptive language**, understanding, memory, processing, planning, executive functioning and expression all support effective cognition and the demonstration of that cognition. There can be problems with any of these processes, which can hinder learning. While reading the following paragraphs, consider how either proficiency or difficulties with any of the processes described could influence students' learning.

> **Receptive language** is the ability to understand or comprehend language heard or read.

Learning environments are busy and complex. There is an overwhelming amount of information available to us at all times through mobile technology. Effective learners have developed skills in filtering out information and stimuli that are not directly relevant to the task at hand so they can focus on what is important and useful. This can range from dealing with the multitude of links on a webpage to concentrating on one question on a page of 20. Such skills are crucial for efficient learners.

Some learners have difficulty giving the right amount of sustained attention to a learning activity and instead focus on anything that presents itself. A pervasive and significant level of this tendency to pay attention to just about everything can mirror the criteria used to diagnose ADHD. Rather than these students having an attention deficit, however, they in fact have an over-attentive mind. Such students pay attention to everything without discrimination and find it very difficult to sort out and focus on things that are relevant.

Seeing and hearing differently can also affect learning. When we hear or see something, our brain converts the signals into perceptions that, through experience and teaching, we match to words and ideas. Colour blindness is also a perception issue that may be very relevant for some learners. It is a genetic variation linked to a recessive gene that is most commonly passed on to sons by their mothers. It is determined by self-report, which becomes problematic for some children, who have only ever seen their world this way. In practical terms, it means that teachers have to be careful about the use of information colour coding. Some students cannot discriminate between different colours, with red–green colour blindness most common. Such a perceptual difficulty is also associated with rare visual dyslexia, which can become more complicated by psychological factors usually associated with failure at school. In such cases it can be nearly impossible to determine what is physiological, what is psychological and what is the result of an inadequate opportunity to develop age-appropriate skills.

Reflection 4.2: Perception and learning

Our perception is extremely powerful. Consider, for example, the experience of a new resident in New Zealand, where there are no snakes. Driving home one day this person is certain she can see a snake on the side of the road. Although it is not a snake, the new resident interprets the item's shape and position in meaningful ways based on her previous experiences. A mixture of physiological and psychological functioning takes in the visual information and makes 'sense' of it.

Our world is alive with complicated sounds, the most sophisticated of which is speech – one of the vital tools for sociocultural functioning and classroom learning. Over time, listeners develop skills in putting together bits of speech, because they do not always catch everything everyone says. This is accomplished through the psychological processes that help us make sense of language based on who is speaking, what the topic is, what the context is and what we know about how language fits together. We also use our phonemic awareness skills to help us hear, remember and interpret the sounds that make up words. We can often join the dots of incomplete speech in this way, which helps us deal with pairs of speech sounds that 'look' identical except for them being either voiced or voiceless.

Think and do 4.3: Phonemic awareness

Video yourself saying these words, with a slight gap between each pair. Then replay it with the volume off and see if you can see any difference within the pairs.

- fat – vat
- leave – leaf
- big – pig
- good – could

- Ms – Miss
- chin – gin
- doll – toll

If someone is talking with you about their *leave*, you have to decide from the rest of the conversation whether it is *leave* or *leaf*. If there is no context, it is often impossible to perceive what is intended.

Phonemic awareness is the ability to hear, identify and manipulate the smallest units of sound that are meaningful. It is displayed through accurate rhyming, being able to break words into their component sounds (for example, 'cat' has three separate phonemes: 'k', 'æ' and 't') and manipulating sounds in words (for example, saying 'beach' without the 'b'). Phonemic awareness is a key skill underlying reading achievement and, for those students who struggle, reading difficulties. Hearing problems and frequent ear infections can affect the development of phonemic awareness.

Interpreting the cultural tool of language requires a particular type of learnt perception termed 'receptive language'. Proficiency with receptive language becomes increasingly important as learners progress through their formal schooling. Developmental trajectories related to receptive language have been well documented, with early milestones marked by children's responses to language prior to their development of any expressive language. By the time students start school, at five years of age, it is expected that they will be able to respond to the verbal instructions used in classrooms and will have a bank of basic language concepts that will support their early reading and mathematical learning. Facility with receptive language underpins successful communication skills and supports students' effectiveness and efficiency in learning. Alternatively, difficulty with these skills, such as that experienced by students with aphasia (severe difficulty understanding and/or producing language), can become an early barrier to learning that may persist.

Proficiency with memory skills correlates with learning achievement for many students. Students with disabilities or learning difficulties and those experiencing mental illness often have memory difficulties and need to deliberately learn strategies (such as rehearsal and visualisation) to improve their retention of important information so they can recall and process it. Many people have developed unique ways of remembering everything they need in life, from using shopping lists to updating the contacts list in their phones.

In the educational psychology literature, over time there has emerged an increasing number of models that aim to explain cognitive processing. Initially, such models tended to be static, with 'intelligence' thought to be finite and fixed. Now, intelligence is often conceptualised as fluid, practical, multifaceted, emotional and related to wisdom and creativity (Sternberg 2010). In Sternberg's successful intelligence model, thinking is considered in terms of knowledge that is applied practically and creatively, and with wisdom. Such models aim to assist in understanding the sophistication and complexity of thinking and how it is used in learning and in life.

Processing and reasoning relate to the action of fluid intellectual abilities: those that are flexible, adaptable and responsive to opportunities to learn. In general, contemporary views of intelligence (for example, Naglieri and Das's [1997] conception of the cognitive variables of planning, attention and simultaneous and successive processing) consider intelligent functioning to be the result of a complex interaction of processes, which, importantly, can be developed and are responsive to teaching. Models like this provide ways of looking at thinking that involve the processing of and reasoning about ideas, concepts, facts and patterns.

Although school education may have been set up originally to transmit knowledge – to impart facts and ensure students were able to retrieve them – contemporary curricula focus on the development of thinking skills throughout schooling. Teaching aims to be transformative, to develop high thinking levels. For example, thinking is not just the retrieval of factual knowledge. In Bloom's revised taxonomy, thinking is also understanding, applying, analysing, evaluating and creating conceptual, procedural and metacognitive knowledge (Krathwohl 2002). Thinking skills underpin the capabilities signified by ATRiUM. It is impossible to consider any area of human functioning without taking into account what sort of thinking is involved.

Cognitive education and cognitive interventions are based on the same fundamental idea, that teaching can alter thinking or cognition so that individuals can learn to think more effectively and efficiently. For example, research into the learning challenges faced by students who have disabilities or learning difficulties like ADHD or any form of ASD has confirmed the vital role in enhancing learning of teaching students cognitive planning and executive functioning skills (for example, planning, organising, regulating attention and prioritising).

> **Cognitive education** is based on the tenet that everyone can improve their cognitive skills through education.

The complex processes of human thinking have been increasingly analysed in terms of a hierarchy of processes that build up to **higher-order thinking** – the kind of thinking that teachers aim to foster. A useful model of the nature of thinking in classroom learning and assessment activities is Collis and Biggs' (1986) SOLO taxonomy (see also chapter 2). Many teachers find this model helpful in assessing learning from student products such as essays or explanations (the purpose for which the model was developed) and in setting learning tasks. SOLO provides a reliable framework that can be used to adapt tasks and differentiate instruction (see also chapter 7). The model proposes that thinking in any new learning domain begins with the learner grasping one aspect of the new knowledge, followed by multiple aspects. These two

> **Higher-order thinking** involves learning complex judgmental skills such as problem-solving and critical thought.

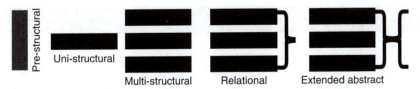

Figure 4.4: *The Structure of the Observed Learning Outcome taxonomy*
Source: Adapted from Collis and Biggs 1982.

steps of gathering information are the quantitative building of knowledge in a particular domain. This is the knowledge limit that is investigated by many assessment tools. However, in order for students to move to higher-order thinking rather than just gathering facts, they need to progress to the next SOLO levels, which mark the qualitative development of knowing, understanding, reasoning and making sense of knowledge.

Figure 4.4 depicts the four steps in this thinking model, as well as the prior step – that is, before thinking is activated in a certain domain. SOLO's stages – pre-structural, uni-structural, multi-structural, relational and extended abstract (Collis and Biggs 1986) – can be mapped over any academic or everyday learning domain, including any area of the school curriculum. Students will come to any new topic with a range of current thinking levels. Teachers need to determine what the students know, what they need to learn and how they can assist them achieve their optimum learning outcomes. In some lessons, teachers might aim for quantitative knowledge development, while in others they may want to focus on qualitative thinking and higher-order skills.

Interpersonal dimensions

As people mature they usually develop tools that support positive interpersonal interactions. By learning the nuances of cultural and social settings, individuals become expert at understanding the verbal and non-verbal languages that allow them to learn together and alone and to share learning and thinking in classroom contexts. Interpersonal skills development takes time, is influenced by the culture of the learning environment and is mediated by others in that environment. Young children gradually learn their home language in response to modelling and explicit teaching by more competent family (*whānau*) members. For example, it is typical for family members to accept different language levels from different children depending on their development level and what is known about their skills. We accept approximations for words and phrases from three year olds and then we model the correct words and phrases in our responses. Parents and carers are teaching in every such interaction. They teach manners (*tikanga*) all the time and model the respect (*mana*) that is key to the broader development of moral and ethical behaviour.

Classrooms and schools have particular interpersonal interactions and social expectations (such as turn-taking, cooperative group work and respectful

Reflection 4.3: Understanding the SOLO taxonomy

The SOLO taxonomy's usefulness can be illustrated through relating it to learning to drive. When considered in these terms, it becomes clear that driving requires a complex set of knowledge and skills. These must be orchestrated relationally and eventually developed further, into the realm of extended abstract activities, so drivers can manage any hazardous situations that arise.

Driving requires, for example, turning the engine on and keeping it running until it needs to be turned off; keeping the car on the road, within the lane; using a foot to apply pressure to the accelerator, the brake and in manual cars coordinating the clutch; manipulating the gear stick, not just when starting the engine but during driving; watching for road signs and lights as well as other hazards, and other vehicles that can be any size or shape; and keeping within appropriate speeds – not too fast, not too slow. Once the driver's decision-making has connected to the appropriate sound of the car's engine and a sense of speed, and when the driver is familiar with a particular journey, they can eventually drive 'without thinking', or automatically. Learning has resulted in automaticity in this domain, which is essential for continued safe driving. If we think of learning to drive with regard to the SOLO categories, it breaks down as shown below:

Pre-structural thinking about driving is like a young child's view that you simply put the key in and the car goes.

Uni-structural thinking is, for example, knowledge that steering keeps the car on the road.

Multi-structural thinking is the accumulation of the multiple ideas already expressed in this list.

Relational thinking is forming connections between all the dimensions of driving a car.

Extended-abstract thinking is being able to drive the car on the road with other traffic and respond appropriately to the many signals in the environment, expected and unexpected, in order to keep everyone safe.

In addition to the thinking involved in learning to drive, there is also often an emotional layer of learning that significantly affects progress and success. Fear, anxiety and parents' or carers' need of control as they teach their children to drive cannot be removed from the situation. This often influences the effectiveness of parents or carers as driving teachers and can result in them choosing not to teach their own children to drive or children seeking instruction elsewhere.

communication) that support effective social group functioning and learning. Inappropriate social interactions in classrooms can severely hinder teaching and learning. In fact, in many classrooms much teacher time is spent managing the social situation rather than teaching. Effective, responsive teachers know how to organise a classroom and set clear expectations for the types of social interactions that support learning. Richmond's (2007) balance model of behaviour management, for example, presents a preventative approach through equalising teachers' use of language between acknowledging and correcting students' behaviour.

In schools and classrooms much effort goes into establishing procedures for managing student behaviour that does not meet the expectations of the setting. Principals and leadership teams in recent times, however, have accepted that part of the reason for behavioural problems may reside in school systems and processes themselves. As a result, whole-school programs such as Positive Behaviour for Learning have become increasingly popular. These have been complemented by approaches within the community to strengthen parenting skills (for example, The Incredible Years Parents, Teachers, and Children Training Series and the Triple P – Positive Parenting Program).

Individual student behaviour is dependent on many factors, not just the effectiveness of teachers' classroom management. It can also be affected by the match between student-learning needs and opportunities for learning, the 'fit' between the school and the cultural dimensions of students' homes, students' emotional functioning and levels of resilience, motivation and relationship skills. Relating to others, for example, is relevant to relationships at different levels in classrooms. Firstly, the relationships between learners and their teachers are crucial to learning. Secondly, teachers need to work productively with other teachers, professionals and support staff to create learning in inclusive classrooms. Thirdly, relationships between the students themselves impact significantly on teaching and learning effectiveness in a classroom, and particularly on collaborative and cooperative **learning strategies**. In contemporary inclusive classrooms, learning is most effective when students *and* collaborative teacher groups can function together as a community of learners.

> **Learning strategies** are used by students to help them understand information and solve problems.

Intrapersonal dimensions

Because classrooms aim to systematically teach cognitive skills, less explicit emphasis is usually placed on other dimensions of individual functioning – in particular, the emotional functioning that is actually inherent in every activity. Thinking and feeling go together, affect one another and need to be considered together. Furthermore, thinking and emotions are connected to behaviour in a manner that is recognised as very powerful. For example, an intervention for anxiety and depression, cognitive behaviour therapy (see Graham and Reynolds 2013; Meichenbaum 1977), makes a difference through focusing on both behaviour and thinking to make changes in how individuals experience the world. Similarly, effective teachers now include consideration of emotional climate in their classroom practice (Evans et al. 2009).

Seligman's (2011) work in developing the field of positive psychology has provided a model that integrates academic achievement with important aspects of human wellbeing. Seligman identifies five aspects – positive emotions, engagement, positive relationships, meaning, and accomplishment – that underpin successful learning and are compatible with the tripartite notion of sustainable learning as learning for all (positive emotions), teaching that matters (positive relationships and accomplishment) and learning that lasts (engagement and meaning). Learning and wellbeing are obviously interrelated, and this fact is increasingly recognised in schools.

The indigenous development models (for example, Mark and Lyons 2010) presented earlier in this chapter share a focus on wellbeing, as do pastoral care and mental health programs like MindMatters and KidsMatter.

Think and do 4.4: Psychology and motivation

Compare Seligman's (2011) aspects of human wellbeing with Maslow's (1954) hierarchy of needs (described in chapter 6). How do these two conceptualisations fit together? Can you construct a model that accommodates both sets of ideas?

Differences in emotional development are part of many disabilities and learning difficulties. For example, students who have profiles that position them on the autism spectrum often have difficulty understanding other people's perspectives, putting themselves 'in their shoes' and acting empathetically. Neuroscientific research evidence about the existence and action of mirror neurons may help explain these differences (see chapter 2).

The previously simplistic 'nature versus nurture' debate is now considered in terms of the interaction between genetic makeup (the unpacking of nature) and environmental conditions (nurture) that switches on or switches off particular genes. Increasingly, as mentioned earlier, teaching and learning will be informed by mapping genetic science and neuroscience onto human behaviour and development, along with emerging understandings of how experiences of culture, society and relationships play out in people's lives.

All humans experience emotional responses to their experiences. As they grow, most individuals are expected to self-manage these responses in socially acceptable ways. Temper tantrums are acceptable in two year olds but not in school-aged children. It is not uncommon for students who have been identified with a learning difficulty to exhibit more extreme responses to emotions than their peers. In many cases, this is what brought these students to the attention of the professionals who formally assessed and labelled them in the first place. Other students will also experience significant intrapersonal difficulties as they mature. In some cases, these may become so persistent or debilitating that they are formally determined to be psychological illnesses. It is usual for many of these conditions to become noticeable during adolescence and early adulthood, a time when students are expected to become increasingly self-sufficient, self-managing and reliable. However, this is exactly the time when they have the least control over themselves.

In terms of intrapersonal functioning, education's aim is to produce self-regulated learners who can manage their own distinctive learning processes and emotional responses and who work towards accomplishments related to their future learning. These learners are motivated, actively engage in learning opportunities, strategically develop skills to support their optimum learning and look for future situations in which to apply and extend their learning. Graham and Berman's (2012)

Table 4.1: *A self-regulated learning model*

PHASES	POSSIBLE AREAS FOR REGULATION			
	COGNITION	MOTIVATION OR AFFECT	BEHAVIOUR	CONTEXT
1 Forethought, planning and activation	Target goal-setting Prior content and knowledge activation Metacognitive knowledge activation	Adoption of goal orientation Efficacy judgments Ease of learning judgments Perceptions of task difficulty Task value activation Interest activation	Time and effort planning Planning for self-observations of behaviour	Perceptions of task Perceptions of context
2 Monitoring	Metacognitive awareness and cognition monitoring	Awareness and monitoring of motivation and **affect**	Awareness and monitoring of effort, time use and need for help Self-observation of behaviour	Monitoring and changing task and context conditions
3 Control	Selection and adaptation of cognitive strategies for learning and thinking	Selection and adaptation of strategies for managing motivation and affect	Increase or decrease effort Persist or give up Help-seeking behaviour	Change or renegotiate task Change or leave context
4 Reaction and reflection	Cognitive judgments Attributions	Affective reactions Attributions	Choice behaviour	Evaluation of task Evaluation of context

Source: Graham and Berman 2012.

self-regulated learning model, shown in table 4.1, illustrates the phases that students go through in becoming skilled at managing their own cognition and behaviour as they work towards their goals, monitor the success of their attempts, select and adjust strategies and evaluate their efforts.

> An **affect** is an emotional component of the intrapersonal dimension of human functioning.

Think and do 4.5: Self-regulation

Consider your own learning in reference to the model in table 4.1. In what ways do you carry out the processes in each phase and across the four areas?

Sustainable learning and learning needs

Teachers, families (*whānau*) and students themselves need to develop a shared understanding of each learner's strengths, weaknesses and current learning needs in order to be able to communicate productively and explore what might be hindering progress at any particular time. Language is necessary that is meaningful but that does not rest on assumptions that can become barriers to learning. For example, most people have skills and abilities within a range that is considered 'normal', 'expected' or 'typical'. Rather than thinking about those who have different ability profiles as belonging to a separate category altogether, such students can be thought of as functioning at different points on the same continuum as everyone else. Students may have gifts, talents or increased sensitivities (hyper-abilities) or they may have lower than usual ability levels (hypo-abilities). There are many reasons that individuals develop different strength and weakness profiles, including genetic makeup, in utero and birth experiences, general health, opportunities to learn, accident and trauma. It is vital for teachers to have confidence that everyone can learn and deserves the opportunity to flourish. The teacher's role is to remove as many barriers as possible so that all students have the best possible opportunities to learn.

Although diagnostic categories can help explain common characteristics of students with particular syndromes or disabilities, much variation is evident between the skill sets of individuals who are 'in' the same category. From a teaching point of view, it is most useful to consider differences in students' learning abilities as resulting from their individual combinations of physiological, psychological, social and cultural factors – factors that either support or hinder learning in the classroom. Teachers need to know, through assessment and observation, what each of their students' learning needs is and whether or not those students have a particular label or diagnosis. Teachers should investigate and make sense of the influences on learning for learners in their classrooms in order to personalise teaching as far as possible and practicable. This is in line with contemporary developments in medicine and exercise, which are both becoming more personalised through the use of assessment and technology, and even genetic testing and analysis (see, for example, Timmons et al. 2010).

To date, many educational systems have relied on classification and diagnostic procedures from outside the field of education to provide structures to allow available resources to be shared equitably for the education of all students. In terms of disability, the primary reference for what 'counts', and therefore attracts funding, comes from the field of psychiatry, in the form of the *Diagnostic and statistical manual of mental disorders* (from 2013 in its fifth edition and known as the 'DSM-5'; APA 2013). This is often used in conjunction with the World Health Organization's *International classification of diseases*. As their titles suggest, both these references are medically oriented and seek to define students' exceptionalities in terms of development and functioning. Tension arises with using such a classification system in inclusive educational settings, because it frames difference in terms of deviation from the norm – primarily as deficit, disease or disorder – in comparison to other groups.

Instead of this orientation, sustainable learning seeks to position differences along continua in order to encourage teachers to work out what any labels actually 'mean' for students and their families in terms of learning and the provision of appropriate opportunities to learn. Observing and assessing in order to ascertain learners' strength and weakness profiles in terms of the ATRiUM capabilities encourages educators to go behind some of the commonly used labels to see what they might mean for individual learners and their teachers.

Summary

This chapter has explored the nature of diversity and how different factors affect learning. These factors can be aspects of individual functioning or can reside outside the learner – within the classroom, family or community. They are defined by the relationship between the learner and the environment. It is vital for any understanding of what supports and hinders learning to be shared and checked with all involved in an individual's learning. It is useful to consider the learning capabilities summarised by ATRiUM during planning and implementing inclusive practices for all learners, irrespective of any disability or learning difficulty. Teachers are responsible for removing as many barriers to classroom learning as possible.

Further reading

Australian Bureau of Statistics. 2011. 'Australian social trends, March 2011: education and Indigenous wellbeing.' Catalogue no. 4102.0. Australian Bureau of Statistics. www.abs.gov.au/AUSSTATS/abs@.nsf/Lookup/4102.0Main+Features50Mar+2011.

Department of Education. 2013. 'School wide positive behaviour support.' Northern Territory Government. 22 May. www.education.nt.gov.au/teachers-educators/students-learning/safe-schools-nt/swpbs.

Department of Education. n.d. 'Positive behaviour support (PBS).' Government of Western Australia. http://det.wa.edu.au/studentsupport/behaviourandwellbeing/detcms/navigation/positive-classrooms/positive-behaviour-support/?oid=Category-id-13613981.

Department of Education and Early Childhood Development. 2013. 'School-wide positive behaviour support.' Victorian Government. 25 November. www.education.vic.gov.au/about/department/vlc/Pages/behavioursupport.aspx.

Department of Education, Training and Employment. 2014. 'Schoolwide positive behaviour support.' Queensland Government. 10 January. http://education.qld.gov.au/studentservices/behaviour/swpbs/.

Education Counts. n.d. 'BES (iterative best evidence synthesis).' New Zealand Government. www.educationcounts.govt.nz/publications/series/2515.

The Incredible Years website: http://incredibleyears.com/.

Itard, E. M. 1802. *An historical account of the discovery and education of a savage man, or of the first developments, physical and moral, of the young savage caught in the woods near Aveyron, in the year 1789.* London: Wilson & Co.

KidsMatter website: www.kidsmatter.edu.au/.

MindMatters website: www.mindmatters.edu.au/.

The New Zealand Curriculum Online. n.d. 'Positive Behaviour for Learning (PB4L) – Incredible Years teacher programme.' New Zealand Government. http://nzcurriculum.tki.org.nz/System -of-support-incl.-PLD/School-initiated-supports/PB4L-Incredible-Years-teacher-programme.

Positive Behavioral Interventions & Supports website: www.pbis.org/.

Positive Behaviour for Learning (PB4L) website: http://pb4l.tki.org.nz/.

Positive Behaviour for Learning website: http://pblsupport.pbworks.com/w/page/47299779/ frontpage.

Triple P – Positive Parenting Program website: www.triplep.net/glo-en/home/.

References

ABS (Australian Bureau of Statistics). 2011. 'Australian social trends, March 2011: education and Indigenous wellbeing.' Catalogue no. 4102.0. ABS. www.abs.gov.au/AUSSTATS/abs@.nsf/ Lookup/4102.0Main+Features50Mar+2011.

APA (American Psychiatric Association). 2013. *Diagnostic statistical manual of mental disorders,* 5th edn. Arlington, VA: APA.

Blakemore, S. J. and S. Choudhury. 2006. 'Development of the adolescent brain: implications for executive function and social cognition.' *Journal of Child Psychology and Psychiatry* 47 (3–4): 296–312.

CESE (Centre for Education Statistics and Evaluation). 2012. 'Student attendance 2012 (Semester 1).' *CESE Bulletin,* no. 3. NSW Government. www.dec.nsw.gov.au/documents /15060385/15385042/Attendance%20Bulletin%202012%20v6.pdf.

Chaffey, G. 2008. 'Is gifted education a necessary ingredient in creating a level playing field for Indigenous children in education?' *Australasian Journal of Gifted Education* 17 (1): 38–9.

——. 2009. 'Gifted but underachieving: Australian Indigenous children.' In T. Balchin, B. Hymer and D. J. Matthews, eds. *The Routledge international companion to gifted education,* 106. Abingdon, United Kingdom, and New York: Routledge.

Chopra, T. 2013. 'Expanding the horizons of disability law in India: A study from a human rights perspective.' *The Journal of Law, Medicine & Ethics* 41 (4): 807–20.

Claiborne, L. B. and W. Drewery. 2010. *Human development: family, place and culture.* North Ryde: McGraw-Hill.

Collis, K. and J. Biggs. 1986. 'Using the SOLO taxonomy.' *SET Research Information for Teachers*, no. 1: 4–16.

Department of Education and Communities. 2013. 'Suspension and expulsions 2012.' NSW Government. June. www.det.nsw.edu.au/media/downloads/about-us/statistics-and-research/key-statistics-and-reports/long-suspension-expulsions-2012.pdf.

Durie, M. 1998. *Whaiora: Māori health development*. Auckland: Oxford University Press.

Education Counts. 2013a. 'Stand-downs, suspensions, exclusions and expulsions from school.' New Zealand Government. August. www.educationcounts.govt.nz/indicators/main/student-engagement-participation/80346.

——. 2013b. 'Attendance in New Zealand schools 2012.' New Zealand Government. July. www.educationcounts.govt.nz/publications/series/2503/attendance-in-new-zealand-schools-in-2012.

Evans, I. M., S. T. Harvey, L. Buckley and E. Yan. 2009. 'Differentiating classroom climate concepts: academic, management, and emotional environments.' *Kōtuitui: New Zealand Journal of Social Sciences Online* 4 (2): 131–46.

Gay, G. 2010. *Culturally responsive teaching: theory, research, and practice*. New York: Teachers' College Press.

Geake, J. 2009. *The brain at school: educational neuroscience in the classroom*. Maidenhead: McGraw-Hill.

Gracey, M. and M. King. 2009. 'Indigenous health part 1: determinants and disease patterns.' *The Lancet* 374 (9683): 65–75.

Graham, L. and J. Berman. 2012. 'Self-regulation and learning disabilities.' *Special Education Perspectives* 21 (2): 41–52.

Graham, P. and S. Reynolds. 2013. *Cognitive behaviour therapy for children and families*, 3rd edn. Cambridge: Cambridge University Press.

Gross, M. U. 1989. 'The pursuit of excellence or the search for intimacy? The forced-choice dilemma of gifted youth.' *Roeper Review* 11 (4): 189–94.

Itard, E. 1802. *An historical account of the discovery and education of a savage man, or of the first developments, physical and moral, of the young savage caught in the woods near Aveyron, in the year 1789*. London: Wilson & Co.

Krathwohl, D. 2002. 'A revision of Bloom's taxonomy: an overview.' *Theory into Practice* 41 (4): 212–18.

McAllister, G. and J. J. Irvine. 2000. 'Cross cultural competency and multicultural teacher education.' *Review of Educational Research* 70 (1): 3–24.

Mark, G. T. and A. C. Lyons. 2010. 'Māori healers' views on wellbeing: the importance of mind, body, spirit, family and land.' *Social Science & Medicine* 70 (11): 1756–64.

Maslow, A. (1954). *Motivation and personality*. New York: Harper.

Meichenbaum, D. 1977. 'Cognitive behaviour modification.' *Scandinavian Journal of Behaviour Therapy* 6 (4): 185–92.

Naglieri, R. and J. P. Das. 1997. *Cognitive assessment system*. Itasca, IL: Riverside Publishing.

OECD (Organisation for Economic Co-operation and Development). 2012. 'PISA 2012 results.' OECD. www.oecd.org/pisa/keyfindings/pisa-2012-results.htm.

Pere, R. 1997. *Te Wheke: a celebration of infinite wisdom*, 2nd edn. Gisborne: Ao Ako Global Learning.

RANZCP (Royal Australian and New Zealand College of Psychiatrists). n.d. 'The dance of life.' RANZCP. http://indigenous.ranzcp.org/content/view/6/6/.

Richmond, C. 2007. *Teach more, manage less: a minimalist approach to behaviour management*. Sydney: Scholastic.

Sallis, J. F., J. J. Prochaska and W. C. Taylor. 2000. 'A review of correlates of physical activity of children and adolescents.' *Medicine and Science in Sports and Exercise* 32 (5): 963–75.

Seligman, M. 2011. *Flourish: a visionary new understanding of happiness and well-being*. New York: Free Press.

Sibley, B. A. and J. L. Etnier. 2003. 'The relationship between physical activity and cognition in children: a meta-analysis.' *Pediatric Exercise Science* 15 (3): 243–56.

Smith, L. and E. Thelen. 2003. 'Development as a dynamic system.' *Trends in Cognitive Sciences* 7 (8): 343–8.

Sternberg, R. 2010. 'WICS: a new model for school psychology.' *School Psychology International* 31 (6): 599–616.

Timmons, J. A., S. Knudsen, T. Rankinen, L. G. Koch, M. Sarzynski, T. Jensen and C. Bouchard. 2010. 'Using molecular classification to predict gains in maximal aerobic capacity following endurance exercise training in humans.' *Journal of Applied Physiology* 108 (6): 1487–96.

UN (United Nations). 2007. 'Convention of the rights of persons with disabilities.' UN. www.un.org/disabilities/default.asp?navid=15&pid=150.

Chapter 5

Assessment and feedback

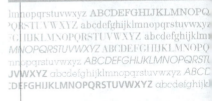

Intended learning outcomes

Engagement with the text in this chapter will enable readers to do the following:

- explain how assessment supports effective teaching and sustainable learning

- compare and contrast assessment *of* learning, assessment *for* learning and assessment *as* learning

- articulate how assessment is embedded in the responsive teaching cycle

- distinguish between various assessment approaches and choose strategies that best fit different educational purposes

- explain the effects of different feedback types on learning

Big ideas

- Teachers' use of assessment and students' involvement with assessment practices should support effective teaching and sustainable learning.

- Assessment information needs to be made available to learners and their families (*whānau*) in the form of feedback and reporting so that responsibility for learning is shared and support for self-regulated learning development is provided.

- Assessment is ongoing throughout the teaching cycle. All classroom decision-making is based on assessment *of* learning, assessment *for* learning and assessment *as* learning (DEECD 2014).

- **Assessment *of* learning** is traditional assessment that identifies and measures what has been learnt. This is important but is no longer enough for responsive teachers.

- **Assessment *for* learning** aims to acknowledge growth and learning, determine achievement, identify current learning needs and necessary adaptations and evaluate the instruction's effectiveness. It ensures that factors that support and hinder learning are investigated in order to personalise learning.

- **Assessment *as* learning** is assessment that creates learning opportunities. A formalised type of this kind of assessment practice is known as **dynamic assessment**.

Introduction

In the more traditional 'transmission of knowledge' educational context, assessment was straightforward – a matter of finding a test that assessed what had been taught and then reporting on the results from that test. As the school curriculum has become more contextualised and process oriented, however, assessment has become more complicated and central to instructional decision-making and seen as integral to the learning process. Every day, teachers are required to make complex decisions about the most appropriate assessments to use in classrooms and schools. Assessment is embedded in and generated by curriculum (ACARA, n.d.; Department of Internal Affairs 2008; Ministry of Education 2007) and has become increasingly sophisticated to reflect the current conceptualisation of teaching and learning and the place of assessment *of* learning (summative assessment), assessment *for* learning (formative assessment) and assessment *as* learning (self-assessment and self-regulation) (Herr et al. 2012).

Contemporary educators understand more clearly the power of assessment as a tool to support learning, and effective teachers ensure that assessment is used as such by constructively aligning it with their teaching (Biggs and Tang 2011). Also, feedback about learning that comes from assessment is now considered one of the most powerful tools teachers can use (van den Bergh et al. 2013). Therefore, it is vital that both assessment and feedback informed by assessment are embedded throughout the responsive teaching framework and recognised as integral to every teaching and learning interaction. This chapter will examine in detail the *why* and the *how* of assessment in contemporary classrooms.

Why do I use assessment?

Assessment can be any opportunity that a learner has to demonstrate learning. Generally, assessment is a response to questioning or some stimulus material through a range of processes (for example, brief or extended oral and written language, graphic representations, creative products and performances or selection of pre-prepared responses). Such episodes can occur in the class, in small groups, in large state- or territory-wide groups or in individual interviews. The assessment can be an extended process (for example, weeks for writing an essay or observation in class over a term) or can be short and sharp (for example, an hour-long exam or 10-minute performance).

Much assessment is used to support decisions about whether a learner should be receiving 'more of the same' or 'something different' in terms of instruction. All of these decisions depend on the particular system and the criteria against which students are assessed:

- Teachers make decisions about providing **differentiated instruction** in the classroom or whether students need separate specialist or individualised teaching.

- Teachers and families make decisions about whether to seek further specialist assessment of students' learning and development.

- School leaders make decisions about class placement, placement in alternative settings or whether outside resourcing is required.

- Educational system personnel make decisions about allocating funding or resources.

- Specialist program leaders make decisions about the kind of support required.

> **Differentiated instruction** provides students with activities and pathways to learning so that everyone within a classroom can learn effectively.

In the context of sustainable learning, the purpose of assessment is to support learning. Assessment that supports learning most effectively is a process embedded in classroom and school programs that aims to achieve the following results:

- Acknowledge growth and learning.

- Determine achievement.

- Identify current learning needs.

- Decide on the instructional adaptations needed.

- Determine the effectiveness of the necessary adaptations.

Responsive teachers also use assessment to constantly evaluate their teaching. Instead of holding a view that a student's success is due to their inherent ability and effort, effective teachers know that the type of teaching provided is vitally important and that indications of a lack of student understanding are opportunities to make changes to their instructional approaches to increase success. Effective teachers evaluate their instruction, the content and their teaching strategies to make considered decisions about what to alter. This happens daily in effective and reflective teachers' classrooms.

Sometimes teachers are closely involved in the investigation of developmental differences for students and can contribute valuable information to inform outside assessment professionals. All diagnoses should be based on the thorough collection of valid data, including how students respond to the school setting and to instruction. As an example, gathering information about the behaviour of students taking medication aimed at changing behaviour is vital to the ongoing medical management of conditions such as ADHD and mood disorders. It is important to have information about behaviour prior to the prescription of medication and then after medication in order to help decide whether the treatment is having the desired effect. It is also valuable for parents and carers, paediatricians, psychiatrists and psychologists to have information about learning and behaviour when conditions such as anxiety and mood disorders, ADHD and ASD are under consideration. The diagnosis of many of these conditions requires evidence of the behaviours' pervasiveness, which means that specialists need to know whether certain behaviours are evident in school, home and community settings.

Contemporary assessment is ecological and draws on conventional and alternative approaches that support assessment of, for and as learning.

In defining and identifying factors that support or hinder learning, sustainable learning guides teachers to keep their investigations ecological – this means that teachers need to look for influences in every aspect of learners' worlds. **Contemporary assessment** continues to look within learners as well as outside them to seek to understand the interaction that certain aspects of the environment may have with individual students' functioning.

Developmental screening

Developmental assessment begins outside school and starts as soon as a baby is born. The general idea is that routine assessments identify children who may have developmental and learning needs that are different from those typically anticipated and for which some support may be appropriate. Babies, even unborn babies, are screened for health, developmental syndromes and conditions for which medical intervention is available. Many such conditions have implications for children's development and learning.

In particular, hearing and vision abilities are routinely screened. If they are found to be outside usual bounds there can be profound implications for individuals' development and for teaching and learning. In New South Wales, specialist teachers with knowledge and skills in early development for children with hearing loss and vision loss begin their support of the family from as early as possible. Early learning within the family is vital for developing the language and experiential foundations for school achievement and lifelong learning.

As young children develop, they are routinely screened for any significant deviation from expected development so that conditions can be identified early and appropriate interventions put in place. All family gatherings to inspect new babies and developing toddlers involve informal assessment that acts as a screening for identifying needs. Visits to the community nurse include measuring children's weight, head size and body length, which are all potential developmental indicators. Visits to playgroups are also opportunities for new families to compare their child's development against that of others.

This community developmental screening becomes more formalised as children move into educational settings. For example, early childhood centres note and keep records on children's development (that is, cultural, linguistic, social and behavioural, cognitive and physical information) and convey information to families about delayed or accelerated development, levels of responsiveness to teaching and reactions to the setting. Preschool and early childhood settings also share information with schools to ensure transitions are effective.

Informal screening is carried out during orientation or transition to school sessions in many settings. School psychologists, for example, spend many kindergarten sessions screening students for any evident developmental issues that may affect engagement and achievement at school. Sometimes, children have not had any formal educational experience prior to school, and their foundation year is the first opportunity for such screening. The aim of this assessment is to prevent or address difficulties so that formal teaching and learning are as effective as possible right from the start. Formal educational screening of pre-academic skills through tests or checklists occurs on entry to school in many educational systems. Following on from these assessments, children can be flagged as at risk for formal academic learning or in need of more intensive or alternative assessment or instruction. Such screening can also act as a baseline assessment against which future learning can be compared.

Another common form of screening assessment is used to select students to be enrolled in particular schools or to receive scholarships. In some educational systems, for example, there is a high demand for the assessment of giftedness in four year olds, who are then able to start school early and can enrol in particular schools that run 'gifted' programs. Similar assessment also happens every year when families go through the screening process for selective high schools or selective classes.

Educational systems offer a range of educational settings and resources for learners who have disabilities or learning difficulties. Assessment information supports the selection of students for separate settings or for services within local schools. Every year, specialist professionals in educational systems work in teams to consider assessment information for selection purposes. Increasingly, their decisions concern the allocation of additional resources to schools rather than the placement of students in special schools, but both types of selection processes still occur.

Assessment of learning

Assessment is an opportunity for learners to demonstrate what they know and understand and for teachers to determine achievement. These assessment purposes work in tandem and are assessment's traditional aims. Opportunities to demonstrate learning are provided throughout school. These can be classroom based or school based or can be formal state- or territory-wide or nationwide written or performance examinations. Such assessment *of* learning is essential to determine whether a learner has achieved the intended learning outcomes required in the current area of study (Biggs and Tang 2011).

Assessment *of* learning in schools describes learning achievement against criteria derived from the curriculum or child development trajectories, known as 'criterion-referenced assessment'. Developmental screening as described above is an example of assessment in reference to criteria defined by typical developmental pathways. Additionally, some test results based on large student samples can provide scores that indicate how a learner is progressing in relation to others of the same age or grade, which is called 'norm-referenced assessment'. Such assessments act like punctuation marks in the learning narrative. They are usually summative; that is, they sum up previous learning. This is the traditional reason for assessment that still has a strong purpose in schools.

The Higher School Certificate in New South Wales and the National Certificate of Educational Achievement in New Zealand are two examples of assessment that aims to 'sum up' what has been learnt during the years of schooling. The results of these achievement tests are also used by universities to make decisions about who will be offered a place. This is based on the idea that assessment results can indicate who is most likely to benefit from tertiary learning. It is one example of assessment's screening and selection function and, in particular, the use of a past-learning measure to make predictions about future learning.

Assessment *for* learning

Assessment *for* learning is achieved when teachers strategically gather evidence of the ways in which their students learn and what has been learnt so that they can make informed decisions about what and how to teach next. Assessment *for* learning informs future teaching and learning: it is the process of gathering and 'interpreting evidence about where learners are up to in their learning, where they need to go next and how best to get there' (ARG 2002). Assessment is only as good as the action that follows it. The 'test' of good assessment is whether it identifies a course of action that supports future learning.

Responsive, reflective teachers are active researchers. They gather data upon which to base the evaluation of their teaching then use that data to support instructional decision-making: not only evidence of student learning is needed, but also evidence of the teaching factors that contributed to learning – in other words, the factors under

Learning trajectories are progressions or descriptions of how students' learning of concepts develops over time.

the teachers' control that either supported or hindered learning. Responsive teachers adapt their teaching by taking into account what they know about their students and their learning processes. Teachers cannot always assume that past learning will be available as a base for future learning; instead, they need to have flexible expectations that can be adapted to accommodate new assessment information. Their overall aim is to teach in order to improve their students' future **learning trajectories**.

The development and implementation of **personalised learning plans**, which are required for all Aboriginal and Torres Strait Island children, shows how assessment can be used in this way (SCEEC 2013). Personalised learning as defined in this process is based on the recognition of 'the individual strengths, needs and goals of students' (DEEWR 2011, 2), which can be accurately determined only through assessment. An example of the personalised learning plan process developed by a small rural school is provided below.

> **Personalised learning plans** map the pathway that a student needs to follow to achieve appropriate individual learning goals.

Learners themselves can also use assessment information to support their decisions about participation in classroom learning. Assessment information can affect how learners frame their self-beliefs and motivation for learning and, thus, how much effort they expend and how much confidence they have when engaging in learning activities.

Personalised learning plans

The traditional context for personalised or individualised teaching was in special education, where individual educational plans and individual learning plans were used as a way to ensure the special needs of students with a disability were considered, either through separate teaching outside the classroom or through adaptations within the classroom. The goal of contemporary personalised learning plans is to meet the needs of all students in a personal and responsive way.

Sustainable learning is in essence personal. It is not about the comparative test results across a learner group but about the learning journey of each learner: where each has come from, where each is going and how to get there. This personalised focus is inherent in responsive teaching, which asks teachers to know each of their students in order to provide the teaching that is needed for individual learners.

At the same time, sustainable learning is communal. It both depends on partnerships and contributes to those partnerships. The 'Aboriginal and Torres Strait Islander Education action plan 2010–2014' recognised this when it focused on engagement and connections to support learning and explicitly directed teachers to go outside their classrooms to partner with families to support better learning for Indigenous students (Department of Education 2013). Many schools have created processes for this active engagement with families in order to personalise learning for each student. Such processes need to be developed with particular school resources and personnel in mind. It is highly likely that those developed in one school will not work in another school. The commitment of the school to connecting with families will determine the success of any processes. Partnership with families is vital in supporting steps 3 to 8 of the RTF, from finding out about learners and their family contexts, and working out what to teach now and how to teach it to seeing what was learnt, how best to provide feedback on learning and evaluating teaching strategies.

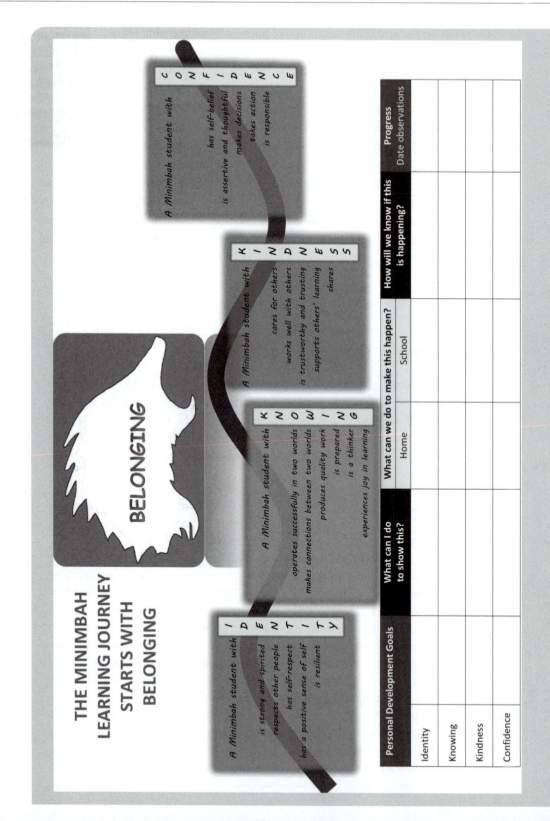

THE MINIMBAH
LEARNING JOURNEY
STARTS WITH
BELONGING

BELONGING

A Minimbah student with
IDENTITY

is strong and spirited
respects other people
has self-respect
has a positive sense of self
is resilient

A Minimbah student with
KNOWING

operates successfully in two worlds
makes connections between two worlds
produces quality work
is prepared
is a thinker
experiences joy in learning

A Minimbah student with
KINDNESS

cares for others
works well with others
is trustworthy and trusting
supports others' learning
shares

A Minimbah student with
CONFIDENCE

has self-belief
is assertive and thoughtful
makes decisions
takes action
is responsible

Personal Development Goals	What can I do to show this?	What can we do to make this happen?		How will we know if this is happening?	Progress
		Home	School		Date observations
Identity					
Knowing					
Kindness					
Confidence					

THE MINIMBAH LEARNING JOURNEY STARTS WITH BELONGING AND LEARNING THE CULTURE WAY

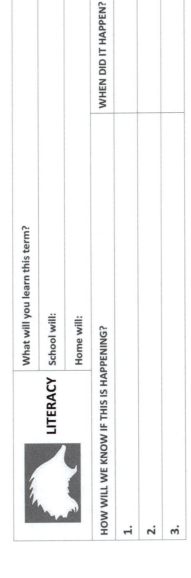

Story sharing

Learning maps

Think and do

Draw with symbols

Link to the land

Try a new way

Watch and do

Community links

Figure 5.1: *Two pages from the 'Minimbah learning journey' (a personalised learning plan) using the '8 Aboriginal ways of learning'*
Source: Minimbah Aboriginal Primary School.

An example of the process and documentation in one small independent Aboriginal school is provided below to illustrate how this particular community followed through with their commitment to personalised learning. The school developed a personalised learning plan process (which in this case was called a 'learning journey') that reflected its core values, starting with 'belonging to the mob'. The process involved a meeting with each family and student to yarn, or discuss, the learning needs of each student. This allowed teachers to gather information and to collectively, with the family and student, set goals for development and learning, which were then written into the student's personal learning plan (see figure 5.1).

The process's initial focus was to find out from the student and family perceptions of talents and strengths, interests, goals, role models and personal qualities. After that, a series of prompts further explored students' perceptions:

- My favourite thing to do is...
- My favourite place is...
- I am good at...
- I would like to be better at...
- I feel good about myself when...
- What I like about school is...
- What I dislike about school is...

- I feel happy when...
- I feel proud when...
- I worry about...
- I like to relax by...
- These people make me laugh...
- Other things you should know about me are...

The next part of the discussion was spent exploring how 'belonging' involves identity, knowing, kindness and confidence and from this shared understanding identifying personal development goals. These were described so that they were clear to everyone, and a shared understanding was developed about how everyone would know when each goal had been achieved. The discussion involved talking about how success might be achieved and what people at school and at home needed to do to make it happen. The meeting then moved on to look at key academic goals in literacy and numeracy and what they were for each student.

The process described here prefaces the typical school record of achievement. The remaining pages of the learning journey included school and national assessment results, data about attendance patterns, records of any other agencies involved with the student and notes from all meetings concerning this student's learning journey.

Other schools are finding their own ways of responding to the necessity of providing a personalised focus in education. Some schools are using Aboriginal mentors or educational assistants to facilitate the personalised learning plan process, while others are using executive teachers' time and expertise. It is traditionally difficult to engage families of Aboriginal students, as there is distance between them and schools. As one Aboriginal mentor interviewed in an evaluative study stated, 'Most families expect that contact from the school will be negative and this will take a long time to change' (Graham and Berman 2013, 36). The use of the personalised learning plan process is a way to actively and positively engage families in their children's schooling.

Assessment *as* learning

Assessment *as* learning provides opportunities for learning at the same time as assessment; that is, the assessment activity is also a learning activity. It becomes learning about learning, or meta-learning: an opportunity for students to learn about themselves as learners, with a focus on self-reflection, becoming metacognitive and thus self-regulating. An assessment activity can also be an opportunity to learn curriculum content. Smart teachers can use this dual focus so that every opportunity for learning in a classroom is also an opportunity for assessment and every assessment activity is a learning activity.

Teachers make many educational decisions based on assessment *of* student learning aside from the core teaching and learning decisions, including determining achievement, screening and selecting students who may require instructional adaptations or targeted interventions and evaluating instruction and programs. These decisions require different approaches, and teachers need to make choices about the best ways to assess learning, to have that assessment inform their teaching and to use assessment activities *as* opportunities to learn.

How do I approach assessment?

Contemporary assessment strategies and approaches provide many options for teachers and meet different purposes at different times. As used by responsive teachers, contemporary assessment acknowledges the complexity and sophistication of learning and human functioning. It brings together a range of assessment approaches and draws on the huge bank of conventional tests available. It is a collaborative process that takes into account many perspectives and voices as well as the complexity of the context of the assessment. Instead of trying to eliminate the social, emotional and cultural variables that affect learning, it accepts their richness and tries to make sense of how they interact with that learning. Contemporary assessment also views cognitive functioning as modifiable – students can be taught how to think and learn (Wong et al. 2008).

All assessment can be positioned along the continua shown in figure 5.2. While conventional assessments are placed towards the left, contemporary assessment procedures, on the right, tend to be less formal, and can be continuous, more formative and focus on what can be done to support future learning. They tend to emphasise the processes used by learners in their classrooms rather than the products of test-taking. Reflecting this, contemporary assessment is a more **idiographic assessment** than conventional assessment. Contemporary assessment includes tests that conform to conventional assessment standards but places them within a more complex ecological context.

> **Idiographic assessment** (also called 'ipsative assessment') is individually focused evaluation in which the only comparisons made are between an individual and themselves (at another time, in a previous assessment and so on).

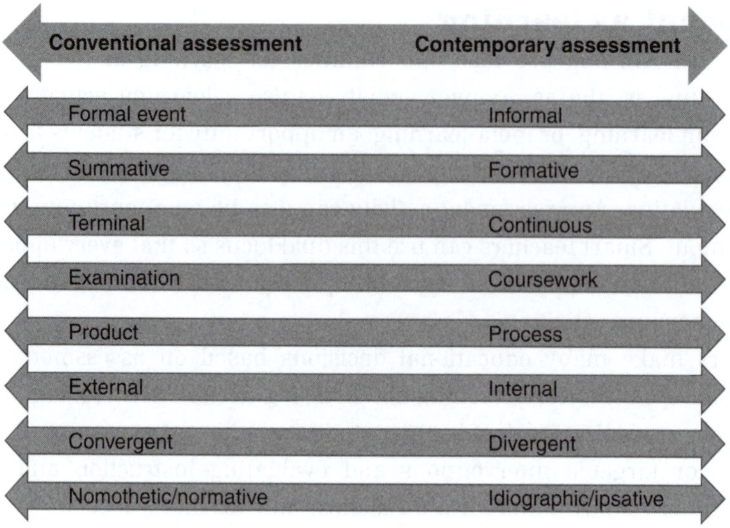

Figure 5.2: *Dimensions of assessment*
Source: Adapted from Berman 2001.

Contemporary assessment in the classroom and beyond underpins effective teaching and learning. Key approaches to assessment that responsive teachers need to consider are outlined below.

Ecological assessment

Ecological assessment recognises that student learning and behaviour are defined through interaction with the ecology or environments in which students function. It has long been understood that it is not possible to understand students' behaviours without looking at what happened prior to those behaviours (the antecedents) and what happened after them (the consequences). The focus of ecological assessment is much more sophisticated; it centres on the complex interplay between individuals and their environments, which include other people, activities, physical objects, space and time.

For example, it is only recently that systemic learning assessment has deliberately considered aspects like opportunity to learn. Previously, assumptions were made that all students had equal opportunity to access instruction, and these suppositions underpinned the comparative assessment of learning achievement and definition of disabilities. Such assumptions resulted in consequences like the invalid assessment of intellectual disability and the over-identification of students from disadvantaged backgrounds whose opportunities to learn had been limited by poverty. Responsive teachers make sure they take an **ecological view of learning** and do not assume that influences lie solely within the learners.

An **ecological view of learning** recognises that learning is influenced by school, family (*whānau*), community and the larger social, structural, political, economic and cultural environment.

Naturalistic and narrative assessment

Traditionally, learning and behaviour assessments in schools were carried out during a contrived assessment event – and often they still are. Such events are not natural. In contrast, naturalistic assessment studies learners in their natural settings – for example, during day-to-day school tasks – and tries to identify factors in those settings that are affecting learning as well as noticing how the student responds to those factors. Narrative assessment, which is used to assess young children and students with significant disabilities, is an extension of this assessment approach (Ministry of Education, n.d.). In narrative assessment, stories are developed that demonstrate development and learning within natural contexts suited to that learning. In the case of students with significant disabilities, their learning and development may seem to occur in such small steps that they can be missed unless this type of detailed assessment procedure is used to focus on and illuminate important evidence of learning.

E-assessment

Assessment is carried out in many different ways and uses all educational tools. Just as contemporary teaching and learning rely on electronic technologies for communication and accessing information, assessment is also increasingly using these technologies. Educational psychologists are beginning to use clinical assessment tools within an online environment. Electronic technology can provide modern stimulus material – bright, shiny, up-to-date text and graphics that can be easily shared with many people. In this way, electronic technologies provide the opportunity for standardised assessment across large populations. Electronic assessment, or e-assessment, which is 'the use of information technology for any assessment-related activity' (NVES, n.d.), can also be accessed from multiple sites so that large groups of geographically disparate people can be assessed simultaneously. E-assessment has thus been introduced for the large-scale screening of beginning school students as well as for the assessment of student learning at all levels of formal education; for example, there are plans for online NAPLAN testing in Australia.

Learning capabilities are used in different ways depending on the technology being employed, and there is longstanding acceptance that some technologies assist students to demonstrate their learning more effectively. This assumption underpins processes such as the NSW Board of Studies Disability Provisions for the Higher School Certificate (BOS, n.d.) and the Special Assessment Conditions in New Zealand (NZQA, n.d.), which allow some students to use electronic technology to support the demonstration of their learning. Of course, learners who have significant impairments in sensory or physical capabilities often rely on **assistive and augmentative technology**, and this must be considered in all assessment.

Assistive and augmentative technology supplements or replaces speech or writing for those with impairments in the production or comprehension of spoken or written language.

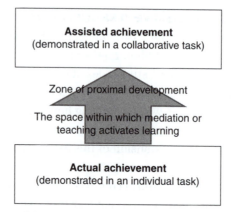

Figure 5.3: *A representation of dynamic assessment*

Dynamic assessment

Dynamic assessment is based on the idea that if teachers want to observe how their students learn, they should activate learning and be with them while it is happening. Dynamic assessment is based on Vygotskian theory and is designed to explore what occurs within what Vygotsky calls the students' **zone of proximal development** (see figure 5.3) – the gap between what learners can do themselves and what they can do with the help of a person who is more competent (Rogoff and Wertsch 1984).

> The **zone of proximal development** is the space between what learners can do alone and what they can do with the assistance of others.

Dynamic assessment deliberately incorporates a teaching phase so that learners' responses to teaching can be explored. Three types of information are accessed in this way: measures of actual (or unassisted) achievement, measures of assisted achievement and information about factors that support and hinder individuals' learning. Dynamic assessment allows investigation of how to help learners as well as information about how learners respond to teaching (Lauchlan and Carrigan 2013; Lidz 2003). Not only is it appropriate for teachers to use this form of assessment; it is also a useful part of the assessment repertoire of other assessment professionals, particularly educational psychologists.

Conventional assessment

Conventional assessment in education is generally referred to as 'testing'. Testing is grounded in psychometric theory and behaviourist learning theories and is focused on behaviours and products (for example, written responses) that are easily observable and measurable. There are many beautifully constructed, statistically reliable and valid tests that have assumed a significant status in education, but they contain only items that are easily measurable and therefore do not necessarily reflect the full range of difficulty inherent in any particular curriculum domain. Assessment professionals today try to use the best aspects of conventional testing as tools to support decisions about teaching and learning.

Conventional assessment is formal rather than informal, using tasks designed specifically and exclusively for assessment and presented as an 'event'. It can be used for groups or for individuals, in schools or elsewhere, and often for learners who have disabilities or learning difficulties, in clinical settings. This assessment type is summative, in that it provides information about prior learning. It is also often terminal – at the end of a course of learning – and has generally been presented in the form of examinations or tests in which students' performances are written responses, with the product marked. It can be external or internal to schools; however, external tests have been seen to be more objective and fair and carry significant status. Most conventional assessments use convergent tasks designed to have only one correct response. Conventional assessment is concerned with relating an individual's results to the group's results by comparing the performance of specific students to that of people in general. This approach is in contrast to the use of idiographic assessment, which seeks to understand unique individuals.

Conventional testing specifically aims to filter out factors that affect learning to try to find some 'pure' or 'true' measure of what students know. For example, many conventional assessments do not take into account cultural and linguistic differences among test-takers, even though it is clear such information is important in the interpretation of test results and developing an understanding of learners and how they respond to their environments. Results of conventional assessments always need to be carefully interpreted within the context of learning for each student.

Is my assessment fit for purpose?

Often, the decision about what assessment strategy to use is determined by factors that are not pedagogical but logistical. Assessment strategies may be chosen because they are easy to administer, score and record, or because it is relatively easy to rank and order students against each other. However, much of what is needed to assess learning is complex and not amenable to simplistic procedures. The result of a mismatch between the approach chosen and the target of assessment is that assessment can easily become too removed from the authentic learning process and thus be invalid. Teachers need to be on the lookout for invalid assessments and assessment that is not fit for its purpose. A framework that supports the careful use of assessment in schools and classrooms is shown in figure 5.4. Three key dimensions of assessment – the purpose, the content and the procedure – are reflected in the three prompt questions 'Why?', 'What?' and 'How?' Assessment professionals, including teachers, need to consider each of these dimensions when making decisions about what assessment strategy to use in their classrooms.

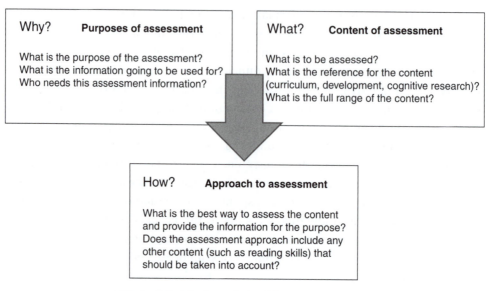

Figure 5.4: *A framework for classroom assessment*
Source: Berman 2001.

Consider the process of a primary-school teacher wanting to select a strategy for assessing students' understanding and application of place value in numeration. There are commercial tests able to be photocopied and available for this part of the curriculum, and it would be relatively easy to print these, supervise class administration, mark them and tally up the scores. However, is this the best way to assess students' understanding of place value?

The first question for classroom teachers is whether the performance during assessment is valid: is it a true measure of the student's learning, or is it a measure of performance at that time but not aligned with other indicators of learning or development in the domain of interest? Also, is the assessment information reflective of what is occurring in the classroom and in alignment with the other assessments that have been done?

If the assessment is in line with what is already known, then results tend not to be questioned. But what if scores are consistently low but inaccurate? Chaffey's (2008, 2009) work in identifying 'invisible' gifted Aboriginal children through the use of dynamic assessment reminds teachers that it is possible for classroom and school

Think and do 5.1: Classroom assessment

How could you use the framework for classroom assessment in figure 5.4 to support your use of assessment in the classroom? Interview one or more teachers about their use of assessment methods in the classroom. How do they use assessment results as feedback about their teaching? Access some form of conventional assessment test and consider it in response to each of the questions in the assessment framework.

assessments to underestimate student potential. Responsive classroom teachers have a responsibility to question all the assessment information collected or shared about students. In interrogating assessment results, it is important for teachers to ask, 'How does this information contribute to my understanding of these learners?' Responsive teachers have the task of combining the different pieces of assessment information available into a meaningful picture that makes clear the learning needs of their students.

Reflection 5.1: Assessment-capable students

Students' learning is enhanced by their progress towards becoming competent strategy-users and '**assessment-capable** learners'. According to Hook, who has developed extensive teacher resources informed by the SOLO model, assessment-capable learners share five characteristics (HookED, n.d.; see also Hattie 2009; Hattie and Timperley 2007): they know what quality work looks like, are familiar with the criteria for task success, can compare and evaluate their own work in terms of these criteria, share a concept of quality that is aligned to their teachers' thinking and are able to monitor the quality of their work and improve it when necessary by drawing from a repertoire of appropriate actions and strategies.

Responsive teachers have considerable responsibility for setting up the conditions necessary for their students to become assessment capable. They can do so by providing experiences focused on examining quality work and carefully structuring and making explicit to the students in their classes the learning intentions and success criteria for major tasks.

> **Assessment-capable** students ask themselves, 'Where am I going?', 'How am I going?' and 'Where to next?'

Assessment within the responsive teaching framework

Assessment is inherent in each step of the RTF (introduced in chapter 3 and shown in figure 3.1). Specifically, it is vital to information-gathering in each step and to the establishment of reference points for the explicit assessment involved in steps 3 and 6. Figure 5.5, derived initially from a framework for developing inclusive classroom programs, shows a sequence of assessment questions and information sources essential to support teachers in making informed professional decisions at every point of the RTF (Graham, Berman and Bellert 2002).

These questions underpin the actions of reflective teachers and those concerned with **action research**. Effective teachers continually question and gather information to help them understand their learners and to evaluate the effect of teaching on student learning, so that informed decisions can be made about future instruction. This process is not only about the learners. Classrooms are ecological contexts in which learning behaviours and teaching decisions affect each other. All factors impacting on the teaching's effectiveness in relation to student learning need to be considered.

> **Action research** is a cycle of reflection on practice and subsequent changes in practice based on that reflection.

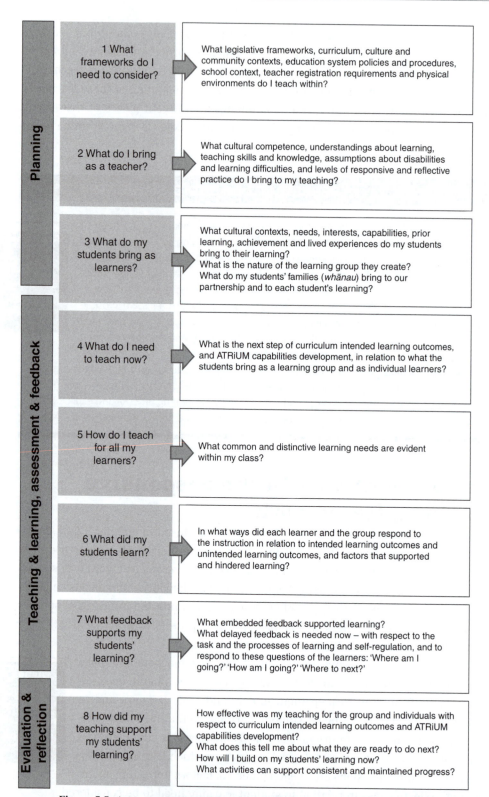

Figure 5.5: *Assessment questions within the responsive teaching framework*

Assessment is vital to such responsive instruction and occurs throughout the RTF, but most explicitly at steps 3 and 6. Both assessment *of* learning and assessment *for* learning are used to greatest effect when they are instrumental in deciding how to provide the next learning opportunities. Teachers have to select the most appropriate form of assessment to support their teaching and their students' learning. A way to determine the purpose of assessment is to work out where the assessment fits in the RTF. Assessment *of* learning, for example, is essential in step 3 and implicit in step 6. When assessment is targeted at future learning, it is assessment *for* learning, which provides teachers with information that helps them to respond meaningfully to each of the other steps in the RTF cycle. The RTF as it underpins assessment decisions is discussed in the following sections.

1 What frameworks do I need to consider?

The frameworks within which teachers teach have much to contribute to assessment plans and procedures. This section is not meant to be exhaustive; it is able only to prompt teachers' thoughts about the frameworks within which all their teaching is planned. Effective teachers set up and manage their own ways of accessing relevant information at this step, and it is upon this foundation that all their teaching is planned and organised.

Within government legislation, each educational system has its own assessment plan that culminates in some end-of-school assessment event, such as the NSW Higher School Certificate or the New Zealand National Educational Achievement Certificate. Governments are also increasingly requiring state- or territory-wide or national assessment at other points in students' schooling. The purposes of such assessment can be blurred, as the results can become high stakes and used for political purposes. Teachers have a responsibility to consider how such assessment information (for example, the analysis of NAPLAN data) can be used to support learning for their students.

School systems have built-in student assessment procedures on school entry that are used as a baseline against which teaching and learning can be assessed and, as previously discussed, to screen for children who may need specific classroom teaching and specialist support immediately, because they bring a particular profile of capabilities that are less than expected or advanced. Additionally, some schools provide a firm structure for assessment, including the specific strategies to be used and student records that are to be completed each term or year based on the prescribed assessment procedures. In most instances, curriculum defines the learning that is to be the focus of assessment. There are often accompanying support documents and resources that more explicitly articulate teaching, learning and assessment activities and expectations. Cultural and community contexts affect how assessment is carried out and how results are shared with learners and their families. Teachers also work within guidelines for the development of their professional competencies in selecting and using assessment (AITSL 2014; NZTC 2009).

Another consideration relevant to assessment relates to the ICT demands inherent in lessons. Schools and systems manage this aspect of teaching and learning – which is of high expense and becomes quickly out-of-date – in different ways, from dedicated computer laboratories to flexible classrooms that require each learner to bring their own device. There are implications related to professional development and technological expertise that accompany both extremes and can make or break a lesson.

A final consideration is the physical environment within which teaching and learning happen. Schools and educational settings vary enormously in terms of the facilities and resources available, and this affects the decisions teachers can make about learning activities. Some schools are more adequately resourced than others, and the buildings and grounds also influence the types of learning activities that a teacher can realistically facilitate. For example, it is interesting to see the changes in architecture and classroom organisation that are evident in schools built at different times. In 2014 in New Zealand there was a push for 'modern learning environments' that to teachers who had been working since the 1970s looked like retro settings (Ministry of Education 2014). Such trends in the design of learning spaces have profound effects on what learning and teaching can be like and how teachers work beside and with other teachers.

2 What do I bring as a teacher?

As reflective practitioners, teachers are constantly thinking about their own professional skills and knowledge in reference to frameworks for registration, accreditation and career progression. Teacher registration provides one of the frameworks identified in step 1 of the RTF that is expanded in step 2. The teacher registration guidelines clearly articulate the skills and knowledge that beginning teachers should continue to develop throughout their careers. There are other powerful factors that individuals bring to teaching, however, that are related to the less conscious perspectives they may have developed from their own life experiences and contexts. It is vital for responsive teachers to be aware of what they bring to the classroom and the possible effects of their attitudes and values on learners.

One factor that has a profound impact on classrooms is cultural competence. This affects individuals' language, actions and responses to learners with similar and different cultural backgrounds. It is important that responsive teachers assess their own cultural competence so that as far as possible differences in culture do not become a barrier for any of their learners. The New Zealand Teachers Council offers a resource called 'Tātaiako: cultural competencies for teachers of Māori learners' (NZTC 2011), while educational systems in most Australian states and territories also offer similar supports. For example, the Northern Territory Department of Education and Training has developed a 'Pedagogical framework for cultural competence' based on the work of Perso (2003), that advocates as a basic principle that teachers should not 'assume anything other than these three truths … (1) your students know a lot,

(2) they are capable of learning a whole lot more in an environment where high expectations abound and, (3) they bring a rich background and knowledge to the learning environment' (Northern Territory Government 2010, 3).

In the context of inclusive teaching, teachers' knowledge about and attitudes towards a wide diversity of learners and their particular learning needs are obviously important. Responsive teachers also assess what they bring to their teaching when working with students who have disabilities or learning difficulties and plan for appropriate professional development experiences so they can optimise the effectiveness of their teaching for all learners.

3 What do my students bring as learners?

Class groups are made up of individual learners who bring their own world views, cultural backgrounds, previous learning experiences and school histories to the classroom. It is not possible to know everything about all students; however, getting to know learners helps establish trust and allows teachers to match their teaching to students' learning needs. The term 'learning needs' is not necessarily a description of deficits; it is meant to refer to what students 'need' at any particular time. Students' learning needs could just as easily relate to their superior competence and ability to do more advanced work as to their need for smaller steps to build knowledge and more content repetition to consolidate learning. Some students will enter the classroom accompanied by a folder of individual assessment information, medical and psychological reports. Others will have no documentation but will be involved in specialist assessment during their school years.

Some students will have been identified at birth with particular conditions that have implications for their development and learning trajectories. For example, Down syndrome, spina bifida, cerebral palsy and vision loss are often identified at birth or soon after, and each of these diagnoses has implications for children's development and learning at school. Other conditions, such as ASD and hearing loss, are often identified in the preschool years.

In all these cases, students are likely to arrive at school with substantial information about their development and learning so far. As schooling becomes increasingly formal, the assessment documents for some students accrue, and by the time they reach high school some students have a thick wad of reports that document their development assessment at particular stages. What is most important from these reports is what has 'worked'. It is important to remember that all assessments are anchored to the developmental stage and time they were completed and so may, or may not, be relevant to the current context.

Diagnostic labels are a 'shortcut' way to communicate that a student has a condition or way of behaving or learning that is different from most other students. Dramatically, labels can be the first thing teachers hear about their students. A colleague may say, 'You are getting a new student in your class. She has ASD'. Such an introduction can be a challenge, as it effectively hides the person and foregrounds the diagnostic label. This can create a fear of the known or the unknown, depending on experience. It is vital for teachers to go past labels and get to know individual students and how their behaviour patterns or physiological conditions play out in everyday life.

While it is not possible or necessary to know about all labelled diagnoses, it is possible to access and filter relevant information that can inform instructional decision-making. A label can be thought of as a handle on a door that can be opened to invite conversation with students, their families and any previous professionals who worked with them, as well as a keyword for teachers' own research. Teachers need to remember that significant differences can be evident between people who have the same label and that the use of labels remains fluid and changeable.

Reflection 5.2: Exploring labels with an open mind

Labels are important and serve some purposes well. They support a level of shared understanding, as they encapsulate assumptions, can indicate similarities and relationships among educational problems and provide a common language. For example, 'cerebral palsy' will mean something to a teacher depending on that teacher's knowledge and experience of cerebral palsy, and that meaning will be related to physical mobility and speech. But that is the limit of the label's usefulness. Without further information it is impossible to know whether cerebral palsy for a particular child is a little difficulty in the classroom or whether it impacts on every aspect of learning from physically accessing the classroom to interacting through language. Responsive teachers dig below the labels to find out what they mean for individual students' learning.

A key purpose of labels in education, as in other social systems, is to support priorities for services. In this context, labels are used to sort people, so that the available resources are allocated in some systematic way. The labels usually focus on negative aspects of ability or disability and divide people into 'mutually exclusive' groups, even though the reality is often more complex than this. Used for this purpose, labels can take on a permanence that may not be valid. Because they tend to be deficit focused, labels can become stigmatising over time and then may be discarded and replaced with new terms – which in turn develop stigma. An example of this is the replacement of 'mental retardation' with 'intellectual disability (intellectual developmental disorder)' in the DSM-5 (APA 2013). 'Mental retardation' is a term that has been considered inappropriate in Australia for decades yet was still in use in the United States until 2013.

Identification of some conditions can happen early in childhood, while others are determined at later stages of childhood or even in adulthood. Some disabilities are not identified at all during students' school years. Different professionals are responsible for identifying different disabilities and conditions. Families, nurses and early childhood teachers usually pick up the first signs of the atypical attainment of developmental milestones. Referral to a paediatrician explores the child's developmental history and screens for known medical conditions. Sometimes this leads to the identification of a disability; however, in many cases no medical syndrome is found.

If a particular condition is identified, this can provide an anticipated development trajectory and associated early intervention. If no known syndrome is identified, then the child's development should be closely monitored to try to understand what the developmental pathway will be. In both cases, specialists in early childhood development (for example, speech pathologists, physiotherapists, psychologists, occupational therapists and paediatricians) ideally become involved in early intervention and monitoring of the student's development.

Overall, students in schools who present with learning needs that look different from those of most other students rely on assessment to support appropriate learning experiences. This assessment is usually carried out by their teachers and specialist teachers but can also include assessment by outside professionals. This kind of assessment can help define and clarify students' developmental and learning needs, determine whether students meet the eligibility criteria for specific educational or social provisions and assist families and students themselves to understand and support their developmental, learning, health, physical, social and emotional aspects of functioning.

Not only do teachers need to know individual students as learners; they also have the task of getting to know their classes as groups of learners. Different assessment strategies support this assessment task, with much of this kind of assessment embedded in everyday interactions with the class. While teachers may think that individual learners are hard to get a handle on, a learner group can be even more difficult to understand, as there are so many variables affecting their functioning at any one time. Developing a **sociogram** of class interactions is illuminating in terms of students' connectedness and isolation and can underpin some of the decisions that teachers need to make about grouping their students. A procedure for making a simple sociogram is given below.

> A **sociogram** is a graphic representation of the structure of interpersonal relations and social links in a group situation.

Knowing what learners bring to the classroom is never a fully completed task! Teachers will always be able to find out more about their students and their families. A responsive teacher puts labels in perspective and digs beneath them to understand students as people first and then in terms of their functioning in the classroom. The sustainable learning framework for this kind of investigation into classroom capabilities is encapsulated in the acronym **ATRiUM**: investigate how students actively learn, think, relate to others, use language, symbols and ICT systems and manage themselves. The goal is to be flexible and adaptable and to take into account new information as part of what informs responsive teaching at any particular time.

> **ATRiUM** Active learning; Thinking; Relating to others; Using language, symbols and ICT; and Managing self.

Constructing a classroom sociogram

A sociogram is a diagram that shows the social links between students, constructed from information gathered about students' perceptions of their peers. Sociograms provide important information about the connections and tensions between students in a class and can support decisions about grouping and organising students for the most productive learning and social outcomes.

Sociograms used for research purposes often ask for information about both 'likes' and 'dislikes', but gathering this information can be difficult in classrooms. Sociograms that ask for positive information only can still be revealing and give teachers useful information to assist in their professional decision-making. The procedure for constructing a classroom sociogram is explained below:

1 Decide on the purpose for constructing a sociogram and what questions the students need to be asked. Gather this information in a casual, low-key manner. Some examples of purposes and sample questions follow:

   - Tap into the friendship groups. ('List all your friends in the class.')

   - Organise groups for a particular learning activity. ('Who would you most like to work with this week on mathematical problems?')

   - Construct informal activity groups. ('List three people who you would like to spend free time with.')

   - Establish seating arrangements for a term. ('List five people who you would like to sit with this term.')

2 Organise the collected information into a table or spreadsheet to identify the pattern of responses.

3 Translate this information into a map or diagram. (Photographs can be used instead.) There are a great number of ways in which to display sociogram results, as an online search will demonstrate, but it helps to start simply.

4 Use arrows to show which students have been chosen by whom. Try to arrange students so the resulting diagram has the least possible number of crossed lines, to make the map easy to read.

5 Consider what this sociogram says about the classroom's emotional dynamics. Who are the social 'magnets'? Which children are isolated in the class? Identify the 'mutual choice pairs'. Are there any surprises in the data collected? How can the information be used to improve students' grouping and performance?

4 What do I need to teach now?

Having gathered information during the first steps of the RTF, responsive teachers determine what their students need to learn by considering this information in relation to the curriculum and what they know about learning and development. This may be quite straightforward for many students because the curriculum is written in line with their needs. However, this is only the beginning of class planning and assessment for a class of diverse learners. It is important to teach the students who actually are in the classroom, and not those teachers might 'think' (or wish) are in front of them. Responsive teachers also have responsibility for creating a new learning community in their classrooms. What learning is needed around the processes and expectations of the classroom or school? Do these students know each other? Have they learnt together before? Are they aware of the classroom expectations and of the types of learning tasks to be used? (Such classroom-level instructional strategies are discussed in detail in chapter 6.)

5 How do I teach for all my learners?

Responding to this part of the RTF draws on teachers' skills and knowledge of teaching, their efficient use of the curriculum and its supporting documents and the physical and personnel resources available in their classrooms. Teachers need to consider these resources in light of what they know about what their students bring to the classroom. The students themselves are often the most valuable 'resources' available. It is not just about what students need to learn but what they can teach others and how they can develop into sustainable lifelong learners.

Within this step of inclusive teaching is the corollary question 'How will I know what has been learnt?' It is integral to planning a teaching sequence that teachers obtain some indication of the learning that has happened (or has not taken place). Teaching does not necessarily result in learning, so the effect of teaching needs to be closely monitored to ensure informed decisions about future instruction. (Specific strategies for differentiated teaching and assessment are discussed in chapter 7.)

6 What did my students learn?

While effective teachers employ assessment strategies throughout the RTF, this question cues the place of traditional assessment and testing of achievement. There are many ways in which this assessment can be done. Teachers can consider the basic assessment *of* learning – the assessment of achievement in relation to the curriculum taught. This type of assessment looks at changes in achievement and what factors may have supported or hindered students' learning. Teachers' main tasks here are to be clear about what it is they are assessing and to make sure that this is not confounded. The curriculum has defined intended learning outcomes for students, and these are the first reference point. The focus of assessment *for* learning is on the processes used in learning (both with and without assistance) and the key competencies (New Zealand curriculum) and cross-curricular capabilities (Australian curriculum) that support learning. Another layer to consider in making assessment decisions is that assessment *of* learning, in reference to the curriculum, the context of educational settings and the provision of appropriate learning opportunities.

Teachers need to assess against the intended learning outcomes of their teaching and to notice and explore any unintended outcomes for their students. The latter often come in the forms of behavioural strategies that are used by discouraged students to protect themselves from further failure or experience of 'difference' from their peers. For example, it can be quite common for gifted students to deliberately choose to underperform or engage minimally with learning tasks. Teachers need to be aware that these unintended outcomes related to assessment can occur and have strategies to address them (for example, offering a supportive cooperative classroom environment, setting achievable clear goals, focusing on mastery, providing appropriate feedback and encouraging risk-taking).

Teachers traditionally compare student assessment results on a periodic basis. There are some assumptions underlying this practice that require discussion. For example, if teachers keep a record of spelling test scores each week, they will have a set of scores measuring the same spelling processes but with different content on each occasion. Students who score 10 out of 10 each week can be assumed to have effective spelling skills, but the scores themselves do not help teachers understand how learners are mastering their spelling words. A student who scores erratically, with 4 or 5 out of 10 in some weeks and 10 out of 10 in other weeks is an inconsistent speller. This pattern raises questions about the learner and their engagement, as well as about the assessment. The scores could reflect teachers' choices of words or assessment activities rather than students' spelling skills.

Past achievement does not completely predict future achievement, particularly for students who learn in an individual way. For example, students who score 4 out of 10 or less in weekly spelling tests might be thought of as consistently poor spellers. This interpretation could become a prediction about future learning: these students will always have trouble with spelling. However, such a conclusion is a misuse of the assessment results, because it limits the possibilities of future learning. Instead, an effective, responsive teacher might ask, 'What errors are these students making? What assistance do they need to improve their spelling scores?'

From the students' perspectives, these teaching actions are also very powerful. Success is the best generator of success. To provide assessment that results in failure is as good as telling learners that they are failures. Feedback, whether deliberately given or implied through assessment results, profoundly affects students' future learning. Consistently low or erratic performances in assessments can create an expectation from students that 'I cannot do this!'

Instead of accepting poor performance, a responsive teacher will delve underneath superficial assessment results to understand more about what is going on for learners, to explore what factors supported and hindered their learning or the demonstration of their learning. Questions teachers need to ask themselves following poor assessment results include the following:

- Is the assessment reliable?
- Is the assessment valid?

- Were any particular factors affecting performance at this time?
- Are there factors that affect performance each time in this type of assessment? If so, how can I change the activity to allow a better demonstration of achievement?
- If this assessment type generally leads to failure, how else can I validly assess this area without affirming expectations of low achievement for my students?
- How can these students be supported to become more assessment capable?
- How can I make this assessment more successful for these students? Is it a matter of allowing more time to complete the test, or do the students need assistance in decoding the questions or recording answers?

A focus on student-learning processes allows additional important information to be gathered. Such assessment measures the capabilities related to learning in general, which in this book we call the ATRiUM capabilities. These learning processes are activated within the zone of proximal development – that space between what learners can do alone and what they can do with the assistance of others. The general idea underlying this social mediation of learning is that what learners can do with assistance today is what they will be able to do independently tomorrow. Responsive teachers activate the zone of proximal development and engage with these processes while learning is in progress. In this way, they continuously monitor their students' learning, evaluate the impact of current learning opportunities and make decisions about how to better support learning.

7 What feedback supports my students' learning?

This step of the RTF is inherently connected to the previous step and is usually planned in tandem with teaching and assessment approaches. Not only will feedback be a key part of daily in-class interactions, but in a formal mode it will provide feedback about students' learning to their families (*whānau*), the school and the system. As well, an effective scaffold for delivering daily feedback carries over into written reporting.

In Hattie's (2009) broad meta-analysis of the factors that affect learning, feedback stands out as one of the most powerful. Feedback is information about learning and task success gathered through assessment and provided to learners. It supports future learning, and it is therefore vitally important for teachers to know that some types of feedback are more effective than others. Feedback can be provided in many ways, either deliberately or implied. Effectively utilised, it works to assist students to reduce the gap between their current performance and the intended learning outcomes.

Giving effective feedback is a skill that teachers need to develop. In sustainable learning, feedback language is introduced by the teacher and then gradually internalised by effective learners so they become self-regulating and eventually provide supportive feedback to themselves. There is a cultural dimension to giving feedback that also has to be acknowledged: some cultures are very effusive in giving feedback, while others are more subdued. How teachers give feedback will depend to some extent on their cultural expectations and experiences as well.

The challenge for teachers is to give honest feedback that helps students' future motivation and learning. Appropriate feedback helps learners set up their own framework for self-feedback. Feedback about a task is most effective when it incorporates reference to the task, the cognitive processes and the self-regulation strategies needed for the task.

Feedback about cognitive processes and self-regulation is most powerful in supporting learning. Feedback about the task that is linked to feedback about process and self-regulation also has a strong impact. Despite this, most feedback heard in classrooms and homes is directed at the learner's self. Feedback about the self, however, is the least effective feedback type for supporting learning and is best used sparingly. This feedback type does not directly support motivation for learning or achievement, in contrast to feedback about task, process and self-regulation, which is more likely to positively affect both motivation and achievement. Even if the feedback is not explicitly about the self – that is, about the learner's worth – many children interpret such feedback as being about themselves. Teachers need to distance the self from the other feedback dimensions so learners can feel safe to try new things, to take risks in learning and to make mistakes. Feedback about a student's value needs to be positive irrespective of learning outcomes. If students feel good about themselves, the other feedback types are easier to receive and to use to support learning.

An extension of this effective feedback model is based on the notion that important feedback is also provided by the learners themselves as they self-assess their efforts. Consequently, teachers have the role of modelling effective feedback forms so that learners can begin to internalise this type of self-talk and use it to guide their own learning. Teachers' use of feedback targeted at the task, the processes needed for the task and self-regulation supports students' use of the same feedback types. This is very powerful for sustainable learning, as it supports students as they move towards becoming independent learners.

Feedback can be communicated as statements or as questions. Statements seem absolute; it is preferable to use a gentle mixture of statements and questions to give feedback and help learners develop their own feedback strategies. As learners mature, they internalise feedback and often use the same words teachers have given them while providing external feedback. This is why teachers often hear their own words repeated when students play schools! Teachers need to work out what scripts will be most appropriate for their students then use these consistently as a core of their feedback statements so that they become the language of feedback and the language of thinking about learning in the classroom. Some scripts for giving feedback are suggested in table 5.1, with statements on the left and questions on the right.

Table 5.1: *Scripts for feedback about task, process and self-regulation*

	STATEMENT	QUESTION
Task (How well the task is understood or performed)	That's right. That's wrong. That's nearly right. You could use the dictionary.	Was that right? Was it wrong? Which parts are correct? Which parts are not right yet? Could you use a dictionary?
Process (The process needed to understand or perform the task)	You did that well, by counting backwards. You remembered the list correctly. You followed the procedure step by step to get the answer. You used trial and error well in that problem. You asked intelligent questions.	How did you do the counting in that? How did you remember them all? What steps did you use to get there? Did you use trial and error? Did it help with that problem? What questions did you ask during that task?
Self-regulation (Self-monitoring, directing and regulating thinking and actions)	You are getting more consistent in your answers. You did that confidently. You changed your thinking in that question. You moved your hand in a different way then and it worked. You really stuck at that difficult question.	Are your answers more consistent? Why is that? What is working well for you? Did you feel confident during that question? How did you change your thinking for that one? What did you do differently to make that section work? How did you keep at that question and not give up?

Source: Adapted from Hattie and Timperley 2007.

Think and do 5.2: Feedback

1   Using the protocol for giving feedback provided in table 5.1 as a guide, practise providing different feedback types.

2   Observe a teacher in action and take note of the kind of feedback provided to students and its visible effect on learning.

3   Consider your experiences of receiving feedback at different stages of your educational experience in terms of the discussion presented in this chapter. Where in your life can you, or do you, use the guiding questions of 'Where am I going?', 'How am I going?' and 'Where to next?' How would you teach the value of these questions to students in your classroom?

Traditionally, feedback has been given through the allocating of marks, grades or rankings, and these strategies are still prevalent in schools and educational systems. They are used primarily not to support learning but to sort people, so that limited resources can be distributed in a way that is seen to be fair. This happens at all educational levels, from offers of places at universities to funding for students who have significant disabilities. It is important to be aware that teachers' efforts at employing feedback that supports learning, motivation and achievement will be affected by the use of marks and grades. This is because learners, particularly those who receive low marks, often interpret such results in terms of the self. It is not uncommon to hear this illustrated through statements such as 'I am dumb'. Even adult learners focus on assignment grades and tend to discount elaborated professional feedback.

A related issue in Australian schools is that of mandatory A to E grading. This practice was begun to ensure families received valid reports about their children's learning and were not misled by less direct forms of reporting. However, such a system means that learners who have any developmental delays or intellectual disability will almost always receive the lowest grade. If the research showing that grades discount any other feedback is correct, then these students are being given damaging self-focused feedback throughout their schooling (Carless 2006; Smith and Gorard 2005). This type of feedback, over time, can reduce motivation for learning, self-esteem and mental wellbeing.

8 How did my teaching support my students' learning?

This is a reflective and evaluative step in which teachers analyse the assessment information they have gathered to determine the effectiveness of their teaching and assessment activities in preparation for the next planning for teaching phase, in which preparation for how to build on learning occurs. In this phase, teachers revisit the questions 'What do the learners need to learn?' and 'How do I intend to teach and assess?'

The self-assessment by teachers that was needed in step 2 is revisited here. Not only does a teaching experience affect learners; it also contributes to teachers' expertise development. Self-assessment is essential for supporting responsive teachers' reflective practice. Considering the development of professional skills and knowledge and their application in classroom teaching is necessary during this phase; it is important to take stock of what both students and teachers have learnt and how this learning will affect future teaching.

Evaluative use of assessment information happens most often in the classroom as part of an action research cycle. It also happens on a wider scale, across schools and educational systems in the evaluation of educational programs based on assessment information (since it is not appropriate to allocate resources to or include students in programs that are not effective) and in relation to intervention programs developed for learners with specific needs. The evaluative use of assessment information can be problematic, however. For example, many teachers who teach advanced high-school classes in New South Wales feel that their students' Higher School Certificate results are increasingly used to make evaluative comments about them as teachers, without taking into account the nature of the particular learner group. Assessments in contemporary educational assessment have been increasingly used to compare schools.

Efficacious intervention programs, like *QuickSmart*, also use embedded assessment procedures (such as pre-tests, post-tests, monitoring performance through recording and graphing results and follow-up maintenance testing) to ensure they are making a difference for learners. Such assessments *of* learning provide evidence of the efficacy of interventions for individual students across school settings and contexts.

Summary

Assessment is a process that works in tandem with teaching and learning. It is no longer the end-of-year examination or a weekly classroom test; it is now a process that starts the learning and teaching cycle and is integral throughout that cycle. Assessment supports educational decision-making throughout the responsive teaching cycle. It is the gathering of information that determines achievement, informs teaching, guides the selection and screening of students and evaluates teaching. Teachers use assessment as an integral part of their periodic planning for teaching. In fact, assessment allows teachers to make sure their teaching and learning activities meet student's learning needs and abilities. Valid individual assessment supports the personalising or individualising of teaching and learning activities in order to take into account individual learners' idiosyncrasies.

Responsive teachers use assessment strategies every day in their interactions with students. Every interaction in a classroom can be seen as an assessment opportunity, a chance for teachers to provide an opportunity for students to demonstrate their learning, processing and competencies. This is informal assessment, but it is no less important than formal assessment events. Teachers who use assessment moments to underpin their teaching decisions encourage their students to become assessment capable. Teachers need to act as detectives, using assessment strategies and the interpretation of results to make sense of student learning and provide appropriate feedback that enhances students' demonstration of their own learning.

Further reading

ACT Government. 2011. 'Teachers' guide to assessment.' ACT Government. www.det.act.gov.au/__data/assets/pdf_file/0011/297182/Teachers_Guide_to_Assessment_Web.pdf.

American Psychiatric Association. n.d. 'DSM-5 development.' American Psychiatric Association. www.dsm5.org/Pages/Default.aspx.

Assessment Reform Group. 2002. *Research-based principles to guide classroom practice.* London: Assessment Reform Group.

Australian Curriculum, Assessment and Reporting Authority. 2011. 'National assessment program – literacy and numeracy (NAPLAN).' ACARA. www.nap.edu.au/naplan/naplan.html.

Australian Institute of Teaching and School Leadership. n.d. 'Australian professional standards for teachers.' AITSL. www.aitsl.edu.au/australian-professional-standards-for-teachers.

Australian State (for advice about assessment and the Australian curriculum, for example): www.qsa.qld.edu.au/13634.html.

Department of Education and Communities. n.d. 'Kindergarten assessment.' NSW Government. www.curriculumsupport.education.nsw.gov.au/beststart/assess.htm.

Education and Training Directorate. n.d. 'Early years assessment.' ACT Government. www.det. act.gov.au/teaching_and_learning/assessment_and_reporting/early_years_assessment.

McLachlan, C., S. Edwards, V. Margrain and K. McLean. 2013. *Children's learning and development: contemporary assessment in the early years.* Melbourne: Palgrave MacMillan.

Ministry of Education. 2007. 'Key competencies.' New Zealand Government. 14 September. http://nzcurriculum.tki.org.nz/The-New-Zealand-Curriculum/Key-competencies.

——. n.d. 'Assessment online.' New Zealand Government. http://assessment.tki.org.nz/.

Northern Territory Government. 2010. 'Pedagogical framework for cultural competence.' Northern Territory Government. www.education.nt.gov.au/__data/assets/pdf_file/0017/15218/PedagogicalFrameworkCulturalCompetence.pdf.

Nuffield Foundation. n.d. 'The Assessment Reform Group.' Nuffield Foundation. www.nuffieldfoundation.org/assessment-reform-group.

QuickSmart website: http://simerr.une.edu.au/quicksmart.

Weeden, P., J. Winter and P. Broadfoot. 2002. *Assessment: what's in it for schools?* London: Routledge Falmer.

Wyatt-Smith, C. and J. Cummings, eds. 2009. *Educational assessment in the 21st century: connecting theory and practice.* Dordrecht: Springer.

References

ACARA (Australian Curriculum, Assessment and Reporting Authority). n.d. 'Australian curriculum.' ACARA. www.australiancurriculum.edu.au/.

AITSL (Australian Institute for Teaching and School Leadership). 2014. 'Australian professional standards for teachers.' AITSL. www.aitsl.edu.au/australian-professional-standards-for-teachers/standards/list.

APA (American Psychiatric Association). 2013. *Diagnostic statistical manual of mental disorders,* 5th edn. Arlington, VA: APA.

ARG (Assessment Reform Group). 2002. 'Assessment for learning: 10 principles.' ARG. http://assessmentreformgroup.files.wordpress.com/2012/01/10principles_english.pdf.

Berman, J. 2001. 'An application of dynamic assessment to school mathematical learning.' PhD thesis, University of New England.

Biggs, J. and C. Tang. 2011. *Teaching for quality learning at university.* Maidenhead: McGraw-Hill.

BOS (Board of Studies NSW). n.d. 'Disability provisions.' BOS. www.boardofstudies.nsw.edu.au/disability-provisions/.

Carless, D. 2006. 'Differing perceptions in the feedback process.' *Studies in Higher Education* 31 (2): 219–33.

Chaffey, G. 2008. 'Is gifted education a necessary ingredient in creating a level playing field for Indigenous children in education?' *Australasian Journal of Gifted Education* 17 (1): 38.

——. 2009. 'Gifted but underachieving: Australian Indigenous children.' In T. Balchin, B. Hymer and D. J. Matthews, eds. *The Routledge international companion to gifted education*, 106. Oxford and New York: Routledge.

DEECD (Department of Education and Early Childhood Development). 2014. 'Assessment advice.' DEECD. www.education.vic.gov.au/school/teachers/support/Pages/advice.aspx.

DEEWR (Department of Education, Employment and Workplace Relations). 2011. *Guide to developing personalised learning plans for Aboriginal and Torres Strait Islander students: a professional learning resource*. Canberra: Australian Government.

Department of Education. 2013. 'Aboriginal and Torres Strait Islander Education action plan 2010–2014.' Australian Government. https://education.gov.au/aboriginal-and-torres-strait -islander-education-action-plan-2010-2014-0.

Department of Internal Affairs. 2008. 'Official version of Te Aho Matua o Nga Kura Kaupapa Māori and an explanation in English.' *Supplement to the New Zealand Gazette*, no. 32: 735–46. Available at New Zealand Curriculum Communities. https://nzccs.wikispaces.com/ file/view/Supplement_TeAho32Feb08.pdf.

Graham, L. and J. Berman. 2013. *Final project evaluation: closing the gap in NSW independent schools*. Report presented to the Association of Independent Schools of NSW, Sydney.

Graham, L., J. Berman and A. Bellert. 2002. 'Practical literacy programming for students with disabilities: making IEPs work in the classroom.' In B. Gordon, ed. *Practical literacy programming*, 121–35. Sydney: Primary English Teaching Association.

Hattie, J. 2009. *Visible learning: a synthesis of over 800 meta-analyses relating to achievement*. London and New York: Routledge.

Hattie, J. and H. Timperley. 2007. 'The power of feedback.' *Review of Educational Research* 77 (1): 81–112.

Herr, N., M. Rivas, B. Foley, V. Vandergon, M. d'Alessio, G. Simila, D. Nguyen-Graff and H. Postma. 2012. 'Employing collaborative online documents for continuous formative assessments.' In P. Resta, ed. *Proceedings of the Society for Information Technology and Teacher Education* 2012, 3899–903. Chesapeake, VA: Association for the Advancement of Computing in Education.

HookED. n.d. Website. Pam Hook. http://pamhook.com.

Lauchlan, F. and D. Carrigan. 2013. *Improving learning through dynamic assessment: a practical classroom resource*. London: Jessica Kingsley.

Lidz, C. 2003. *Early childhood assessment*. Hoboken, NJ: John Wiley.

Ministry of Education. 2007. 'The New Zealand curriculum.' Wellington: Learning Media. Link to document at 'The New Zealand curriculum.' New Zealand Government. http://nzcurriculum. tki.org.nz/The-New-Zealand-Curriculum.

——. 2014. 'Modern learning environment.' New Zealand Government. www.minedu.govt.nz/ NZEducation/EducationPolicies/Schools/PropertyToolBox/StateSchools/Design/Modern LearningEnvironment.aspx.

——. n.d. 'Narrative assessment.' New Zealand Government. http://assessment.tki.org.nz/ Assessment-tools-resources/Tools-for-Learners-with-Special-Education-Needs/Narrative -assessment.

Northern Territory Government. 2010. 'Pedagogical framework for cultural competence.' Northern Territory Government. www.education.nt.gov.au/__data/assets/pdf_file/0017/15218/Pedag ogicalFrameworkCulturalCompetence.pdf.

NVES (National VET E-learning Strategy). n.d. 'E-assessment.' http://flexiblelearning.net.au/ tools-and-resources/assessment/.

NZQA (New Zealand Qualifications Authority). n.d. 'Special assessment conditions guidelines.' NZQA. www.nzqa.govt.nz/providers-partners/assessment-and-moderation/managing-national -assessment-in-schools/special-assessment-conditions-guidelines/.

NZTC (New Zealand Teachers Council). 2009. 'Registered teacher criteria.' NZTC. www. teacherscouncil.govt.nz/rtc.

——. 2011. 'Tātaiako: cultural competencies for teachers of Māori learners' NZTC. www. teacherscouncil.co.nz/sites/default/files/Tataiako%20Cultural%20Competencies%20 for%20Teachers%20of%20Maori%20Learners.pdf.

Perso, T. F. 2003. *Improving Aboriginal numeracy*. Adelaide: Australian Association of Mathematics Teachers.

Rogoff, B. and J. Wertsch. 1984. *Children's learning in the 'zone of proximal development'*. San Francisco, CA: Jossey-Bass.

SCEEC (Standing Council on School Education and Early Childhood). 2013. *Aboriginal and Torres Strait Islander education action plan 2010–2014*. Melbourne: SCEEC.

Smith, E. and S. Gorard. 2005. '"They don't give us our marks": the role of formative feedback in student progress.' *Assessment in Education: Principles, Policy & Practice* 12 (1): 21–38.

van den Bergh, L., A. Ros and D. Beijard. 2013. 'Teacher feedback during active learning: current practices in primary schools.' *British Journal of Educational Psychology* 83 (2): 341–62.

Wong, B., L. Graham, M. Hoskyn and J. Berman. 2008. *The ABCs of learning*, 2nd edn. Burlington, MA: Elsevier Academic.

Chapter 6

Learning for all

Intended learning outcomes

Engagement with the text in this chapter will enable readers to do the following:

- utilise the ATRiUM capabilities to focus on the strengths and needs of individual students when planning and implementing responsive teaching for effective learning

- explain the limitations of using labels to categorise the learning needs of students with disabilities or learning difficulties and understand that responsive teachers focus on learning, not labels, in order to best provide learning for all

- describe key aspects of some major disability categories and identify capabilities on which to focus when planning learning support for students with disabilities or learning difficulties

- reflect on how collaboration with families and systematic frameworks for intervention inform and support responsive teaching

- distinguish how key strategies and instructional approaches support teaching for learning for all

Big ideas

- In learning for all, responsive teachers strive to provide teaching and learning that meet the needs of all learners. This requires insight into the needs of all students in the class and knowledge about evidence-based strategies and approaches to teaching.

- All learners have similar fundamental learning needs, yet every learner is different. These differences matter, especially in terms of planned, responsive teaching and effective learning.

ATRiUM Active learning; Thinking; Relating to others; Using language, symbols and ICT; and Managing self.

- By viewing students with disabilities or learning difficulties through the lens of **ATRiUM** capabilities, teachers can gain valuable insights that provide important information for teaching and learning.

- Although knowing about disability categories may provide teachers with useful information about student learning, an overt focus on disabilities or learning difficulties can lead teachers to view students in terms of what they *can't* do rather than what they *can* do.

- Collaboration with the families of students with disabilities or learning difficulties facilitates information-sharing that is beneficial to all.

- Early intervention is predicated upon the assumption that providing timely, appropriate support for learning can reduce the impact of disability, with long-term benefits for individuals, their families and their communities.

- Research has validated some key instructional approaches that lead to improved learning outcomes for students with disabilities or learning difficulties. Combining direct instruction and strategy instruction is a fundamentally effective approach for supporting learning for all.

Introduction

When the wide range of developmental domains are considered – such as language, visual processing, sensory integration, physical growth, coordination, memory, self-regulation of emotion and attention, motivation and social skills – then every individual has a unique profile of capabilities and differences, mediated by factors such as personality and experience. This diversity is based on differences, and in the context of responsive teaching and effective student learning, students' differences *matter*.

Sustainable learning focuses on the capabilities and learning needs of all students and the professional capabilities and professional learning needs of all teachers. In order to sustain learning, both teachers and students need to develop knowledge, skills, strategies and attitudes that will equip them to negotiate the contemporary world's increasingly complex and uncertain circumstances. Inclusive practices lie at the heart of learning for all; therefore, the knowledge and practices most relevant to inclusion are the focus of this chapter. Teaching for sustainable learning requires teachers to make instructional plans and decisions based on the needs of the learners about what to teach and how to teach it effectively. Specifically, this chapter relates to

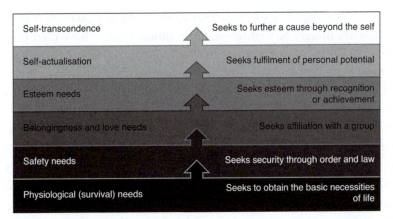

Figure 6.1: *Maslow's expanded hierarchy of needs*
Source: Adapted from Maslow 1954, 1987. Printed and electronically reproduced by permission of Pearson Education, Inc.

the identification of students' learning needs and consequent intentional planning by the teacher to provide learning opportunities for all.

What do all students need?

What do all students need in order to learn? Although teachers must identify the particular learning needs of individual students, it is useful to reflect that in many ways all students have similar needs, both in general and in regard to learning.

A well-known framework for considering human needs in general is Maslow's (1954, 1987) hierarchy of needs, which examines human behaviour from a holistic perspective. It proposes that people's behaviour and motivation can be understood as the processes of striving to meet universal human needs. Accordingly, human needs are arranged in a hierarchy of physical, emotional, social and intellectual needs. Maslow's theory includes the premise, disputed by some, that survival needs must be satisfied before it is possible to progress to higher-level, or growth, needs. An extended hierarchy is represented in figure 6.1 (Koltko-Rivera 2006).

Think and do 6.1: Hierarchy of needs

Using the stages of need depicted in figure 6.1, describe Maslow's (1954, 1987) hierarchy of needs in the context of student learning in contemporary classrooms. Make sure you think inclusively; for example, consider multicultural perspectives and disability perspectives.

1   What are the basic student needs to which teachers can contribute?

2   How can teachers ensure their students' psychological and cognitive needs are met in the classroom?

3   What does self-fulfilment mean in an everyday classroom setting?

Maslow's hierarchy theory has obvious applications in classroom teachers' work. Students who are hungry or frightened, for example, need to have their physiological needs met in order to fully participate in classroom activities and learning. Similarly, students need to feel comfortable within the classroom and know that their contributions and efforts are valued if they are to progress academically to the best of their potential.

Once certain environmental and affective conditions within the classroom and school environment are in place, what do all students need in order to learn? An obvious response is 'Good teaching!' Hattie's (2003, 2009) work provides key information about 'good' teaching by identifying influences most likely to have a positive impact on the nature and quality of effective student learning. In reporting over 800 meta-analyses relating to student achievement, Hattie (2003, 2) differentiated the major sources of variance in student performance and discovered that teacher-mediated factors account for about 30 per cent of these, noting that 'it is what teachers know, do, and care about which is very powerful in this learning equation'. According to Hattie's analysis, the areas under teachers' control that are most likely to influence students' achievement include feedback and remediation with feedback, instruction and direct instruction, class environment, the challenge of goals, peer tutoring and mastery learning. (The question of what constitutes 'good' teaching is also discussed in chapters 3 and 7.)

Think and do 6.2: Teaching influences

1   All students need 'good' teaching in order to learn to the best of their potential. Research the teacher-mediated influences that Hattie (2003) identified as most beneficial for improving student-learning outcomes.

2   Think about teaching and learning experiences that 'worked' for you at school or university or in other learning environments. Putting aside the personality of the teacher, identify the teaching approaches and strategies that were most helpful to you as a learner. Can you relate these strategies and approaches to the teacher-mediated influences shown to have a large impact?

Teachers can derive a lot of useful information about their students – what they need to learn and how best to teach it – by first gathering information about their capabilities and learning needs. Using information-gathering and evaluation of student needs based on the ATRiUM capabilities can provide a lens through which to look for deeper understandings about the capabilities and learning needs of all students, as well as for identifying areas for pedagogical and instructional supports that individual students may require. Figure 6.2 shows some key areas to consider when identifying students' capabilities and learning needs.

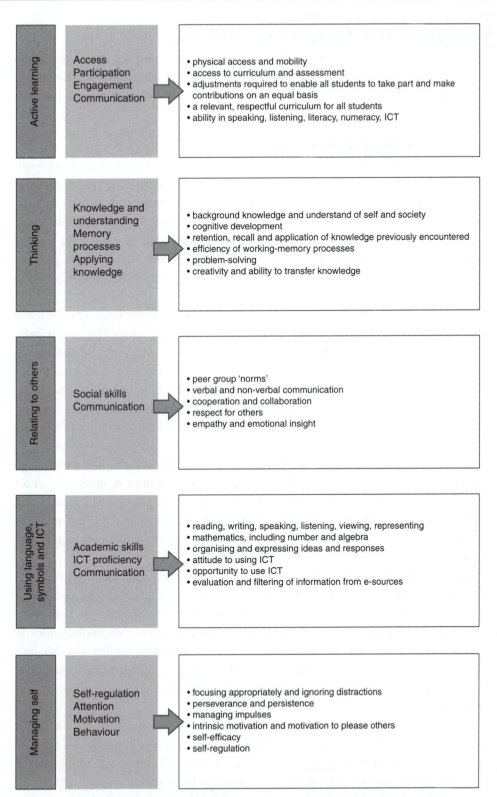

Figure 6.2: *Using ATRiUM to identify students' capabilities and learning needs*

Supporting learning for all

There is much that a classroom teacher can do to support learning for all, but in the context of sustainable learning, such support is maximised when it takes place within a broader framework that effectively draws upon family, community and systemic structures.

Home–school partnerships

Students do not leave their home and community when they come to school but begin to belong to another community and face the challenge of reconciling similarities and differences between these communities. Teachers can expand and enrich students' day-to-day interactions by fostering family–school partnering practices that empower families to support students at home and in school (Lines, Miller and Arthur-Stanley 2011). Nurturing respectful relationships with families and developing a genuine sense of shared responsibility are seen as fundamental to providing better learning outcomes for all students.

Schools can provide details about available community services and facilities and information that have the potential to help families with issues they face in relation to parenting, understanding child and adolescent development and supporting learning in the home. Parents or carers are the 'experts' on their children and can provide invaluable information for teachers about their children, their history and their personal characteristics, all of which help teachers better understand the children as learners. Families can also help teachers to understand children's family backgrounds, cultures and goals.

Schools and teachers need to communicate with families about a wide range of matters, but especially about school programs and student progress. In order for communication to remain open, it is important that parents and carers are informed about a student's successes as well as their challenges and that teachers and school leaders are available and approachable so parents and carers can initiate communication.

Learning does not stop with the last lesson of the school day, and many parents and carers are keen to support their children by discussing, practising and applying their academic skills at home. Parents and carers can be encouraged to support their children in applying 'school learning' in reading, writing or mathematics to everyday literacy and numeracy tasks, such as writing a shopping list and calculating costs. It is also important for parents and carers to continue to value informal learning that occurs through play, social events, household tasks and other aspects of daily life.

Both school and home can benefit when schools provide opportunities for family and community members to volunteer. This enables members of the broader school community to make a contribution at a level they are comfortable with and gives the school access to resources that would otherwise not be available.

Intervention planning

Many, but not all, students with disabilities or learning difficulties display learning patterns that are different or delayed when compared to those of their peers. A common response is to provide some kind of intervention to support students' learning of the desired knowledge or skills. Early intervention – that is, intervention offered when the learning delays first become apparent – is thought to be the most effective approach, because it can prevent more long-term and serious impacts of disability or learning difficulty, potentially improving learning outcomes and reducing the need for costly ongoing support. For example, when formative assessment early in the school year indicates that a student is experiencing difficulty in writing sentences, a brief and well-targeted intervention program implemented at the time has greater potential to help the student 'catch up' with their peers than waiting until the delay is 'proven' by formal testing or end-of-year reporting (the wait-to-fail approach). The long-term benefits of such interventions are obvious: the costs of timely short-term intervention are far outweighed by the costs of not intervening and waiting until the student has 'failed'. Early identification of delays in learning followed by focused short-term or long-term instructional interventions can significantly decrease the impact of learning problems during school and for the whole of an individual's life.

The duration and frequency of early intervention are variable, depending on the level of need and the complexity of the condition. Importantly, in order to maximise the effective use of available resources to achieve educational outcomes, it is essential that intervention approaches are based on evidence of best practice rather than on a whim of what might work. Such an approach is also relevant to systemic considerations – that is, school and system planning – about how to provide timely, effective and efficient academic, social or behavioural support to students.

An influential model that can be used to guide such intervention planning and resource allocation considerations is **response to intervention** (often abbreviated to RtI and also referred to as responsiveness to intervention and response to instruction). Response to intervention is an approach that advocates systematic attention to both early identification of emerging learning delays through screening and classroom assessment, and early intervention using planned and evidence-based approaches (Gersten et al. 2009). It combines screening and high-quality instruction for every student with regular monitoring and assessment to identify learning difficulties as soon as they emerge and timely, effective intervention to prevent students from falling behind (see Fuchs and Fuchs 2006).

> **Response to intervention** is a multi-level approach for aiding students that is adjusted and modified as needed.

Consistent with the least intensive to most intensive design of the multi-tiered response to intervention model, at tier 1 students are provided with effective, evidence-based instruction in their classroom with information from universal, curriculum-based assessment and monitoring used to inform instructional decision-making. Students who do not demonstrate anticipated progress in response to this

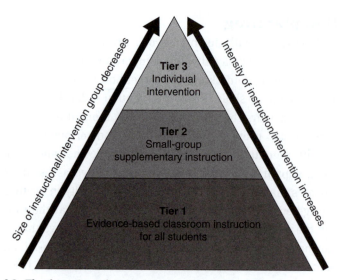

Figure 6.3: *The three tiers of response to intervention*
Source: Adapted from Vaughn 2003. Reproduced with permission of the RTI Center.

core, universal instruction are identified through assessment and monitoring. They then participate in small-group supplementary tier 2 interventions and, when necessary, more intensive tier 3 interventions (Vaughn 2003; see figure 6.3).

Research on multi-tier implementations in the United States has indicated evidence of growth in student performance, increased task completion and reduction in special educational referrals (Glover and Di Perna 2007). Response to intervention has been influential in the United States in recent decades, particularly as it applies to identifying low-achieving students soon after learning delays or problems emerge and providing them with timely, appropriate intervention (Fuchs and Fuchs 2006). In Australia, where formal diagnosis of students experiencing learning difficulties is not routinely required to access school learning support services, the construct of response to intervention is more relevant as a framework for systematic planning for curriculum-based assessment and monitoring and appropriate intervention (Graham and Bailey 2007). Although response to intervention is yet to be widely implemented in Australia, it is relevant to this discussion of intervention because of its emphasis on quality-first teaching, and due to its potential to inform a responsive, systematic, data-driven approach to the planning and provision of appropriate support for those students experiencing persistent learning difficulties.

Disabilities and learning difficulties

So far in this text, we have not explicitly described categories of disabilities or learning difficulties, as we wanted to delay this discussion until it could be framed within broader considerations about sustainable learning and responsive teaching. Using disability or learning difficulty labels to describe and understand students and their learning needs is of limited value for teachers working towards providing learning for all. The notion of sustainable learning implies a commitment to perceiving each student as an individual who is developing – seeing students holistically, as learners with unique characteristics, rather than recognising them according to labels or categories of limitation. In this way, the learners themselves – their capabilities, talents, experiences, background knowledge and motivations – are acknowledged and respected. Knowing about students' interests, motivations, ability to use and understand language and levels of proficiency in academic and social skills provides teachers with far more information to work with in developing responsive teaching than knowledge about the causes and characteristics of a particular disability or learning difficulty – although this information does have relevance, as discussed below.

Think and do 6.3: Capabilities and differences

Think about a person you know whose development and/or learning was delayed or notably different in some way compared to that of their peers. You may have encountered the person during your schooling, in the community, in your family or while teaching. Without using any disability or learning difficulty labels or referring to what the person 'couldn't do', briefly describe the person, their capabilities and differences and what their strengths and needs as a learner might be. Repeat this three-step process to describe yourself.

Students' capabilities and differences and the distinctions between difference and disability or learning difficulty are complex matters. They are also very relevant matters for teachers to consider and frequently reconsider, because students with disabilities, learning difficulties or other additional learning needs, all of whom require adjustments, differentiation or a different approach to enable learning, are present in almost all classrooms. In many ways, as we have seen, these students have the same fundamental learning needs as their peers, but in some unique ways their needs are different from those of their peers. Many students, with disabilities or without, will require additional assistance and support for learning from their teachers during their school lives. The responsibility to provide learning for all means that teachers acknowledge differences in their students' capabilities and plan for, resource and deliver learning experiences that intentionally and respectfully develop the capabilities of the learners.

In particular contexts, including the educational planning necessary for learning for all, differences do have to be acknowledged, and student needs in academic, social and lifelong learning skills, when divergent from those of their peers, need to be identified.

In preparing to teach students with disabilities or learning difficulties, teachers need to make sure they don't rely on formulaic responses – for example, that students who have spina bifida require a certain set of supports and teaching, while learners who have ASD require a different set. This is true only to a certain extent and can be quite misleading. It also suggests that the process of understanding what each student brings to their learning is simple, when in fact it is very complex. Responsive teachers question assumptions around a label and find out what it means for *this* learner, in *this* school context, at *this* time.

Online research

There is an overwhelming body of accessible knowledge about disabilities and learning difficulties – too much to know and too much to cover in detail in this book. Instead, a useful approach is to access and filter the information available online. For example, the NSW Department of Education and Communities' online resource Physical as Anything is an informative and reliable starting point for research. It contains information about a wide range of medical, developmental and psychological conditions, with pages on specific conditions and related information under the tabs 'Schools and teachers', 'Implications for schools' and 'Classroom support' (Department of Education and Communities, n.d.). Similarly, New Zealand's Ministry of Health (2014) website contains information about some common disabilities and learning difficulties.

However, when researching online, significant caution is needed, as there are many websites promoting commercial programs and educational approaches promulgated for specific disabilities and learning difficulties that do not have a sound evidence base. Bourke and Loveridge (2013) suggest useful criteria for evidence-based research and stipulate finding a balanced view by looking at research, practice and personal perspectives on the topic. The following access tips and filtering parameters are also helpful.

Access tips

- Define your search by identifying keywords, for example, 'students' 'spina bifida' and 'learning' (and, perhaps, 'Australia' or 'New Zealand').
- Use double quotation marks to search for an exact phrase.
- The Boolean search terms 'AND', 'OR' and 'NOT' help refine a search.

Filtering parameters

Authority: Who is the author? Do you know the author? Does the page express fact or opinion? Are other viewpoints acknowledged?

Objectivity: Does the information seem to be biased? Are all perspectives represented in a balanced way? Is the information actually intended to be humorous or a parody instead of serious?

Timeliness: How current and timely is the information? Does the page provide specific dates? Does it matter how current the information is for this topic?

Efficiency: Is the information worth the effort necessary to access it? Is it well organised – for example, is there a table of contents, menu, index and other navigational tools? Is the information presented in simple and effective way?

Authenticity: Is the information authentic? Is it from a credible organisation? Has its accuracy been confirmed by others? Does it come from a primary or secondary source? Are original sources provided and are they clearly documented? Is there a bibliography?

Relevance: How helpful is the information? Is it written in a useable form, and is it sufficiently detailed?

Oneness: Does the source 'fit' with the other information gathered, enabling alignment and summarising of facts?

Accuracy: Is this information accurate? Is it possible to know?

Disability categories

Disability categories are broad and include quite heterogeneous populations. For example, the ASD diagnosis includes highly intelligent and competent people and people who experience profound impairment. The adage used by ASD educators 'if you know one person with autism, you know one person with autism' certainly applies to other conditions as well, because many disability categories encompass significant variability in their impact on individuals. Inconsistency in language concerning both disability and the impact of disability supports the argument that disability labels or categories yield little information for teachers about individuals, how they learn and how to effectively teach them. Hence, in the context of sustainable learning we suggest that teachers focus on their students' *learning*, not labels.

Teachers need to be aware that the term 'disability' means different things in different contexts, so the labels and categories used to identify students with disabilities are quite variable. Similarly, while some syndromes identified in medicine or psychology necessarily imply a disability, many do not. The profusion of terms such as 'disability', 'delay', 'disorder' and 'syndrome' makes defining disability in a school context a challenging endeavour. For example, in Australia, the *Disability Discrimination Act 1992* defines disability quite broadly, but in some Australian states a student can have a disability according to the Disability Discrimination Act yet not meet criteria that would enable their local school to access extra funding for them. Further, understandings of disabilities and their classifications change over time, and disability categories overlap, as evidenced by complex disabilities or dual diagnoses.

Many of the labels for disabilities that teachers encounter are those defined in the DSM-5 (APA 2013a) and the World Health Organization's (2010) *International statistical classification of diseases*. The diagnostic labels listed in these works are constructed in response to recognised behaviour patterns and physiological symptoms and are written for the purpose of guiding diagnosis by medical practitioners. The descriptions and labels alter over time, as different patterns and hypotheses are developed and framed by new knowledge or ways of seeing differences in human functioning. There is an assumption that there is an underlying physiological basis for recognised behaviour patterns; however, this has not been established in many cases. The list below describes the evolution of the DSM criteria in relation to ASD from 1952 to 2013 and shows how this diagnostic label has changed over time.

DSM-I (1952): Children who exhibited autistic-like symptoms were diagnosed under the label 'schizophrenic reaction, childhood type'.

DSM-II (1968): Children who exhibited autistic-like symptoms were diagnosed under the label 'schizophrenic, childhood type'.

DSM-III (1980): Young children who exhibited autistic-like symptoms were diagnosed under the label 'infantile autism'.

DSM-III-R (1987): Children who exhibited autistic-like symptoms were diagnosed under the labels 'autistic disorder' or 'pervasive developmental disorder not otherwise specified (PDD-NOS)'.

DSM-IV (1994): Children who exhibited autistic-like symptoms were diagnosed under the label 'Pervasive developmental disorder', which had several subtypes: autistic disorder, Asperger's disorder, Rett's disorder, childhood disintegrative disorder and pervasive developmental disorder not otherwise specified (PDD-NOS).

DSM-5 (2013): Children who exhibit autistic-like symptoms are diagnosed with the umbrella diagnosis of 'autism spectrum disorder' (APA 2013b, 1).

Despite the limitations of diagnostic criteria, it is important to acknowledge that some specific information about disabilities is informative for teachers, because they can benefit from knowing about general behaviour or development patterns associated with the conditions. In turn, this information may help teachers identify evidence-based strategies and approaches suitable for their students. Accordingly, summary information is given below about selected disabilities, described in generic categories commonly recognised in educational settings. Importantly, this information is linked to suggested areas of consideration for instructional support. The descriptions here are brief, because information about disabilities (and learning difficulties) is readily available elsewhere – for example, in developmental psychology texts, special educational books and online. Each description is followed by lists of key ATRiUM capabilities, differentiation approaches and on-the-spot adjustments on which focus should initially be placed when planning and delivering responsive teaching.

Autism spectrum disorder

ASD is a lifelong neurodevelopmental disorder that manifests with varying degrees of severity. It can influence how a person processes information, communicates and relates to other people, thereby impacting on their understanding of the social world and what is happening around them. It is more prevalent in males than in females but occurs with equal frequency within all ethnic and socioeconomic groups.

People living with ASD commonly have impairments in three development areas: social communication, social interaction, and imagination and thought (Wing and Gould 1979). Some people experience substantial difficulties in all areas, while for others the impact may be subtle and more evident in some development areas than in others. Related factors include sensory sensitivity, restricted and repetitive interests, anxiety, executive functioning constraints and learning difficulties. Many people with ASD have intellectual capacities in the average range (some with particular strengths or specific weaknesses in cognitive domains), some have advanced intellectual capacities, and some have profound intellectual disability.

In the school setting, students experiencing ASD often benefit from structured classroom routines, with advanced warning of impending changes and a well-organised learning environment, including clearly articulated, regularly referred to and consistently enforced rewards and rules. The use of social stories, social scripts and visual representation, such as comic-style drawings, is an often-cited strategy for supporting understanding about social skills, desirable and undesirable behaviours and developing insights into others' emotions.

ATRiUM capabilities
- active learning (curriculum access)
- relationships (empathy, emotional insight)
- managing self (self-regulation)

Differentiation approaches
- varying the participation mode – for example, using an ICT application rather than a written task to show understanding
- planning further to support students in group work contexts – for example, giving students specific roles within a group
- providing scaffolds for tasks – for example, breaking down tasks into step-by-step components
- using visual schedules and reminders to support learning, organisation and behaviour
- adjusting the level of task difficulty to suit students' academic and social capabilities

On-the-spot adjustments
- using preferential seating or a seating plan for the whole class
- giving opportunities for lesson breaks
- using 'fiddle toys' or other small items to help regulate sensory issues or anxiety
- allowing students the option to move away from or otherwise manage a potential source of anxiety or sensory overload – for example, wearing headphones to block out noise

Intellectual disability

People with an intellectual disability experience limitations in some aspects of daily functioning and in their ability to learn and use new information. Terms commonly used synonymously for intellectual disability include 'cognitive disability', 'developmental delay' and 'learning disability' (Hinckson and Curtis 2013). The terminology is ambiguous and caution is required, as not all students who are described as having a developmental delay or a learning disability actually have an intellectual disability. It can be a stand-alone condition, a symptom of a syndrome (for example, Down syndrome) or the impact of a condition such as cerebral palsy (although not all people with cerebral palsy have an intellectual disability).

Intellectual disability results from a wide range of possible impairments or conditions, and its impact varies with individuals and their context. Some people with mild intellectual disability are able to complete regular educational courses, including senior school courses, when supported by appropriate differentiation and adjustments. Although a person with intellectual disability may become competent in academic skills such as reading, writing and arithmetic, they are likely to experience difficulty with learning new information, especially higher-order concepts or complex ideas, and with generalising information between contexts to solve novel problems. Others, especially those with a moderate or severe intellectual disability, require a pattern of study quite different from the regular curriculum, with a greater focus on functional skills.

In the school setting, students with an intellectual disability often benefit from some extra small-group or individual instruction to develop academic skills, either in the classroom or in a withdrawal setting. Additional support in developing age-appropriate social skills and in learning about child protection and anti-bullying strategies can be beneficial.

ATRiUM capabilities

- active learning (curriculum access, communication)
- thinking (knowledge and understanding, memory)
- using language, symbols and ICT (academic skills)

Differentiation approaches

- modifying the task difficulty level
- providing scaffolds or proformas for tasks
- pre-teaching and reteaching
- allowing for additional practice
- breaking down tasks into achievable steps
- facilitating alternative response formats – for example, a poster presentation rather than an essay

On-the-spot adjustments
- reducing the quantity of work
- providing additional simplified demonstrations or explanations
- using visual representations for ideas and routines

Language disorders

Students experiencing difficulties with understanding language and formulating and expressing ideas may be assessed by a speech therapist as having a language disorder in expressive or receptive language, or both. An expressive language disorder means that the person has difficulty formulating and sequencing ideas, while a receptive language disorder indicates difficulty processing and understanding others' language. Difficulties with articulation may also present as part of a language disorder, although many people with expressive or receptive language difficulties speak with no apparent impediment in their speech, and, conversely, many people who experience articulation difficulties do not have a receptive or expressive language disorder. Pragmatic language – the use of language in social communication – may also be impaired in some individuals and is commonly found in those with ASD. Many people with an intellectual disability can also be considered to have a language disorder because of the difficulties they experience in understanding communication and expressing their ideas.

In the school setting, the presence of a language disorder impacts on individuals' abilities to access and participate in classroom learning and social interactions, as well as on aspects of daily living. Students with a language disorder often experience a barrier to learning with high levels of verbal interactions in a classroom, because they cannot adequately process or respond to ideas being discussed. Many also experience difficulty comprehending texts and following instructions. Students with a language disorder may have the intellectual capacity to access and participate in the curriculum but experience learning difficulties because of the impact of their condition. Students with a language disorder often benefit from extra instruction and practice opportunities to develop literacy and numeracy skills and concepts, as well as from some support for appropriate social interactions with peers.

ATRiUM capabilities
- active learning (curriculum access, communication)
- thinking (memory, problem-solving)
- using language, symbols and ICT (academic skills, communication)

Differentiation approaches
- modifying the task difficulty level
- adjusting the way information is presented – for example, by providing alternative texts with simplified language
- providing step-by-step instructions for tasks

On-the-spot adjustments

- rephrasing explanations and instructions in simpler language
- limiting the amount of teacher talk when presenting new information
- providing a glossary of key terms
- allowing more time to process information and complete tasks

Vision loss and hearing loss

Significant restrictions in the ability to hear or see can be due to a wide range of factors, including congenital or developmental conditions, health conditions or accident or trauma. Such restrictions can have a major impact on how students learn and participate at school.

In the school setting, teachers of students with vision loss or hearing loss need to engage in significant collaboration with specialists, family members and the students themselves in order to understand and provide for the students' learning needs. The input of specialist teachers is often required to help students access curricula and class teachers and school communities provide appropriate adjustments and modifications. Such requirements may mean that the curriculum needs to be presented in alternative formats or with significant modification of materials and activities. Technology can play a significant role in enabling learning and participation, and options for use of adaptive, assistive and specialised technology applications should be fully explored. The learning needs of students with vision loss or hearing loss are unique to the individual and the context, so no specific suggestions for differentiation or adjustments are given below.

ATRIUM capabilities

- active learning (curriculum access, participation)
- using language, symbols and ICT (ICT proficiency)

Physical disability

Physical disability has many different causes and manifestations and impacts on each individual quite differently, even with people affected by the same condition. It can affect a person's gross and fine motor movements, coordination and stamina. People with a physical disability most often do not also have an intellectual disability, vision loss or hearing loss, and teachers need to ensure they do not make such assumptions by, for example, talking loudly and slowly to a person in a motorised scooter.

In the school setting, the effects of physical disability can impact across the curriculum and in many other school contexts. Students can experience difficulty with physical access to the school and classrooms, participation in sport and physical education and reaching or carrying equipment. More subtle impacts can be found in everyday school activities, such as handwriting, tying shoelaces, changing clothes, using the toilet, unpacking lunch, judging personal space in lines, closing zippers in bags, sitting on chairs or on the floor, folding notes to take home and putting books back on shelves. Some students with a physical disability require assistance with eating, drinking or personal care. Often, there are implications for socialisation as well.

Students with a physical disability may require the support of additional personnel, such as a teacher assistant, and additional planning and modifications to allow access for mobility devices. Whole-school planning may also be required for the location of classrooms a student with physical disability needs to access, as well as for the time and distance required to transition between locations in the school. Planning for excursions requires particular consideration, as students with a physical disability need to be able to access excursions on the same basis as other students. Consequently, if a planned excursion involves sites or activities not accessible to students with a physical disability when adequate supports are provided, alternative options for the excursion for the whole cohort of students should be considered.

ATRiUM capabilities

The main capability for the teacher's focus is active learning, particularly with regard to access to and participation in learning, which need broader consideration than physical access and must allow students to fully participate in learning activities and demonstrate knowledge and skills in assessment tasks. Equitable access and participation can be enhanced, at least in part, by appropriate use of assistive technologies.

Differentiation approaches

- presenting information in a form that is accessible to students
- planning learning activities and assessment in which students can fully participate, which may include effective use of additional personnel
- additional planning to ensure that learning activities in sport, physical education and hands-on technology subjects provide opportunity for students with physical disabilities to practise the same skills as their peers, at a level appropriate to the students' ages and capacities to perform the skills

On-the-spot adjustments

- facilitating the use of a reader or writer
- reducing the quantity of work required
- providing additional time to complete tasks
- accepting different formats for responses

Mental health disorders

Mental health disorders encompass a wide range of conditions that can have significant impacts on the learning, participation and wellbeing of students. Such conditions include anxiety, behavioural, mood and psychotic disorders. The most common mental health disorders are anxiety and depressive illnesses, which hinder active learning through passive or active non-participation and at their extreme result in non-attendance and eventually school refusal. Mental health disorders interfere with thinking skills; they have been described as like 'white noise' in between the learner and everything that is going on in the classroom. They can affect perception, attention, planning and processing, as well as demonstration of thinking and learning. Quite often, the experience of living with a mental health disorder impacts on socialisation and self-confidence.

In the school setting, students experiencing a mental health disorder often benefit from access to school psychologists who can work with them, their teachers, their family members and other mental health professionals to ensure that they feel safe and ready to learn at school. School personnel such as trusted teachers, teacher aides or peer mentors can provide additional everyday support for students when needed. Students experiencing mental health disorders may be particularly vulnerable to bullying, and this requires close monitoring by staff and supportive peers.

ATRiUM capabilities

- active learning (curriculum participation)
- managing self (self-regulation, motivation)

Differentiation approaches

- varying the task demands and participation expectations to suit students' current capacity
- avoiding or modifying at times written tasks, performance tasks and activities that require sustained attention or extensive planning

On-the-spot adjustments

- varying the timetable
- planning preferential seating
- allowing for frequent lesson breaks
- reducing the amount of content in learning and assessment tasks

Attention deficit hyperactivity disorder (ADHD)

ADHD can significantly impact a student's learning and participation. As mentioned in an earlier chapter, contrary to the implication of the disorder's name, students experiencing ADHD often appear to have too much attention – they can pay attention to everything and consequently have difficulty filtering out irrelevant stimuli and constraining impulses. The disorder commonly affects organisational and planning skills, such that students with the condition frequently struggle with organising them-selves, their possessions and their thinking, which can lead to difficulties in learning and socialisation.

In the school setting, students with ADHD benefit from teachers having knowl-edge about the condition and proactively responding to their learning needs – this can sometimes be a challenge, as students with ADHD can be more impulsive, disruptive or disengaged than other students. Additionally, some children who have diagnoses of ADHD are in receipt of medical intervention. Schools may have to play a role in the management of this intervention and, through communication with parents or carers and health professionals, to contribute to informed decision-making around the use and evaluation of the effectiveness of medication.

ATRIUM capabilities

- active learning (curriculum access)
- thinking (memory)
- managing self (self-regulation, attention, behaviour)

Differentiation approaches

- limiting the duration of learning tasks and activities
- reducing expectations of the quantity of work to be completed
- providing a variety of tasks using different modes of responding
- incorporating students' strengths or interests in learning activities

On-the-spot adjustments

- breaking down tasks into achievable steps
- supplying an external representation of time passing – for example, an eggtimer or digital timer with a visual representation, not just a clock
- providing organisational supports
- demonstrating planning strategies and scaffolds and encouraging students to use them
- setting appropriate work targets or goals
- implementing an individual reinforcement or reward schedule

This brief review of disabilities and learning difficulties presents different conditions as discrete entities when in fact students may experience coexisting disabilities and learning difficulties or complex conditions that present new and unique challenges for teachers.

Complex learning difficulties and disabilities

Students may experience coexisting disabilities, learning difficulties or complex conditions that present teachers with novel and unique challenges. In recent research, Carpenter and his colleagues identified 'complex learning difficulties and disabilities' as a 'new frontier' in education (see Carpenter et al. 2014; Blackburn, Carpenter and Egerton 2012; Carpenter 2010).

Students who can be described as having complex learning difficulties and disabilities include those with coexisting conditions such as ADHD, complex medical disorders or profound and multiple disabilities as well as those with disability caused by parental substance abuse (for example, foetal alcohol spectrum disorder), those with difficulties arising from premature birth and those who, due to advanced medical interventions, have survived illness and trauma. Increasing numbers of children and young people are affected by such conditions.

Complex learning difficulties and disabilities can result in students displaying complex learning patterns, very challenging behaviour and extensive learning and social needs that are unfamiliar to many educators and at times not easily accommodated in mainstream educational settings. In fact, Carpenter (2010) posits that educators are currently 'pedagogically bereft' and that affected students are educationally vulnerable because of the novel, unfamiliar and unique challenges they present.

There is a need for new, dynamic, personalised approaches to learning for children who have complex disabilities and learning difficulties. In the United Kingdom, the Complex Learning Difficulties and Disabilities Research Project has developed resources to support teachers in developing learning experiences that reflect the strengths and interests of affected students (see SSAT, n.d.).

Learning difficulties in basic academic skills

Experiencing delays or difficulty in learning basic academic skills is perhaps one of the most common impacts, or side effects, of having a disability or learning difficulty. There are also students who do not have a diagnosis but similarly experience difficulties or delays in learning and applying basic academic skills. In fact, students who do not have a disability or other condition and yet experience difficulties in learning basic academic skills comprise the largest group of students with special needs, and the size of this group continues to grow (Kavale and Forness 2000; Westwood 2003). In Australia, at least 20 per cent of all school students are considered to have problems in academic areas, most commonly in reading (Westwood and Graham 2000). This difficulty in learning and applying basic academic skills is referred to generically in education and psychology literature as 'learning disability' or, more commonly in Australia and New Zealand, 'learning difficulty'. For the purposes of the discussion to follow in this section of the text, to be consistent with the literature the term 'learning difficulties' is used to refer to students with or without a disability or learning difficulty who experience difficulties or delays in learning and applying basic academic skills (Westwood and Graham 2000).

Effective recall and application of basic academic skills are key prerequisites for school learning across the curriculum in primary and secondary schools. Students who have problems with the basics of literacy and numeracy face myriad difficulties in accessing the curriculum, especially after the first few years of school, when the educational focus shifts from learning basic academic skills to using them as tools for further inquiry and learning. Limitations in basic skills impede progress and development in many aspects of learning. They can also have devastating effects on students' self-efficacy and consequent motivation and application; to experience failure or to underachieve in almost every lesson, every day, due to poor literacy and numeracy skills is a daunting prospect indeed.

Students experiencing learning difficulties are part of almost every school community, and understanding of their needs and constraints and knowledge of supportive strategies are highly relevant for all classroom teachers. If certain students cannot read, write or calculate well – that is, they have difficulties in basic academic skills – this does not necessarily mean it is not possible for them to learn new concepts or participate in higher-order learning. Rather, the teachers of such students need to see learning difficulties as a barrier that for many students can be overcome or worked around so that they can access the curriculum.

There are some common **learner characteristics** and barriers to learning exhibited by many students experiencing learning difficulties. Generally, students with learning difficulties are inefficient in the ways they go about the process of learning (Westwood 1993), demonstrating cognitive behaviours such as using inappropriate or inefficient strategies that produce high error rates (Bellert 2008) and undermine confidence; having difficulty with storing, accessing and coordinating knowledge encountered previously and with the flexible use of that knowledge; and displaying behaviour and thinking patterns detrimental to learning, including effective and well-practised avoidance strategies (Chan and Dally 2001; Westwood 1993). Constraints in working-memory function form a key underlying characteristic of many students experiencing learning difficulties (Swanson and Sachse-Lee 2001; Swanson and Siegel 2001), and this has far-reaching implications, making the processes of learning, retaining and using new information difficult.

> **Learner characteristics** are the traits possessed by learners that could affect their ability to learn, such as an ability to stay on task or apply appropriate strategies.

While factors within learners and learners' environments can feasibly be attributed as causes of learning difficulties, it is important for teachers to acknowledge that inefficient or insufficient teaching, poor curricula and poor teacher–student relationships also contribute to and exacerbate such difficulties (Westwood 2004).

Learning difficulties and component skills

Students experiencing learning difficulties can have problems with some or all of the component skills of reading, writing and mathematics, including those listed below.

Reading

- phonological awareness (knowledge of sounds in words)
- phonics (knowledge of letter sounds and blends)
- recognition of previously encountered words
- decoding of unfamiliar words
- reading fluency
- vocabulary knowledge
- comprehension
- application of effective strategies

Writing

- physical formation of letters and legible writing achieved with appropriate speed
- organisation and sequencing of ideas
- expression of ideas in conventional formats (sentences, paragraphs, extended responses)
- vocabulary knowledge
- spelling
- stamina and persistence with writing
- application of effective strategies

Mathematics

- number sense (understanding numbers and how they are affected by mathematical operations)
- counting sequences and numerical identification
- language and literacy skills
- use of number knowledge to solve problems
- application of effective strategies

Teaching for learning for all

As we have seen, teacher proficiency and other teacher-controlled factors can and do have influence on students' attainment levels at school and beyond; educational effectiveness for all students is crucially dependent on the provision of quality teaching by competent teachers (Hattie 2003, 2005; Hill and Crévola 2003). Accordingly, regardless of student and environmental factors, classroom instructional processes form a major variable influencing student achievement (Hattie 2005; Mastropieri and Scruggs 2002; Sanders and Rivers 1996; Schacter and Thum 2004). This is particularly the case for students with disabilities or learning difficulties. Therefore, teachers must have knowledge and understanding about effective, evidence-based instructional practices if they are to meet their professional obligations to provide learning for all. This section presents information about broad strategies and approaches shown by research and evaluation to be effective in improving learning outcomes for all students (Vaughn, Gersten and Chard 2000).

Direct instruction and strategy instruction

One key approach, direct instruction, involves explicit, systematic, step-by-step instruction led by teachers (see chapter 3). It has a focus on content and requires explaining and demonstrating with examples, teacher-directed discourse, discussion and learning from texts and media. Direct instruction is especially applicable when teaching new or difficult information and when content is critical to subsequent learning (Mercer, Jordan and Miller 1996). Another important approach, strategy instruction, involves providing students with information about ways to learn, procedures for approaching learning, self-regulation and 'doing' learning tasks (see chapter 7). In a series of influential meta-analyses, Swanson and colleagues established that direct instruction and strategy instruction have the greatest potential to improve learning outcomes for students with 'learning disabilities' (interpreted here to apply to students experiencing learning difficulties) and that when combined these approaches are particularly powerful and effective (for example, see Swanson 1999; Swanson, Carson and Sachs-Lee 1996; Swanson and Hoskyn 1998). Direct instruction and strategy instruction are generally effective for students with disabilities or learning difficulties, regardless of the content area (Swanson 1999).

Task difficulty, grouping and questioning

In further analysis, Swanson and colleagues discerned three instructional components common across various instructional models and content areas as the most effective approaches for improving students' academic skills, problem-solving, behaviour and social skills (Swanson 1999; Swanson, Hoskyn and Lee 1999). The first of these is control of task difficulty by scaffolding learning – for example, using activities with the level of difficulty adjusted (easier, harder or more specific to the needs of the learner), the teacher providing extra assistance or simplifying demonstrations, and sequencing the procedure in steps from easy to difficult tasks. The second is teaching students in small interactive groups of five or less, and the third is directed response questioning – using interactive questions and answers as well as teaching students to generate questions as they work. The latter is also related to 'think aloud' procedures (Vaughn, Gersten and Chard 2000), during which teachers or peers verbalise questioning, thinking and problem-solving as they read or problem solve.

Deliberate practice

Deliberate practice, another strategy for improving student achievement, uses well-structured activities that allow for repeated experiences of critical aspects of a task (Ericsson 1990; Pegg 2013). Deliberate practice is different from rote content repetition. Rote repetition simply requires repeating a task, and while it may result in the ability to perform the task in the short term and within the same context, it is different from and less effective than deliberate practice, which supports students to develop automaticity and to transfer knowledge across settings. Within deliberate practice, specific activities focus on identified errors or weaknesses, and its implementation involves attention, rehearsal, repetition and feedback, resulting in new knowledge or skills that can later be further developed (Brabeck and Jeffrey 2010). Access to adequate practice opportunities is particularly important for some students with disabilities or learning difficulties, as they may need to rehearse strategies and information more frequently than other learners. Importantly, deliberate practice can improve student motivation to learn information and procedures, because the focused practice improves performance (Pegg 2013).

Feedback

The benefits of deliberate practice are enhanced when students are provided with timely and descriptive feedback. Feedback can be summative – for example, a percentage rank or grade on a test – or formative, when it is ongoing and communicated to the learner in order to improve learning (Shute 2009). Educators have understood the potential for feedback to positively influence performance for some time (for example, Fuchs and Fuchs 1986; Lysakowski and Walberg 1982), and its importance as a key instructional strategy has gained prominence since the publication of Hattie's work supporting the idea that it is the most powerful influence in enhancing student achievement (for example, Hattie 2003, 2005, 2009).

Feedback is considered in detail in chapter 5, but in summary, teachers improve student outcomes by initiating effective feedback practices that provide information about how and why students understand or misunderstand a specific task or content area and what steps they must take to improve (Hattie 2003). Feedback is most effective when it directly relates to the task and provides students with different, additional or enhanced information. It is also powerful when it relates to self-regulation and task completion. Least effective feedback is that which is about the self and is unrelated to performance of a task (Hattie and Timperley 2007).

Reciprocal teaching

Reciprocal teaching is an instructional approach that features a dialogue, most commonly in the form of questions and answers, between the teacher and a small group of students (Palincsar and Brown 1984). However, in this approach it is not necessarily the teacher who asks the questions; rather, students are scaffolded to ask and answer questions of each other. It is a well–known instructional routine that has been shown, through research, to improve text comprehension (see Rosenshine and

Meister 1994). Although reciprocal teaching was designed as a reading strategy, it is included in this section describing generic strategies because it has broad application to learning, not only in reading but in other content areas, such as social studies and mathematics problem-solving, and is applicable to students with different ability levels across all grades (Lederer 2000; van Garderen 2004).

In reciprocal teaching, the adult and students take turns assuming the role of 'teacher' (Palincsar 1986). They interact by predicting, questioning, summarising and clarifying information from a text.

When students engage in predicting what will happen or what information the author wants them to understand from what they are about to read, they are activating their background knowledge. They also learn to use the text's structure to help them make defensible predictions. The questioning part of the strategy provides students with opportunities to identify the kind of information that forms the basis of a good question, to frame their own questions and then to engage in asking themselves and their peers what their answers might be. Summarising is often a challenging task for students with disabilities or learning difficulties. Many find it hard to condense information and to determine which parts of a text are important and which can be omitted without losing key concepts. Teaching summarising requires modelling and practice before students experience independent success. Clarifying, the final aspect of the reciprocal teaching strategy, encourages students to identify difficult vocabulary and parts of the text where the meaning is unclear and gives them practice at implementing 'fix up' strategies to address comprehension breakdowns. Once students are taught in a structured and direct way to clarify their understanding of text through re-reading, reading ahead, using pictures or structural clues and asking for help, the conditions are set for them to read meaningfully and to engage thoughtfully with both narrative and factual texts (Graham and Bellert 2004, 2007).

Classroom management

While the idea that providing students with relevant, respectful curricula and educational tasks that will enable them to succeed reduces the need for conversations about classroom management certainly has merit, the reality of complex contemporary classrooms requires teachers to also develop, implement and refine a set of skills and approaches for managing classroom interactions and organisation. The aim of implementing such skills is to reduce the likelihood of disruptive behaviour occurring or reoccurring. In order to establish and maintain a positive learning environment, teachers need to prevent and minimise the impact of disruptive student behaviour. Richmond (2007) has developed a set of generic classroom management skills relevant to a wide range of approaches that can support teachers in promoting a classroom environment that facilitates learning. The key premises of the approach are that teacher language in the classroom should be predominately about learning, not management, and that teachers can practise a range of skills that minimise teacher management talk. Richmond's 'essential skills for classroom management' are given below and are listed from least intrusive to most intrusive, carrying the implication that teachers should predominately rely on least intrusive skills and implement the more intrusive skills only when earlier approaches have not been effective in changing student behaviour.

Establishing expectations: Clearly articulate rules for prosocial behaviour and check student understanding of these rules in the current context.

Giving instructions: Concisely and effectively describe or show what students are expected to do.

Waiting and scanning: After giving instructions, stand still, stop talking and start looking! Allow students time to process the information and scan the group for indications of non-understanding or reluctance.

Cueing with parallel acknowledgment: Acknowledge the on-task behaviour of a student or group with the intention of prompting others to behave in the same manner.

Encouraging with body language: Use the power of body language to encourage students to stay on task or get on task by making eye contact, touching student work, walking near students or making discreet nodding movements or finger signals.

Encouraging with description: Describe a desired learning behaviour seen or heard, either to an individual or the whole group. In the absence of desired learning behaviours, describe them anyway (rather than describing undesirable behaviours).

Attending selectively and ignoring tactically: To avoid unintentionally reinforcing off-task behaviour that is not seriously disturbing others, keep visually scanning to monitor the student who is of concern. (Do not ignore very inappropriate behaviour.)

Giving a choice: Respectfully challenge the student's persistent off-task behaviour by describing available choices and their logical consequences.

Following through: Firmly deliver a pre-planned action – that is, do what was planned and explained when the student was given a choice. Act calmly and with confidence.

Debriefing: After a behavioural incident, provide an opportunity for those involved and witnesses to say what happened. Avoid dramatising or sanitising the event; rather, simply talk it through and reflect upon what happened. (Richmond 2007)

Think and do 6.4: Classroom management

Microskills are discrete capabilities that teachers can use to promote student behaviours that support learning.

Research further Richmond's (2007) 'essential skills for classroom management' (sometimes referred to as **microskills**). For each skill, do the following:

1 Consider why it is useful in promoting a learning-focused classroom environment.

2 Give an example of what a teacher would say or do when implementing the skill.

3 Think of an example of when you have used the skill or when you have observed another teacher using the skill.

Summary

Learning for all focuses on student capabilities rather than on disability or learning difficulty labels. This strengths-based perspective acknowledges differences in student capabilities and proposes that such differences provide vital information for teachers as they plan and implement responsive teaching for effective learning. Purposeful, open communication and information-sharing with students and their family members support a holistic approach to understanding the learning needs of students. Educational research over the past half-century has identified evidence-based strategies and approaches that responsive teachers can utilise in their endeavours to authentically provide learning for all.

Further reading

Attwood, T. 2008. *The complete guide to Asperger's syndrome*. London and Philadelphia, PA: Jessica Kingsley Publishers.

Australian Institute of Health and Welfare. 2008. 'Disability in Australia: intellectual disability.' Bulletin no. 67. Australian Government. November. www.aihw.gov.au/WorkArea/Download Asset.aspx?id=6442452891.

Autism New Zealand Inc. website: www.autismnz.org.nz/.

Education Queensland. n.d. 'Better behaviour better learning: essential skills for classroom management; core learning component.' Queensland Government. http://edgd801.csc4 learning.com/801images/corelearningessentialskills.pdf.

Frith, U. 1991. *Autism and Asperger syndrome*. Cambridge: Cambridge University Press.

New Zealand Education. 2014. 'Supporting children with Autism Spectrum Disorder (ASD).' New Zealand Education. 26 June. www.minedu.govt.nz/NZEducation/EducationPolicies/ SpecialEducation/OurWorkProgramme/SupportingChildrenWithASD.aspx.

Physical as Anything.com website: www.physicalasanything.com.au/.

SSAT. n.d. 'Complex learning difficulties and disabilities research project.' SSAT. http://complex ld.ssatrust.org.uk/project-resources.html.

Sue Larkey – Australia website: www.suelarkey.com.au/.

Sue Larkey's New Zealand website: www.suelarkey.co.nz/.

References

APA (American Psychiatric Association). 2013a. *Diagnostic statistical manual of mental disorders*, 5th edn. Arlington, VA: APA.

——. 2013b. 'Austism spectrum disorder.' Fact sheet. APA. www.dsm5.org/Documents/ Autism%20Spectrum%20Disorder%20Fact%20Sheet.pdf.

Bellert, A. 2008. 'Narrowing the gap: a report on the *QuickSmart* mathematics intervention.' *Australian Journal of Learning Difficulties* 14 (2): 171–83.

Blackburn, C., B. Carpenter and J. Egerton. 2012. *Educating children and young people with fetal alcohol spectrum disorder.* Oxford: Routledge.

Bourke, R. and J. Loveridge. 2013. 'The role of systematic reviews in exploring possibilities for evidence-based practice.' *New Zealand Journal of Teachers' Work* 10 (1): 1–3.

Brabeck, M. and J. Jeffrey. 2010. 'Practice for knowledge acquisition (not drill and kill).' American Psychological Association. www.apa.org/education/k12/practice-acquisition.aspx#.

Carpenter, B. 2010. 'Disadvantaged, deprived and disabled.' *Special Children*, no. 193: 42–5.

Carpenter, B., J. Egerton, T. Brooks, B. Cockbill, J. Fotheringham and H. Rawson. 2014. *Children and young people with complex learning difficulties and disabilities: a resource book for teachers and teaching assistants.* Oxford: Taylor & Francis.

Chan, L. and K. Dally. 2001. 'Learning disabilities and literacy and numeracy development.' *Australian Journal of Learning Disabilities* 6 (1): 12–19.

Department of Education and Communities. n.d. Physical as Anything.com. Website. NSW Government. www.physicalasanything.com.au/.

Ericsson, K. A. 1990. 'The scientific study of expert levels of performance: general implications for optimal learning and creativity.' *High Ability Studies* 9 (1): 75–100.

Fuchs, D. and L. Fuchs. 2006. 'Introduction to response to intervention: what, why, and how valid is it?' *Reading Research Quarterly* 41 (1): 93–9.

Fuchs, L. S. and D. Fuchs. 1986. 'Effects of systematic formative evaluation on student achievement: a meta-analysis.' *Exceptional Children* 53 (3): 199–208.

Gersten, R., D. Compton, C. M. Connor, J. Dimino, L. Santoro, S. Linan-Thompson and W. D. Tilly. 2009. 'Assisting students struggling with reading: response to intervention and multi-tier intervention for reading in the primary grades; a practice guide.' National Center for Education Evaluation and Regional Assistance, Institute of Education Sciences and US Department of Education. http://ies.ed.gov/ncee/wwc/pdf/practice_guides/rti_reading_pg_021809.pdf.

Glover, T. A. and J. C. Di Perna. 2007. 'Service delivery for response to intervention: core components and directions for future research.' *School Psychology Review* 36 (4): 526–640.

Graham, L. and J. Bailey. 2007. 'Learning disabilities and difficulties: an Australian conspectus; introduction to the special issue.' *Journal of Learning Difficulties* 40 (5): 386–91.

Graham, L. and A. Bellert, 2004. 'Reading comprehension for students with learning disabilities.' In B. Y. L. Wong, ed., *Learning about learning disabilities*, 251–79. San Diego, CA: Academic Press.

——. 2007. 'Effective reading comprehension instruction for students with learning disabilities.' *Australian Journal of Dyslexia and Specific Learning Disabilities* 2 (spring–summer 2007–2008): 7–15.

Hattie, J. A. 2003. 'Teachers make a difference: what is the research evidence?' Paper presented at the ACER Research Conference. Melbourne. 19–21 October. Text available at SA Department for Education and Child Development. www.decd.sa.gov.au/limestonecoast/files/pages/new%20page/plc/teachers_make_a_difference.pdf.

——. 2005. 'What is the nature of evidence that makes a difference to learning?' Australian Council for Educational Research. http://research.acer.edu.au/cgi/viewcontent.cgi?article=1008&context=research_conference_2005.

——. 2009. *Visible learning: A synthesis of over 800 meta-analyses relating to achievement.* Oxford: Routledge.

Hattie, J. and H. Timperley. 2007. 'The power of feedback'. *Review of Educational Research* 77 (1): 81–112.

Hill, P. W. and C. A. M. Crévola. 2003. 'The literacy challenge in Australian primary schools.' In V. Zbar and T. Mackay, eds. *Leading the education debate.* Melbourne: Incorporated Association of Registered Teachers of Victoria.

Hinckson, E. A. and A. Curtis. 2013. 'Measuring physical activity in children and youth living with intellectual disabilities: a systematic review.' *Research in Developmental Disabilities* 34 (1): 72–86.

Kavale, K. and S. Forness. 2000. 'What definitions of learning disabilities say and don't say: a critical analysis.' *Journal of Learning Disabilities* 33 (3): 239–56.

Koltko-Rivera, M. E. 2006. 'Rediscovering the later version of Maslow's hierarchy of needs: self-transcendence and opportunities for theory, research, and unification.' *Review of General Psychology* 10 (4): 302–17.

Lederer, J. M. 2000. 'Reciprocal teaching of social studies in inclusive elementary classrooms.' *Journal of Learning Disabilities* 33 (1): 91–106.

Lines, C., G. Miller and A. Arthur-Stanley. 2011. *The power of family-school partnering (FSP): a practical guide for school mental health professionals and educators.* New York: Routledge.

Lysakowski, R. S. and H. J. Walberg. 1982. 'Instructional effects of cues, participation, and corrective feedback: a quantitative synthesis.' *Educational Research Journal* 19 (4): 559–78.

Maslow, A. 1954. *Motivation and personality.* New York: Harper and Row.

——. 1987. *Motivation and personality*, 3rd edn. New York: Harper and Row.

Mastropieri, M. A. and T. E. Scruggs. 2002. *Effective instruction for special education.* Austin, TX: Pro-Ed.

Mercer, C. D., L. A. Jordan and S. P. Miller. 1996. 'Constructivistic math instruction for diverse learners.' *Learning Disabilities Research & Practice* 11 (3): 290–306.

Ministry of Health. 2014. Website. New Zealand Government. 9 July. www.health.govt.nz/.

Palincsar, A. S. 1986. 'Metacognitive strategy instruction.' *Exceptional Children* 53 (2): 118–24.

Palincsar, A. S. and A. L. Brown. 1984. 'Reciprocal teaching of comprehension-fostering and comprehension-monitoring activities.' *Cognition & Instruction* 1 (2): 117.

Pegg, J. 2013. 'Building the realities of working memory and neural functioning into planning instruction and teaching.' Australian Council for Educational Research. http://research.acer. edu.au/cgi/viewcontent.cgi?article=1179&context=research_conference.

Richmond, C. 2007. *Teach more, manage less: a minimalist approach to behaviour management.* Sydney: Scholastic Australia Pty Limited.

Rosenshine, B. and C. Meister. 1994. 'Reciprocal teaching: a review of the research.' *Review of Educational Research* 64 (4): 479–530.

Sanders, W. L. and J. C. Rivers 1996. *Cumulative and residual effects of teachers on future students' academic achievement.* Knoxville, TN: University of Tennessee Value-Added Research and Assessment Center.

Schacter, J. and Y. M. Thum. 2004. 'Paying for high- and low-quality teaching.' *Economics of Education Review* 23 (4): 411–30.

Shute, V. J. 2009. 'Simply assessment.' *International Journal of Learning and Media* 1 (2): 1–11.

SSAT. n.d. 'Complex learning difficulties and disabilities research project.' SSAT. http:// complexld.ssatrust.org.uk.

Swanson, H. L. 1999. 'Reading research for students with LD: a meta-analysis of intervention outcomes.' *Journal of Learning Disabilities* 32 (6): 503–34.

Swanson, H. L. and C. Sachse-Lee. 2001. 'A subgroup analysis of working memory in children with reading disabilities: domain-general or domain-specific deficiency?' *Journal of Learning Disabilities* 34 (3): 249–63.

Swanson, H. L. and L. Siegel. 2001. 'Learning disabilities as a working memory deficit.' *Issues in Education* 7 (1): 1–48.

Swanson, H. L. and M. Hoskyn. 1998. 'Experimental intervention research on students with learning disabilities: a meta-analysis of treatment outcomes.' *Review of Educational Research* 68 (3): 277–321.

Swanson, H. L., C. Carson and C. Sachs-Lee. 1996. 'A selective synthesis of intervention research for students with learning disabilities.' *School Psychology Review* 25 (3): 370–91.

Swanson, H. L., M. Hoskyn and C. Lee. 1999. *Interventions for students with learning disabilities: a meta-analysis of treatment outcomes.* New York: Guilford Press.

van Garderen, D. 2004. 'Reciprocal teaching as a comprehension strategy for understanding mathematical word problems.' *Reading & Writing Quarterly* 20 (2): 225–9.

Vaughn, S. 2003. '3-tier reading model: reducing reading difficulties for kindergarten through third grade students.' Paper presented at the Celebrating Inclusive Catholic Schools Conference. Broadbeach. July.

Vaughn, S., R. Gersten and D. J. Chard. 2000. 'The underlying message in LD intervention research: findings from research syntheses.' *Exceptional Children* 67 (1): 99–114.

Westwood, P. 1993. 'Striving for positive outcomes for students with learning difficulties.' *Special Education Perspectives* 2 (2): 87–94.

———. 2003. *Commonsense methods for children with special educational needs*. London: Routledge Falmer.

———. 2004. *Learning and learning difficulties: a handbook for teachers*. Melbourne: Australian Council for Educational Research.

Westwood, P. and L. Graham. 2000. 'How many children with special needs in regular classes: official predictions vs teachers' perceptions in South Australia and New South Wales.' *Australian Journal of Learning Disabilities* 5 (3): 24–35.

Wing, L. and J. Gould. 1979. 'Severe impairments of social interaction and associated abnormalities in children: epidemiology and classification.' *Journal of Autism and Developmental Disorders* 9 (1): 11–29.

World Health Organization. 2010. *International statistical classification of diseases and related health problems*, 10th revision. World Health Organization. http://apps.who.int/classifications/icd10/browse/2010/en.

Chapter 7

Teaching that matters

Intended learning outcomes

Engagement with the text in this chapter will enable readers to do the following:

- describe the kind of teaching that is effective for students in inclusive classrooms

- understand the organisation and actions involved in differentiating instruction and making educational adjustments

- define and discuss the 10 essential skills that guide differentiated instruction for teaching that matters

Big ideas

- Teaching that matters recognises that although all learners have similar types of learning needs, every learner is different. These differences matter in terms of effective teaching.

- Whole-school and classroom approaches should be coordinated to support the most effective teaching that matters.

- Differentiated instruction can be implemented in a simple but systematic way.

- Using pre-testing and post-testing to inform inclusive planning and differentiating instruction gives teachers more information to use in tailoring instruction.

- Planning instruction is important because differentiation should be considered in terms of intended learning outcomes.

- The **simplicity principle** means that differentiated instruction should occur only when necessary. It is important to maintain realistically high expectations for all students' performance.

- Evidence-based practices that underpin teaching provide ways in which to address problems in literacy, numeracy and other areas experienced by students with disabilities or learning difficulties.

> The **simplicity principle** is a philosophy of making things uncomplicated and as easy to understand and accept as possible.

Introduction

Sustainable learning depends on teaching that matters. This chapter builds on the content of chapter 6 to focus on the differentiation of instruction in inclusive classrooms. With a growing evidence base of effective teaching practices available from websites like the What Works Clearinghouse (n.d.), the BES (Iterative Best Evidence Synthesis) Programme (Education Counts, n.d.) and Scootle (2014), teachers have an ever-expanding choice of effective strategies to utilise when learners need a different way to master a lesson's learning intentions. In terms of teaching that matters for students with disabilities or learning difficulties, such a repertoire of teaching strategies means that students should experience different instructional approaches if they need them – not more of the same kind of instruction that has already not 'worked' for them. Teaching that matters relates to the fifth step of the RTF ('How do I teach for all my learners?') and, importantly, covers the occasions of responsive teaching that are at the heart of the RTF model.

General orientations to instruction

Teachers' success at providing teaching that matters is influenced by general orientations to instruction and by the **mind frames** that teachers bring to the classroom. Of particular note are culturally responsive teaching orientations, programs like Sternberg's (2003) successful intelligence,

> **Mind frames** are ways of thinking about teaching roles that help educators to make decisions in the classroom and school.

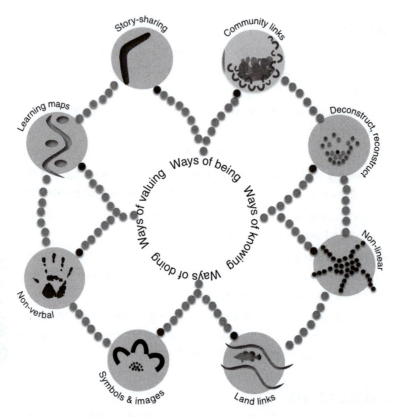

Figure 7.1: *'8 Aboriginal ways of learning'*
Source: Adapted from WNSWRAET, n.d.

which aims to teach the interrelated higher-order skills that individuals need to lead fulfilling lives, and Hattie's (2012) eight professional mind frames for teachers.

Culturally responsive teaching

General approaches to teaching that matters include those developed to facilitate understanding of Indigenous peoples' ways of knowing and understanding. A prime example is '8 Aboriginal ways of learning', developed between 2007 and 2009 by the Western New South Wales Regional Aboriginal Education Team. This program is holistic in the integrated way depicted in figure 7.1. The Aboriginal ways of learning identified are 'interconnected pedagogies involving narrative-driven learning, visual-ised learning processes, hands-on/reflective techniques, use of symbols/metaphors, land-based learning, indirect/synergistic logic, modelled/scaffolded genre mastery, and connectedness to community'. From this perspective, the learning is in the doing. The actions fundamental to learning through the '8 Aboriginal ways' are: 'Tell a story. Make a plan. Think and do. Draw it. Take it outside. Try a new way. Watch first, then do. Share it with others' (WNSWRAET, n.d.).

Think and do 7.1: '8 Aboriginal ways'

1   Explore the teaching ideas documented on the 8 Aboriginal Ways of Learning website (WNSWRAET, n.d.). How can you use some of these ideas in your teaching?

2   Give eight examples of how you could use the '8 Aboriginal ways of learning'. What evidence would you accept to judge whether the approach is having a positive impact on your students' efficiency or effectiveness of learning?

Teaching for successful intelligence

Another way of thinking about how effective teaching underpins teaching that matters is to draw from Sternberg's (2010, 603–4) model of 'wisdom, intelligence, creativity synthesised', or successful intelligence, whose fundamental idea is that humans need a set of interrelated higher-order skills to lead fulfilling lives. They need creativity to guide their actions and assist in managing changing circumstances, analytical skills to judge whether their creative responses are appropriate, practical skills to apply their ideas and convince others that they are worthwhile and 'wisdom to ensure that the ideas they pursue will help achieve some ethically-based common good over both long and short terms'. Sternberg's ideas are compatible with the sustainable learning concept because what teachers do can affect their students throughout their lives, not just in the immediacy of classrooms. For example, teachers who have the sorts of mind frames suggested by Hattie (2012; see below) can draw upon Sternberg's (2013) successful intelligence and teach practically and creatively towards 'wisdom', as outlined in figure 7.2.

Looking at school learning with the aim of developing successful and intelligent behaviours for all students provides a fresh way of considering student performance that is not constrained by self-fulfilling prophecies (Sternberg 2003). Categorical thinking (for example, 'This student has an attention disorder and therefore can't sustain attention and won't do well at school or after it') is limiting for many students experiencing disabilities or learning difficulties, as well as for students with or without disabilities from minority groups, especially involuntary minorities (Ogbu 1992).

Professional mind frames

Work by Hattie (2012), who analysed the evidence base from existing meta-analyses to answer the question 'What works best in education?', makes it clear that teachers' mind frames – their ways of thinking about their teaching roles – are instrumental in the success of students' learning. As well as advocating that teachers 'know thy impact' as a foremost tenet of their practice, Hattie (2012, 160–6) distils eight professional mind frames which can be used to guide educators' actions:

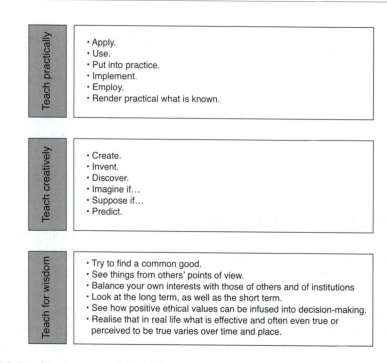

Figure 7.2: *Teaching for successful intelligence*
Source: Adapted from Sternberg 2013. Reproduced with permission of Springer Publishing Company, LLC.

Mind frame 1: Teachers/leaders believe that their fundamental task is to evaluate the effect of their teaching on students' learning and achievement...

Mind frame 2: Teachers/leaders believe that success and failure in student learning is about what they, as teachers or leaders, did or did not do... We are change agents! ...

Mind frame 3: Teachers/leaders want to talk more about the learning than the teaching...

Mind frame 4: Teachers/leaders see assessment as feedback about their impact...

Mind frame 5: Teachers/leaders engage in dialogue not monologue...

Mind frame 6: Teachers/leaders enjoy the challenge and never retreat to 'doing their best'...

Mind frame 7: Teachers/leaders believe that it is their role to develop positive relationships in classrooms and staffrooms...

Mind frame 8: Teachers/leaders inform all about the language of learning.

In a similar way, the RTF's guiding questions lead teachers to seek and consider evidence of their students' growth, and the broader conceptualisation of sustainable learning acknowledges the importance of practices like collaboration and using a specific and shared vocabulary to discuss learning with colleagues, students and their parents or carers.

Think and do 7.2: Mind frames for teachers

1   How many of Hattie's (2012) mind frames do you have? Give examples of how are they evident in your teaching practice.

2   How do the mind frames complement Hattie's description of 16 prototypic attributes of excellent teachers, listed below?

A1. Expert teachers have deeper representations about teaching and learning...

A2. Expert teachers adopt a problem-solving stance to their work ...

A3. Expert teachers can anticipate, plan, and improvise as required by the situation ...

A4. Expert teachers are better decision-makers and can identify what decisions are important and which are less important decisions ...

B5. Expert teachers are proficient at creating an optimal classroom climate for learning ...

B6. Expert teachers have a multidimensionally complex perception of classroom situations ...

B7. Expert teachers are more context-dependent and have high situation cognition ...

C8. Expert teachers are more adept at monitoring student problems and assessing their level of understanding and progress, and they provide much more relevant, useful feedback ...

C9. Expert teachers are more adept at developing and testing hypotheses about learning difficulties or instructional strategies ...

C10. Expert teachers are more automatic ...

D11. Expert teachers have high respect for students ...

D12. Expert teachers are passionate about teaching and learning ...

E13. Expert teachers engage students in learning and develop in their students self-regulation, involvement in mastery learning, enhanced self-efficacy, and self-esteem as learners ...

E14. Expert teachers provide appropriate challenging tasks and goals for students ...

E15. Expert teachers have positive influences on students' achievement ...

E16. Expert teachers enhance surface and deep learning (Hattie 2003, 5–9)

The importance of positive relationships between teachers and their students has been discussed to some extent in chapter 3, but it is worth emphasising here as a key factor in setting the conditions for teaching that matters. Hattie and others view positive student–teacher relationships as a necessary foundation for building trust in classrooms (for example, see Cornelius-White 2007; Hattie 2012; Hughes, Cavell and Willson 2001). Trust is also fundamental in setting the conditions necessary for students to take risks with their learning. This is important so that students can make errors that they can learn from and grow to independently seek help if they are confused or become 'lost', for whatever reason.

In addition, high expectations for student performance are extremely important. Expectations cannot be separated from the learning environment in which they exist and are, therefore, vital for teachers to hold as part of providing a supportive learning environment. Classrooms suffused with high expectations and a sense of challenge stand to optimise the achievement of all learners (Hattie and Anderman 2013). High expectations are particularly important for Aboriginal students. They are, for example, key in Sarra's Stronger Smarter (n.d.) philosophy, which promotes high expectations and relationships and leadership styles that acknowledge individuals' strengths, capacities and rights to opportunity. Luke et al. (2013, 39), in a comprehensive evaluation of the Stronger Smarter Institute's impact, identified three areas which need strong emphasis in order to improve the achievement of Aboriginal students:

> **Whole-school curriculum planning** allows schools to develop and maintain curricula, assessments and reporting plans which address all learning areas for the entire school as well as at year and unit levels.

- understanding, engaging with and acknowledging the cultural and linguistic resources of Indigenous students and communities
- Indigenous staff and leadership within the school and engagement with community
- building teacher capacity and quality pedagogy across the curriculum through **whole-school curriculum planning** in key areas

Whole-school methods resonate with the approach taken in this book. Teaching for sustainable learning is not just about passing on knowledge and skills; it is about teachers' use of systems of ideas like the '8 Aboriginal ways of learning', successful intelligence and Hattie's mind frames in their classrooms. Sustainable learning is also about encouraging teachers and teacher candidates to exercise and evaluate their professional judgment as action researchers who use evidence-based practices in their classrooms.

Evidence-based practice

'Is that approach evidence-based practice?' is a common contemporary question in education. The reasonable premise for asking such a question is that it is best to use teaching strategies that have been shown to be effective in supporting student learning. There are, however, different levels of effectiveness and different types of evidence that can be used by teachers to make informed decisions about their teaching practice. It is not always practical for classroom teachers to sift through extensive scientific evidence and draw their own conclusions about what is effective practice. Even if research is 'gold-standard' science (that is, research that offers a rigorous level of proof and is often conducted using a randomised controlled trial), an approach may not 'work' in particular classrooms for idiosyncratic reasons. Teachers have to make professionally informed decisions about how to teach – judgments informed not only by scientific evidence but by other relevant substantiation from their practice, students and communities.

The scientist-practitioner model of educational psychology practice provides a useful way for teachers to think about what is evidence based and what is not. With this model, professionals use their judgment based on reflection and accessing multiple sources of evidence to decide their future practice. Bourke and Loveridge's (2013, 8) evidence-based practice model involves three types of non-hierarchical 'evidence':

1) Evidence from teaching and professional backgrounds, experience and expertise;

2) Evidence generated from the families and the child/young person regarding their specific and individual circumstances and contexts; and,

3) Evidence from research (national and international; quantitative and qualitative) that informs assessment, intervention, problem solving and decision making regarding practice.

Gathering, analysing and reflecting on information in order to decide 'what to do next' is core to the RTF. Responsive teachers gather evidence every step of the way and then make well-informed decisions about their next actions. The list below positions evidence-based practice within the RTF.

Step 1 Select the frameworks against which all evidence is to be evaluated. Frameworks help define the type of evidence needed and how to talk about it.

Step 2 Gather evidence of your own teacher cultural competence, your assumptions about learning and your skills and knowledge in practice.

Step 3 Gather evidence regarding what the students bring to their learning individually and as a group – cultures, interests, experiences, capabilities, needs, prior learning, family (*whānau*).

Steps 4 and 5 Use the evidence you have from research, from practice and from your students to plan your teaching organisation and actions. Respond to evidence provided during teaching and learning activities to make on-the-spot adaptations.

Step 6 Gather evidence of learners' responses to your teaching against intended learning outcomes, as well as identifying any unintended learning outcomes.

Step 7 Gather evidence of the effect of feedback and the learning experience for each learner.

Step 8 Gather evidence about how teaching supported student learning.

This aligning of evidence-based practice with the RTF emphasises the importance of gathering evidence that shows what has happened, informs teachers about what should happen next and guides them to make that happen.

Transparent and strategic teaching

Teaching that matters and that facilitates sustainable learning is transparent and strategic. How to learn should not remain a mystery for some students. Teachers can model, think aloud or teach explicitly to students what is involved in using both general strategic approaches and task-specific learning strategies. As a first step, articulating intended learning outcomes provides direction for teaching that matters, which then involves selecting and carefully using instructional approaches and teaching learning strategies and combining these with insights from cognitive education so that students can continue to manage their learning independently. A learning-strategies approach also includes the development of shared language that describes what learning 'looks, sounds, and feels like' for students. The general goal from a sustainable learning point of view is to assist learners to internalise a kind of strategic self-talk so they can take control and regulate their own learning.

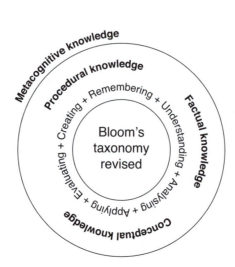

Figure 7.3: *Levels of thinking and knowledge dimensions from Bloom's revised taxonomy*
Source: Adapted from Krathwohl 2002.

Several models are useful for teachers to ensure they clearly state intended learning outcomes. These include the SOLO taxonomy (Biggs and Collis 1982) and the revised version of Bloom's educational objectives taxonomy (Krathwohl 2002). Figure 7.3 shows Bloom's four different types of knowledge (factual, conceptual, procedural and metacognitive) in relation to levels of thinking, from remembering, understanding, analysing and applying to evaluating and creating.

Cognitive education

Explicit teaching of cognitive skills is reflected in cognitive education, the intervention focus of the dynamic assessment movement (see chapter 5). This focus on exploring and teaching students how to think and thus how to learn, through the development of motivational, cognitive and metacognitive processes, has been shown to be effective in supporting learning. Cognitive education is variously known as 'cognitive strategy instruction', 'cognitive skills instruction', 'thinking skills training', 'teaching of thinking skills' and 'self-regulation training'.

Although the first use of the term 'cognitive education', in the 1970s, is attributed to Haywood (1977), there are earlier references to humans' capacity to develop cognitive abilities rather than being assumed to have a fixed level for life. Binet (1909), who constructed an early western intelligence test, referred to 'mental orthopedics', suggesting that he did not see intelligence or cognitive abilities as fixed. Others who have suggested this capacity for growth in cognition include Rey (1934), with a reference to educability, Vygotsky's (1934) concept of the zone of proximal development, Selz's (1935) intelligence-raising and Feuerstein's development of the idea of cognitive modifiability in the 1950s while working with Piaget. Feuerstein, after a long career advocating dynamic assessment and instrumental enrichment, commented that neuroscience and the exploration of 'neuroplasticity' had finally caught up with some of the claims he had made for decades (Feuerstein, Falik and Feuerstein 2013).

As described, cognitive education is most effective when it is curriculum based and integrated within regular school activities and when transfer is explicitly taught through practising processes, cognitive functions and strategies in a range of contexts and situations (Hessels and Hessels-Schlatter 2013). Teaching cognitive skills can be an integral part of classroom teaching. Effective teachers, for example, consistently demonstrate a metacognitive style (for example, planning, monitoring and evaluating) in all domains and throughout the school day. Teachers who have a **growth mindset** and knowledge about concepts such as metacognition, self-regulation, learning to learn and learning strategies see the value of teaching specific strategies for learning and for life, and not just for better academic performance.

> People with a **growth mindset** believe that their capabilities can be developed through engagement in learning and practice.

The effect of cognitive education is greater than most other **educational interventions**, with self-regulation training programs showing strong effects on cognitive abilities and academic performance (Dignath and Büttner 2008; Dignath, Buettner and Langfeldt 2008; Higgins and Green 2005). Larger effect sizes (an indication of 'what works best') have been recorded for interventions that focus on metacognitive processing and meta-knowledge, and not only on cognitive strategies but also for motivational aspects of learning and for programs aimed at high-school students rather than primary-school students (Hessels and Hessels-Schlatter 2013). Further characteristics of cognitive education are that it is learner and knowledge centred; it includes awareness of and attention to cultural, social, cognitive and personal factors that affect learning; it aims to develop learning potential and the motivation to learn; it is based on developmental pathways or trajectories related to specific content that are clearly understood and reflected in educational goals and instructional strategies; it focuses on cognitive and metacognitive process development, and thus further learning; and it establishes an awareness within individuals of their own learning in such a way that it creates momentum for further self-regulated and self-motivated learning (Carlson and Wiedl 2013, 13).

> **Educational interventions** are programs of intense targeted instruction that focus on the needs of the individual child and aim to improve performance and/or behaviour.

General learning strategies

Teaching help-seeking strategies is an example of a specific approach that aims to facilitate learning for all, in terms of self-regulation and ultimately academic progress. Learning strategies – particularly general 'learn to learn' strategies (which focus on helping students to become more active learners by teaching them how to learn, as well as how to use what they have learnt to solve problems and be successful) have an important place in securing outcomes from teaching that persist into adulthood. General learning strategies that students benefit from using independently include rehearsing, organising, self-checking, studying and self-testing (Newman 2002). These strategies act as scaffolds that can be explicitly applied to learning tasks and practised as much as is needed for effective and independent learning to occur. They are useful tools for learning and problem-solving throughout life.

Chapter 6 has already introduced some specific teaching strategies associated with developing the **ATRiUM** capabilities; however, a brief discussion of a general approach towards strategy instruction is warranted here, because the flexible use of learning strategies is key to sustainable learning. Mastropieri and Scruggs (2009, 311; see also Bock 1999) suggest the following seven steps, which combine to guide a thorough approach to teaching learning strategies:

1 Set clear goals that are logically related to the use of each strategy.
2 Follow an effective instructional sequence:
    a State the purpose of instruction.
    b Provide instruction.
    c Model the use of the strategy.
    d Prompt students to use the strategy following your model.
    e Give corrective feedback.
    f Provide guided practice of the strategy.
    g Provide independent practice of the strategy.
3 Inform students of the importance of the strategy.
4 Monitor student performance.
5 Encourage questioning that requires the students to think about the strategies in relationship to tasks.
6 Encourage positive attributions of success to effort and strategy use.
7 Teach for a generalised use of each strategy.

More specific methods for building students' awareness of their own effective learning strategies are provided below. It is particularly important to explicitly highlight the usefulness of specific learning strategies to other applications and domains during their initial instruction and to encourage students to build a flexible repertoire of strategic approaches. The application of knowledge to new situations through transfer and generalisation is a perennial challenge for education and is vitally important for teachers to keep in mind throughout all instructional events.

While most students clearly benefit from learning new strategies and task approaches, some individuals, usually high achievers, already use effective strategies and can become confused or 'slowed down' by unnecessary strategy training. For these students, strategy instruction is not likely to be 'cost effective'. Although it is important that the initial teaching of strategies for most students is explicit and systematic, it should be expected that students will personalise their strategy use to some extent as time passes. This is a component of competent strategy use that does not present a problem unless students' 'tinkering' renders the strategy ineffective. A classroom climate that supports discussion about the various strategic ways that students can approach tasks is likely to increase their awareness of the power of active and involved learning. Such dialogue about learning is the best context for developing students' strategic approaches to learning and for ensuring that these become part of how they tackle current and future challenges.

How to teach learning strategies

Preparation

Develop students' metacognitive awareness and self-knowledge through activities such as the following:

- discussing the strategies students already use to complete specific tasks
- interviewing small groups of students about the various ways in which they complete tasks successfully
- administering simple learning strategy questionnaires to see how often students use particular strategies for particular tasks
- interviewing students using a think-aloud format to observe how they tackle general and specific tasks

Explicit instruction

Teach the strategy explicitly by using the methods below:

- modelling how you use the strategy by thinking aloud through a task (for example, reading a text or calculating an answer)
- naming the strategy and referring to it consistently by that name
- explaining to the students how the strategy will help them
- describing when, how and on what kinds of tasks the strategy is useful

Practice

Provide many opportunities for strategy practice during complex activities like the following:

- solving mathematical problems
- predicting, recalling, questioning and summarising in comprehension exercises
- developing group-assessed oral and written reports
- analysing the results of science experiments
- writing different types of essay responses

Self-assessment

Develop students' metacognitive awareness of what strategies work for them and why by using self-assessment activities like those below:

- debriefing after strategy use
- writing reflections in learning logs about effective strategy use

- comparing students' performance on similar tasks with and without the use of particular strategies

- checking students' confidence levels regarding their strategy use

- reporting on strategy use (for example, 'Why?' 'Why not?') and comparing each student's use of strategies with that of their peers

Support

Provide support for the transfer and generalisation of strategies to new tasks or settings through activities like the following:

- scaffolding, in which reminders to use a strategy are gradually diminished

- giving positive feedback paired with the independent use of a strategy

- analysing and discussing strategies that individual students find effective for certain tasks

- using follow-up activities that encourage students to transfer and generalise their strategy use and report back to the class

- holding 'thought storm' sessions in which students contribute all the possible uses for the strategies they are learning. (Adapted from CARLA, n.d.; Wong and Butler 2012; Wong et al. 2008)

Mindsets

In order to engender the kinds of independent learning behaviours that are important for teaching that matters (and learning that lasts), students and their teachers should be aware of the benefits of embracing a growth mindset in relation to ability and intelligence. Dweck's work in this area has been important in outlining the differences in attitudes and achievements between individuals who have a growth mindset and those with a **fixed mindset** (for example, Dweck 2000, 2006). A fixed mindset stems from the belief that intelligence is determined and static. It is accompanied by the desire to look 'smart' and behaviours such as feeling threatened by others' success, ignoring useful negative feedback, giving up easily when faced with obstacles, risk avoidance and feeling that effort is wasted in trying to accomplish a task – if individuals find tasks difficult, the inference made is that this is because they are not intelligent enough to complete them.

> People with a **fixed mindset** believe their capabilities are at set levels and will always be at those levels.

In contrast, a growth mindset is characterised by the belief that intelligence can be developed through learning. Behaviours associated with a growth mindset include gathering insight and inspiration from others' success, learning from feedback, persisting in the face of setbacks, embracing challenges and feeling that effort is the path to mastery – if these individuals find tasks difficult, the inference made is that it is because they haven't learnt how to be successful at this type of task *yet*.

Risk-taking

One of the most powerful ways that students learn is through making mistakes and then acting on feedback to correct their understandings. Many students who experience difficulty with school learning, however, avoid challenging learning tasks because they want to escape the experience of failure. A fear of risk-taking can seriously limit students' engagement in the classroom and their subsequent success. Encouraging both students and teachers to maintain growth mindsets towards ability makes sense for sustainable learning. It impacts on the way learning is thought about and discussed in classrooms (for example, 'All children can learn', 'Effort and using an appropriate strategy lead to success') and can foster an orientation that encourages the appropriate use of help-seeking and learning strategies. These two important areas combine to equip students, especially those who have particular learning needs or backgrounds, with the skills necessary to behave as active, confident and independent learners throughout their lives.

While school avoidance and resistance issues related to evasion of risk-taking and fear of failure can affect all students, there is evidence that this occurs to a greater extent for Aboriginal and Torres Strait Islander students (Martin 2006). Munns (1998, 179) observed that although Aboriginal students would take risks elsewhere in their lives, they were adversely inclined to take learning-related risks, with the classroom 'the site of their greatest danger' and shame. (Shame used in an Aboriginal sense includes embarrassment in certain situations; it is often caused by unwanted attention or by circumstances rather than as the result of an action.) Shame is explicitly noted for many Indigenous learners and is a core concept that 'can dominate how many Aboriginal children think, talk and behave in the classroom' (Harrison 2011, 179).

A fear of failure and shame and the avoidance of learning risks can lead to Aboriginal students and students with learning difficulties developing 'class-wise' strategies, such as avoiding interaction with teachers, copying, faking and looking busy – behaviours aimed at 'saving face' in the classroom and escaping detection as a student who does not know or understand the class work. Martin's (2006, 39) development of a motivational psychology for Indigenous students suggests that in order to ameliorate students' fear of failure, teachers should be careful with criticism, not single students out, provide a constructive and courageous view of mistakes, remove links between the worth of a person and academic failure and establish a positive cooperative learning climate for learning. Such an approach is likely to be positive for most students.

Help-seeking

An important strategy that supports lifelong learning is seeking help whenever the requirements of a task are not understood or if tasks cannot be completed independently. The ability to recognise when understanding has broken down and the capacity and motivation to take steps to rectify any 'problem' is an example of metacognition in action. This kind of thinking is vital to sustainable learning because it underpins the active problem-solving nature important to engaging with teaching that matters and vital to learning that lasts. Metacognitive skills, as we have seen, are students' thinking about their own thinking and how they identify and then address any breakdowns encountered as they plan, monitor their understanding, evaluate the content they encounter and gauge their performance in responding to learning tasks.

Research into the use of help-seeking strategies indicates that those students who need the most help in classrooms are the least likely to seek it (for example, see Newman 2002; Paterson 2007; Ryan, Patrick and Shim 2005). In fact, the more successful learners are often independent and effective help-seekers. Newman (2002) classified help-seeking as a self-regulatory behaviour that can be explicitly taught and that is a necessary component of independent learners' 'tool kits'. Under Newman's (132–3) model, a self-regulated learner has the following competencies and resources available to support effective and adaptive help-seeking:

a) Cognitive competencies (i.e., knowing when help is necessary, knowing that others can help, knowing how to ask a question that yields precisely what is needed);

b) Social competencies (i.e., knowing who is the best person to approach for help, knowing how to carry out a request for help in a socially appropriate way);

c) Personal motivational resources (i.e., personal goals, self-beliefs, and feelings associated with tolerance for task difficulty; willingness to express to others a need for help; and a sense of personal agency); and

d) Contextual motivational resources (i.e., classroom factors such as goals, grading systems, collaborative activities, student-teacher interaction and teacher expectations for the child that facilitate help-seeking).

While teachers may organise their classrooms in ways that facilitate adaptive help-seeking, students with a disability or learning difficulty may not have the levels of cognitive and social competency necessary to make use of those resources and structures. Help-seeking is enacted through social interaction with others and by students regulating their own learning through obtaining assistance from others. In this way, 'self-regulation' and 'other regulation' are integrally intertwined (see Vygotsky 1978).

This has implications for sustainable learning and suggests that the explicit teaching of help-seeking strategies should accompany the inclusion of students with disabilities and learning difficulties, particularly because adult helpers such as teachers or teacher aides often provide classroom-based instructional assistance to these students. Such help is often long term and can include teachers or aides making decisions about when assistance is needed and the type of support provided, meaning that students with disabilities or learning difficulties may miss important opportunities to learn the skills necessary to act as self-regulating individuals when they finish school. Therefore, a focus on the explicit teaching of adaptive help-seeking strategies, perhaps as part of a broader social skills program, is recommended as a practical way of facilitating learning that lasts.

Social skills programs

Instructional support that improves help-seeking can be part of a broader social skills program. Learning how to be sensitive, responsive and generous when interacting with others is very important for school and post-school life. Social skills programs target the enhancement of students' social competence. Effective social skills programs comprise two essential elements: a teaching process that uses a behavioural or social learning approach and a universal language or set of steps that facilitates the learning of new behaviour (NASP 2002). For example, a social skills program for promoting positive peer interactions could incorporate the following topics:

- general social interaction skills and behaviours (for example, sharing, helping, caring, turn-taking, cooperating)
- skills and behaviours necessary for group cohesion (for example, listening to and encouraging others, respecting opinions, avoiding disruption, understanding roles and the need for order)
- emotions and expressing them appropriately (for example, the cues people give when frustrated, angry, sad and so on)
- strategies for dealing with frustration and anger (for example, asking for help, taking a deep breath, walking away, diverting attention)
- strategies for joining and working within class groups (for example, observing what group members are doing, saying something positive in order to join the group)
- self-management behaviours and techniques to prevent disruption
- simple conflict resolution techniques (for example, talking about problems, compromising, using strategies for controlling one's own behaviour)

Social and emotional skills important for academic success can be taught in a variety of ways, including role-playing; social games; puppetry; using literature, films and videos; discussing real-life experiences; and considering scenario-based problem-solving exercises.

The idea behind all social skills programs is to equip students with the skills they need to work together and accept one another. The mnemonic ACCEPTANCE introduced by Knight, Graham and Hughes (2004, 184) provides a way of presenting some key social skills that can become the focus of classroom programs:

Accepting a realistic view of self and others

Communication and compromise

Changing fixed mindsets

Entry and exit strategies for joining or leaving groups

Promoting prosocial behaviours and strategies for learning

Taking risks and asking for help

Acknowledging individual differences

Negotiation and respect

Cooperative and collaborative learning – the rules of engagement

Expressing emotions in appropriate ways

Teachers can facilitate help-seeking in their classrooms by, for example, providing students with 'permission to ask', supporting their autonomy and growing all students' confidence in their own competence. According to Newman (2002), responsive teachers can protect their students from the embarrassment that typically inhibits help-seeking. Newman maintains that teacher–student relationships that are positive and based on trust and respect influence learners' beliefs about the costs and benefits of approaching the teacher for assistance. Positive peer involvement also provides students with opportunities to experience the constructive social aspects of learning together and sets the conditions for friends to ask one another for help.

Newman (2002) says that adaptive help-seeking appears to be contingent on students' sense of autonomy. When teachers stress the intrinsic value of learning rather than valuing performance in terms of good grades, students are more likely to ask task-related questions to help them really understand their work. Learning goals are especially important for students who might otherwise simply ask for an answer without trying to discover it on their own. Peers either support or discourage student autonomy through social comparisons. When students know how they are doing in relation to their classmates, this can be both positive (for example, the normalcy of needing help) and negative (for example, concern about social status). Teachers can also provide opportunities for students to internalise instructional routines related to growing a sense of competence through help-seeking. For example, in small-group collaborative activities, students can practise the skills of self-monitoring and self-questioning. They can question their peers and learn how asking for and giving assistance to one another are actions related to academic success (Newman 2002).

Differentiated instruction

The kind of teaching that *really* matters for inclusive classrooms is differentiated instruction, a genuine response to diversity in the classroom that can be simply defined as 'teaching things differently according to observed differences in learners' (Westwood 2001, 5). Differentiation addresses the needs of all students – from those who struggle to those who excel – by tailoring instruction according to educationally important student needs. The facets of instructional practice that can be adjusted through differentiation include curriculum content, approaches to teaching content, assessment methods and response modes, classroom organisation procedures, grouping practices and the duration and intensity level of teacher interactions.

Tomlinson (2001, 1), a foremost US author on the topic of differentiation, states that differentiated instruction 'means "shaking up" what goes on in the classroom so that students have multiple options for taking in information, making sense of ideas, and expressing what they learn'. According to Tomlinson, differentiated instruction is a careful combination of individual, group and whole-class instruction that is proactive, student centred and grounded in assessment. It provides multiple instructional pathways related to content, process and product so that students encounter different approaches to what they learn, how they learn it and how they demonstrate their learning.

Differentiation as teaching that matters recognises that important differences exist among learners and that these differences must be responded to so that students can maximise their learning opportunities. It should be acknowledged, though, that teaching increasingly diverse classes is challenging! As Rose (2001, 147) notes, 'The teaching methods and practices required for the provision of effective inclusion are easier to identify than they are to implement'. Taking this further, Westwood (2005, 69) observes that 'in countries where differentiation has been implemented there is accumulating evidence that teachers have great difficulty in applying differentiation strategies in practice, and particularly in sustaining their use over time'.

Although there has been much written about differentiation and ways to implement it in classrooms, it seems that teachers remain somewhat unsure about or reluctant to use these strategies. Research that has examined what happens in classrooms, either through self-report questionnaires or observational studies, confirms that the most commonly used differentiation strategies tend to be those that do not require prior planning (Rose 2001) but instead are instigated as **on-the-spot differentiation** within the flow of a general whole-class lesson – for example, repeating or simplifying instructions, providing extra support or giving specific guidance to some students (Chan et al. 2002; Yuen, Westwood and Wong 2005).

On-the-spot differentiation is the appropriate adjustment of instructional factors at the point of need.

A paradox exists between the variety of differentiation strategies available and the desirability of a simple approach to making decisions about when and how to differentiate to meet students' needs. More than two or three strategies actively in play at the same time in a lesson have the potential to confuse learners unless adjustments are made skilfully. As a general teaching **heuristic**, applying the simplicity principle means that differentiated instruction is provided only when necessary and should be faded as soon as possible (Falvey, Givner and Kimm 1996) to ensure that all students have as much access as possible to the curriculum. As Westwood (2003, 204) wisely advises, it is important to 'ensure a **differentiated curriculum** does not become an impoverished curriculum with the lower-achieving students always assigned less demanding work than the more able students'.

A **heuristic** is a 'rule of thumb', an experience-based technique for learning that results in a solution, though that solution is not guaranteed to be optimal.

An example of this would be the inflexible use of ability groups in the classroom despite the reality of most students' uneven capability profiles. For a student to be in a certain group for some numeracy lessons may be fitting, but for them to stay in the same group for most classroom activities would not allow them to see how different classmates work on a variety of tasks; nor would it set up the conditions for students to ask for or provide help or acknowledge individuality in terms of interests and ability. All students need a chance

A **differentiated curriculum** is the structuring of instruction to meet the needs of all students and to ensure their access to the full course of teaching.

to practise reading comprehension strategies, problem-solving and other higher-order thinking skills. Similarly, the allocation of teacher aide time should be decided on a task-related basis rather than 'welded' to the same student or student group all the time.

The following sections on how to differentiate instruction for sustainable learning constitute a framework that is by necessity somewhat ambiguous. The aim is to provide enough direction and structure and yet flexibility (because classrooms are complex contexts and teachers are individuals) to be useful for most classroom practitioners. In differentiating instruction for sustainable learning, it makes sense to describe what teachers can do differently for individual students in terms of the learning tasks that they design and assign and the intended learning outcomes of these tasks. This kind of general inclusive thinking and planning comes once a classroom organisation approach to delivering responsive teaching is already in place. This means that the learning environment, routines and expectations for working in the classroom are already clear to students and act as foundations for their learning of specific curriculum content. In this way, implementing differentiated instruction is a balancing act between classroom organisational procedures that support a flexible but focused classroom milieu and teacher actions that are planned and those that operate on the spot to maximise student engagement and success.

Classroom organisation for differentiated learning

In order to differentiate instruction, a solid foundation formed by consistent classroom routines and procedures that support students' growing independence in learning and teachers' flexible instruction is necessary. Teachers can reinforce and multiply students' efforts by ensuring that they know how to successfully carry out key classroom behaviours. These include asking for help when it is needed, going on with other related activities if the set learning activity is completed and knowing how to work in groups and contribute to collaborative tasks. Similarly, to operate smooth-running inclusive classrooms, teachers need to be good classroom managers themselves and masters of skills such as giving clear instructions, showing what success looks like, managing transitions between learning activities and providing appropriate feedback. Below is a list of the kinds of classroom routines that support differentiation, including procedures that students should know well:

Asking for help: How to seek assistance without causing disruption to other members of the class (for example, have students ask three peers before the teacher, write their questions down, raise their hand, move to a specific table to signal assistance is required)

Collaborating: How to work in groups and take responsibility for group tasks (for example, ensure expectations are known, assign roles, arrange groups intentionally, give feedback on group processes as well as task performance)

Handing in work: How to check assignments and take them to the teacher for feedback (for example, use coloured folders for the submission of completed work, instigate consistent procedures for collecting homework)

Completing work independently: How to complete contracts or other individual work (for example, negotiate contracts for extra practice or extension, clarify expectations related to independent work, store ongoing projects or activities in a specific place in the classroom from where they can be continued when time is available)

Knowing what's next: How to go on with meaningful work when set tasks have been finished (for example, ensuring all students have access to meaningful work that can be continued when time is available, such as a **Learning in Depth** project [see Egan 2010] with allocated reading and research on specific class topics)

Keeping progress records: How to gather and organise results and examples of progress (for example, show students how to graph their progress on basic skills, select work samples that show evidence of learning, comment on their own progress and that of their peers)

> **Learning in Depth** is a program developed by Kieran Egan and designed to ensure that all students become experts about something during their school years by allocating to each child a particular topic to learn about through their whole school career.

Classroom actions for differentiated learning

The sustainable learning approach to differentiated instruction is guided by step 5 of the RTF, 'How do I teach for all my learners?' and by three sub-questions that focus teachers' actions. Each of these sub-questions and ways of responding to them are discussed below.

How will I teach this content?

First-class instruction that is evidence based and well planned is necessary for all learners to thrive. Such instruction should consider the content and concepts to be taught according to the RTF. To answer this question, teachers can do the following:

- Formulate thoughtful intended learning outcomes.
- Sequence quality learning activities with a rationale for the instructional approach chosen.
- Decide on grouping or individual task structures.
- Consider the lesson from the students' points of view.
- Ensure that students will know what success looks like, through clear and appropriately challenging success criteria.
- Plan what products or outcomes will indicate whether their students' learning trajectories are progressing.

How will I teach this content inclusively?

Answering this question requires thinking about how basic principles of teaching inclusively can be incorporated into the specific lesson plan. The kinds of principles that teachers can consider include those listed below:

- whether cooperative teaching and consulting or co-teaching with colleagues, or a teacher aide or specialist is desirable

- how parents or carers and families might be included in partnership to facilitate learning
- what grouping and effective teaching practices will be chosen
- how students' individual learning plans align with the lesson content

Teamwork and collegial cooperation in planning and problem-solving are hallmarks of inclusive practice. For example, deciding that students may be better served by receiving individual assistance from a specialist teacher or an aide rather than participating in a specific lesson or series of lessons is still inclusive practice.

The thoughtful use of available teacher aide time is an important part of the lesson-planning process. In collaborating with teacher aides, it is important to acknowledge that the responsibility for the progress of all students remains with the class teacher and that aide time is best thought of as available to support all the students in the classroom, not only individuals with disabilities or learning difficulties. The effectiveness of teacher aides' time in the classroom is increased by simple communication-focused measures such as setting aside time for joint planning between teachers and teacher aides, scheduling regular opportunities for reviewing students' progress, providing ongoing informal feedback during and after sessions and instituting a procedure for sharing comments about students' performance (for example, a memo book or computer file).

In addition, there is evidence that small-group intervention programs delivered by trained teaching assistants can significantly impact achievement for those students whose progress is being held back by a lack of fluency in basic academic skills (see Graham et al. 2007). Implementation of the *QuickSmart* basic skills programs in literacy and numeracy, for example, has indicated that such interventions are particularly successful if the following conditions are met:

- The program is evidence based and matched to students' needs.
- The intervention is of a set duration – for example, 30 weeks.
- A specialist or classroom teacher coordinates and supervises the program.
- There is planned time for teacher aides to feed back to class teachers regarding students' progress and to troubleshoot any issues that may have arisen.
- The impact of the intervention is monitored and regularly reassessed as part of a whole-school approach to aligning support programs and identifying where teacher aide time is most effectively employed.

A specific question to consider when planning inclusively is 'If the approach I have chosen doesn't "work" for some of my students, what can I do?' In other words, what alternative instructional strategies would be appropriate if this lesson does not go according to plan? This part of preparing to teach asks teachers to think about how they can plan to use 'different' approaches rather than 'more of the same'.

How will I teach this content to my students?

This question cues teachers to explicitly include their knowledge of their students and how they learn in the planning of instruction, considering which learners may have difficulty and with which content sections. The use of key content pre-tests and post-tests as part of unit planning and evaluation is helpful, because it allows informed planning based on students' results. The key issue here is how the complexity of teaching this content can be considered as simply as possible.

Teachers' knowledge of students' ATRiUM capabilities is important. The general principle is to make the intended learning outcomes accessible to all students as simply as possible; minimal adjustments that take into account students' learning needs are the easiest and the most desirable to implement. The planned learning activities should be appropriately challenging for all students while as far as possible remaining true to the intended learning outcomes of the lesson.

The Structure of the Observed Learning Outcome taxonomy

Developing intended learning outcomes in light of what teachers know about their students can allow differentiation to become more tailored. The adjustments used depend on whether the intended learning outcomes aim to develop (in terms of the SOLO taxonomy) uni-structural, multi-structural, relational or extended abstract outcomes; so in a developmentally appropriate way, the 'level' of learning required is not 'reduced' (Biggs and Collis 1982). This is an improvement to differentiated instruction and means that lower-achieving students, for example, are not assigned 'adjusted' tasks that are peripheral to the learning that the rest of the class is tackling – like a student with language difficulties being asked to make a poster about a 'great debate' rather than participating in an activity that improves speaking and listening skills. Using the SOLO levels can also facilitate multiple entry points to similar tasks (Martin 2012).

In terms of teachers' planning and actions, if the learning outcome focuses on a uni-structural skill, teachers can provide more practice with these foundational skills until students are fluent. For multi-structural outcomes, if students do not have sufficient connections related to the content, teachers can provide enrichment experiences and temporarily decrease the amount of content to be processed until learning becomes more efficient. In order to encourage relational thinking, teachers can point out connections between content and what the students already know and then ask their students to find further connections. Classrooms in which making such connections is encouraged and risk-taking is supported will go a long way towards meeting the learning needs of all students.

Even the use of powerful organising ideas like the SOLO taxonomy, however, comes with a warning: frameworks, like scaffolds, are guides and should be used flexibly, not 'welded' in place. Teaching that is so explicit that students have difficulty tackling learning tasks unless every facet of them is defined risks 'de-skilling' students and preventing them from developing the self-determination and independence required for learning that lasts; and it undervalues teachers' professional knowledge and judgment.

ATRiUM capabilities

In terms of the ATRiUM capabilities, students who have difficulties or who excel in certain areas may require tasks with either simpler or more complex literacy or numeracy demands and more or less scaffolding to complete learning activities independently or through collaborative work. Active learning, for example, can be motivated using students' interests and imaginations and by ensuring that assignments and tasks are meaningful. Thinking can be enabled by constructing intended learning outcomes using the SOLO taxonomy to provide a number of entry points to each lesson for students with different capabilities. Relating to others can be facilitated through establishing clear expectations and classroom procedures pertaining to general conduct, group roles and collaborative work, with extra support provided by the teacher or aide for students who need it. Managing the self can be encouraged by sharing the responsibility for goal-setting and assessment with students, so that they become increasingly in charge of their own learning and management of time, resources and competing demands.

On-the-spot adjustments

Having a repertoire of on-the-spot adjustments that can assist students to reach the learning outcomes of a lesson means considering in advance what is key for students to achieve during the lesson and then differentiating instruction at the point of need in order for them to achieve these results. This may mean, for example, changing the number of examples to be completed, regrouping for immediate reteaching, providing opportunities for further practice of prerequisite skills, organising a specific type of peer support or increasing or decreasing the complexity of the activity for certain students. Other on-the-spot adjustment options include the following:

- selecting and then encouraging other students to provide assistance
- allowing more time to finish written work
- providing more direct teacher help during the lesson (and noting whether or not to make more frequent contact with some students' parents or carers to organise practice opportunities at an appropriate level at home)
- changing the student grouping based on their performance and on the materials or resources they are using or the learning outcomes they are guided to meet
- deciding to use specific technology with some students (for example, having students video or audio record the rest of their answer, use a computer program to reinforce the basics or extend their knowledge by using the internet to expand their answers)

As teachers move around their classes interacting with students engaged in learning activities, they strategically use different types of interactions to check for learning as well as to offer further teaching. Teachers offer these informal interactions at different levels, based on their judgment of the directness required at the time. These spontaneous teaching interactions also function as feedback. Students will draw conclusions about their learning from the teaching type and intensity offered during learning tasks.

Figure 7.4 is an analysis of one teacher's interactions provided within mathematical teaching. It is presented as an example of the types of strategies that teachers and learners rely on throughout daily classroom activities to provide on-the-spot adjustment of instruction. Each of the strategies is defined initially at the lowest support level – that which is often used to check for learning. Responsive teachers do this constantly. There are then two more intensive or supportive levels for each strategy, which can be used if the teacher decides they could guide the most effective interactions at the time.

Think and do 7.3: Teaching interactions

Use figure 7.4 to analyse an observation of a teacher or a video of your own teaching interactions.

1   Identify the types of strategies the teacher is using in interactions with students and the level of each strategy.

2   What was the range of the strategy levels used?

3   Justify, as far as possible, the teacher's selection of particular levels or strategies.

4   Describe how students appear to have interpreted the teacher's interactions as feedback on their learning.

The 10 essential skills that guide differentiated instruction

The previous discussion has sketched the process of differentiation in broad strokes. The 10 essential skills listed here capture more specifically the orchestration, flow and major teaching actions of differentiated instruction. The skills are followed by a series of prompts that can be used in creative ways by teachers of inclusive classes. The skills relate to teaching and learning in general and to the RTF headings of planning, assessment and feedback, and evaluation and reflection, specifically. The essential skills related to planning are planning inclusively, setting clear learning intentions and using routine procedures; to assessment and feedback are using flexible activities, probing understanding, reteaching and extending, using 'different' ways and adjusting on the spot; and to evaluation and reflection are following through with data and reflecting and refining.

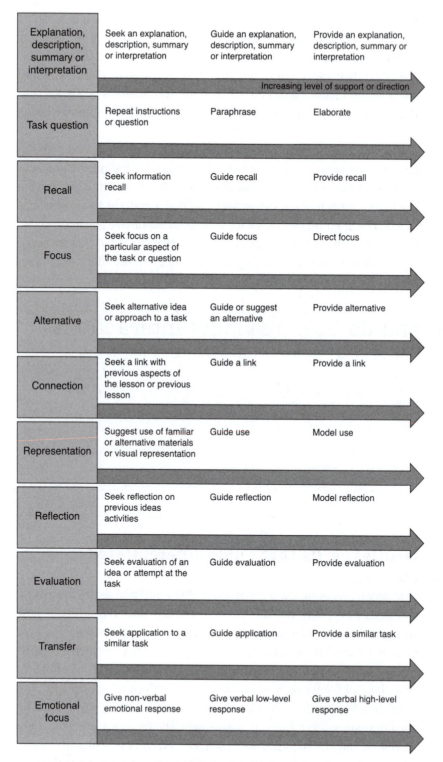

Figure 7.4: *On-the-spot teacher responses*
Source: Berman 2001.

1 Planning inclusively

Structure and sequence content for your class using evidence-based approaches. Build on established classroom routines that facilitate inclusion and differentiated instruction.

Prompts

Establish classroom routines and procedures and structure and sequence content for your class using evidence-based approaches.

- Pre-test to establish prior knowledge and post-test to show growth after instruction.
- Plan to use the best ways to present specific knowledge.
- Decide on the lesson approach and task difficulty variation.
- Be aware of what your students know and their interests.
- Present content using a number of appropriate modes – visual, auditory, kinaesthetic and technological.
- Tailor any adjustments that you make to the learning intentions you set for your students and your teaching.

2 Setting clear learning intentions

Guide the lesson and keep the focus on desired student engagement and outcomes.

Prompts

Set clear learning intentions informed by the SOLO taxonomy. Include multiple entry points to lesson activities.

3 Using routine procedures

Organise students' efforts so that they always know that there are ways of asking for help, accessing feedback, going on with other related learning activities if the set learning activity is completed, working in groups and contributing to collaborative tasks.

Prompts

- Give clear instructions.
- Show what success looks like.
- Manage transitions.
- Provide appropriate feedback.

4 Using flexible activities

Prepare a number of activities that can assist in meeting the needs of all students. Employ the simplicity principle so that minimal adjustments are made and they are made only when needed.

Prompts

In planning flexible activities use the acronym CARE to remember the most common features of instruction that can be adapted. As far as possible, the learning outcomes should remain the same, though the pathway to the outcomes may vary.

Content: More or less content in one lesson, content of the same type but different in terms of complexity or difficulty to decode, content matched specifically to student interest, content very close to a teacher-directed example, content provided using a different modality

Approach: More explicit teaching, students teamed with compatible peers, more opportunity provided for practice, different approaches tried when the 'usual' way isn't 'working'

Relatedness: Instruction related to previous information and to background knowledge, some students provided with more opportunities to develop background knowledge related to the content, students' prior knowledge built upon, pre-test findings used to consolidate or extend learning

Expectations: Expectations altered (to the least degree possible and to support learning and engagement) concerning difficulty level, accuracy, number of examples to be completed, presentation of information, speed, task materials or technology, assessment procedures, response mode, time spent on tasks, scaffolding

5 Probing understanding

Use observations, assessment tasks and questioning to probe students' understanding. Identify students who are having difficulty understanding the lesson and address their learning needs.

Prompts

- Observe.
- Listen.
- Question.
- Notice help-seeking.

6 Reteaching and extending

Identify and address students' learning needs including the need for reteaching to reinforce understanding and eliminate misunderstandings or to extend students whose work shows mastery.

Prompts

Reteaching or extending can be offered to some students in small groups or individually, depending on teachers' observations of students' learning during lessons. Establish routines for transitioning into these small groups:

- Make the formation of a group for reteaching or extending an expected and usual part of classroom instruction, easy for students to join if they think it would benefit them.

- Set clear expectations for how students will transition between activities and monitor behaviour between activities.

- Select an area where reteaching or extending will take place and organise the resources needed in advance.

7 Using 'different' ways

Access a repertoire of teaching approaches and evidence-based interventions which can be used to ensure student learning.

Prompts

Too often, students with learning difficulties are given 'more of the same' when they display confusion or a lack of understanding, rather than a fresh look at the same content using another approach or specific intervention. This situation also applies to students with well-developed academic skills, who also benefit from 'different' ways. Using 'different' ways usually means tinkering with some of the following instruction components:

Grouping: Organise learning as individuals, pairs and small groups; change groups and responsibilities within the group; use reciprocal teaching roles.

Resources and responses: Change the resources or materials used (for example, by providing a worked example); vary the manner in which students respond to learning tasks (for example, orally, in writing, videoed, audio recorded, with a peer).

Engagement: Use different examples that tap into students' interests; encourage active questioning; point out the relevance of the content; use incentives.

Assessment: Allow for different ways to demonstrate learning; give more time to complete assessments; organise different kinds of tests; position fewer items on a page; give more self-assessment and peer assessment opportunities.

Tools: Use different strategies and thinking aids to enhance and enliven explanations (for example, stories; metaphors; binary opposites; rhymes, rhythms and patterns; jokes and humour; images; a sense of wonder; changing the context; relating to the heroic; relevance; meaning).

8 Adjusting on the spot

Address students' needs for differentiation as soon as they are identified.

Prompts

On-the-spot differentiation options include:

Grouping: Change student groupings based on performance, the materials or resources used or required learning outcomes.

Peers: Select and encourage other students to provide assistance.

Time: Allow more time to finish written work or a meaningful individual project if the content has already been mastered.

Teacher attention: Provide more direct teacher help during the lesson.

ICT: Use specific technology with some students (for example, record the rest of an answer; use a computer program to reinforce the basics; extend knowledge through internet research).

9 Following through with data

Assess and monitor student performance and the effectiveness of teaching practices.

Prompts

Students can graph their performance on basic academic skills, collect work examples to illustrate their progress, participate in self-assessment and peer assessment procedures. Teachers can compare pre-test and post-test scores and review anecdotal records, observations, other test scores and work samples to gauge student learning and assess the impact of their teaching.

10 Reflecting and refining

Reflect on all available data and the experience of differentiation to respond to the question 'Was this differentiated instruction effective?' Continuously refine differentiated practice so that it becomes natural, easy to implement and evaluate and resource friendly.

Prompts

Reflecting on and refining practice is continual for effective teachers. Reflection is both 'in action' (thinking on your feet) and 'on action' (retrospective, or thinking after the event). Refining practice is part of teachers 'knowing thy impact' – Hattie's (2012) visible-learning mantra, a call for teachers to always view success in terms of their students' learning outcomes – and can be framed by Hattie's (160–5) eight mind frames for teachers.

Think and do 7.4: 10 essential skills

How would you use the prompts for the 10 essential skills for differentiation to support your practice? Would you share them with your colleagues or your students? Why or why not?

Summary

This chapter has explored in depth teaching that matters. It has discussed general approaches that educators can take to making their teaching transparent and strategic, such as using Sternberg's successful intelligence concept and whole-school approaches to providing culturally responsive and evidence-based instruction. The 10 essential skills for differentiation have been described as teaching that *really* matters for managing inclusive classrooms. This discussion sets the scene for the final chapter, on learning that lasts, because effective and responsive teaching is fundamental to learning that is sustainable. It is through the development of sound basic skills that are mastered and maintained that students become independent learners throughout their lives.

Further reading

8 Aboriginal Ways of Learning website: http://8ways.wikispaces.com/.

BES (Iterative Best Evidence Synthesis) Programme – What Works Evidence Hei Kete Raukura website: www.educationcounts.govt.nz/topics/bes.

Dweck, C. n.d. 'What is Mindset.' Mindset. http://mindsetonline.com/whatisit/about/.

International Association for Cognitive Education and Psychology website: www.ia-cep.org/.

QuickSmart website: http://simerr.une.edu.au/quicksmart.

Scootle website: www.scootle.edu.au/ec/p/home.

Stronger Smarter website: http://strongersmarter.com.au/.

Visible Learning website: http://visible-learning.org/.

What Works Clearinghouse website: www.whatworks.ed.gov.

Wiliam, D. n.d. 'The classroom experiment (ep. 1).' DocZoo. Video published on YouTube, 11 April 2012. www.youtube.com/watch?v=1iD6Zadhg4M.

——. n.d. 'The classroom experiment (ep. 2).' DocZoo. Video published on YouTube, 11 April 2012. www.youtube.com/watch?v=1iD6Zadhg4M.

References

Berman, J. 2001. 'An application of dynamic assessment to school mathematical learning.' PhD thesis, University of New England.

Biggs, J. B. and K. F. Collis. 1982. *Evaluating the quality of learning*. New York: Academic Press.

Binet, A. 1909. *Les idées modernes sur les enfants* (Modern ideas about children). Paris: Flammarion.

Bock, M. A. 1999. 'Sorting laundry: categorization strategy application to an authentic learning activity by children with autism.' *Focus on Autism and Other Developmental Disabilities* 14 (4): 220–30.

Bourke, R. and J. Loveridge. 2013. 'A scientist-practitioner model for inclusive education: supporting graduate students to conduct systematic reviews for evidence-based practice.' *New Zealand Journal of Teachers' Work* 10 (1): 4–24.

CARLA (Centre for Advanced Research on Language Acquisition). 2014. Website. University of Minnesota. 6 March. www.carla.umn.edu.

Carlson, J. S. and K. H. Wiedl. 2013. 'Cognitive education: constructivist perspectives on schooling, assessment, and clinical applications.' *Journal of Cognitive Education and Psychology* 12 (1): 6–25.

Chan, C., M. L. Chang, P. S. Westwood and M. T. Yuen. 2002. 'Teaching adaptively: how easy is "differentiation" in practice? A perspective from Hong Kong.' *The Asia-Pacific Education Researcher* 11 (1): 27–58.

Cornelius-White, J. 2007. 'Learner-centered teacher-student relationships are effective: a meta-analysis.' *Review of Educational Research* 77 (1): 113–43.

Dignath, C. and G. Büttner. 2008. 'Components of fostering self-regulated learning among students: a meta-analysis on intervention studies at primary and secondary school level.' *Metacognition and Learning* 3 (3): 231–64.

Dignath, C., G. Buettner and H. P. Langfeldt. 2008. 'How can primary school students learn self-regulated learning strategies most effectively? A meta-analysis on self-regulation training programmes.' *Educational Research Review* 3 (2): 101–29.

Dweck, C. 2000. *Self-theories: their role in motivation, personality and development*. Psychology Press.

——. 2006. *Mindset: the new psychology of success*. New York: Random House.

Education Counts. n.d. BES (Iterative Best Evidence Synthesis) Programme – What Works Evidence Hei Kete Raukura. Website. New Zealand Government. www.educationcounts.govt.nz/topics/bes.

Egan, K. 2010. *Learning in depth: a simple innovation that can transform schooling*. Chicago, IL: University of Chicago Press.

Falvey, M. A., C. C. Givner and C. Kimm. 1996. 'What do I do Monday morning?' In S. Stainback and W. Stainback, eds. *Inclusion: a guide for educators*, 117–40. Baltimore, MD: Brookes.

Feuerstein, R., L. H. Falik and R. S. Feuerstein 2013. 'The cognitive elements of neural plasticity.' The Neuropsychotherapist. www.neuropsychotherapist.com/wp-content/uploads/2013/03/CognitiveElements.pdf.

Graham, L., A. Bellert, J. Thomas and J. Pegg. 2007. '*QuickSmart*: a basic academic skills intervention for middle school students with learning difficulties.' *Journal of learning disabilities* 40 (5): 410–19.

Harrison, N. 2011. *Teaching and learning in Aboriginal education*, 2nd edn. Melbourne: Oxford University Press.

Hattie, J. 2003. 'Teachers make a difference: what is the research evidence?' Paper presented at the ACER Research Conference. Melbourne. 19–21 October. Text available at SA Department for Education and Child Development. www.decd.sa.gov.au/limestonecoast/files/pages/new%20page/plc/teachers_make_a_difference.pdf.

——. 2012. *Visible learning for teachers: maximizing impact on learning*. Oxford: Routledge.

Hattie, J. and E. M. Anderman, eds. 2013. *International guide to student achievement*. New York: Routledge.

Haywood, H. C. 1977. 'A cognitive approach to the education of retarded children.' *Peabody Journal of Education* 54 (2): 110–16.

Hessels, M. G. and C. Hessels-Schlatter. 2013. 'Current views on cognitive education: a critical discussion and future perspectives.' *Journal of Cognitive Education and Psychology* 12 (1): 108–24.

Higgins, J. P. G. S. and S. Green. 2005. 'Cochrane handbook for systematic reviews of interventions', version 4.2.5 (May). The Cochrane Collaboration. Latest version available at The Cochrane Collaboration. http://handbook.cochrane.org.

Hughes, J. N., T. A. Cavell and V. Willson 2001. 'Further support for the developmental significance of the quality of the teacher–student relationship.' *Journal of School Psychology* 39 (4): 289–301.

Knight, B. A., L. Graham and D. Hughes. 2004. 'Facilitating positive social interactions for children with learning disabilities.' In B. A. Knight and W. Scott, eds. *Learning disabilities: multiple perspectives*, 171–85. Sydney: Pearson.

Krathwohl, D. R. 2002. 'A revision of Bloom's taxonomy: an overview.' *Theory into Practice* 41 (4): 212–18.

Luke, A., C. Cazden, R. Coopes, V. Klenowski, J. Ladwig, J. Lester, S. MacDonald, J. Phillips, P. G. Shield, N. Spina, P. Theroux, M. J. Tones, M. Villegas and A. F. Woods. 2013. 'A summative evaluation of the Stronger Smarter Learning Communities Project: vol 1 and vol 2.' Abstract and link to full documents. Queensland University of Technology. http://eprints.qut.edu.au/59535/.

Martin, A. J. 2006. 'A motivational psychology for the education of Indigenous Australian students.' *Australian Journal of Indigenous Education* 35: 30–43.

Martin, S. 2012. *Using SOLO as a framework for teaching*. Invercargill: Essential Resources Educational Publishers.

Mastropieri, M. A. and T. E. Scruggs. 2009. *The inclusive classroom: strategies for effective instruction*. San Diego: Prentice Hall.

Munns, G. 1998. 'They just can't hack that: Aboriginal students, their teachers and responses to schools and classrooms.' In G. Partington, ed. *Perspectives on Aboriginal and Torres Strait Islander education*, 171–87. Katoomba: Social Science Press.

NASP (National Association of School Psychologists). 2002. 'Social skills: promoting positive behavior, academic success, and school safety.' NASP. www.whrsd.org/uploaded/faculty/wendyprice/socialskills_rk.html.

Newman, R. S. 2002. 'How self-regulated learners cope with academic difficulty: the role of adaptive help seeking.' *Theory into Practice* 41 (2): 132–8.

Ogbu, J. U. 1992. 'Adaptation to minority status and impact on school success.' *Theory into Practice* 31 (4): 287–95.

Paterson, D. 2007. 'Teachers' in-flight thinking in inclusive classrooms.' *Journal of Learning Disabilities* 40 (5): 427–35.

Rey, A. 1934. 'D'un procédé pour évaluer l'éducabilité' (A method for assessing educability). *Archives de Psychologie* 24: 297–337.

Rose, D. 2001. 'Universal design for learning.' *Journal of Special Education Technology* 16 (2): 66–7.

Ryan, A. M., H. Patrick and S. O. Shim. 2005. 'Differential profiles of students identified by their teacher as having avoidant, appropriate, or dependent help-seeking tendencies in the classroom.' *Journal of Educational Psychology* 97 (2): 275.

Scootle. 2014. Website. Scootle. www.scootle.edu.au/ec/p/home.

Selz, O. 1935. 'Versuche zur Hebung des Intelligenzniveaus' (Attempts to raise intelligence levels). *Zeitschrift für Psychologie* 134: 236–301.

Sternberg, R. J. 2003. *Wisdom, intelligence, and creativity synthesized.* New York: Cambridge University Press.

——. 2010. 'WICS: A new model for school psychology.' *School Psychology International* 31 (6): 599–616.

——. 2013. 'What is cognitive education?' *Journal of Cognitive Education and Psychology* 12 (1): 45–58.

Stronger Smarter. n.d. Website. Stronger Smarter. http://strongersmarter.com.au.

Tomlinson, C. A. 2001. *How to differentiate instruction in mixed-ability classrooms.* Alexandria, VA: Association for Supervision and Curriculum Development.

Vygotsky, L. S. 1934. *Myshlenie i rech: psikhologicheskie issledovanija* (Thinking and speech: psychological investigations). Moscow and Leningrad: Sotsekgiz.

——. 1978. *Mind and society: the development of higher mental processes.* Cambridge, MA: Harvard University Press.

Westwood, P. 2001. 'Differentiation as a strategy for inclusive classroom practice: some difficulties identified.' *Australian Journal of Learning Difficulties* 6 (1): 5–11.

——. 2003. *Commonsense methods for children with special educational needs*, 4th edn. London: Routledge.

——. 2005. *Reading and learning difficulties: approaches to teaching and assessment.* Melbourne: Australian Council for Educational Research.

What Works Clearinghouse. n.d. Website. Institute of Education Sciences, What Works Clearinghouse and US Department of Education. www.whatworks.ed.gov.

WNSWRAET (Western New South Wales Regional Aboriginal Education Team). n.d. 8 Aboriginal Ways of Learning. Website. WNSWRAET. http://8ways.wikispaces.com.

Wong, B. and D. Butler, eds. 2012. *Learning about learning disabilities*. San Diego, CA: Elsevier.

Wong, B., L. Graham, M. Hoskyn and J. Berman. 2008. *The ABCs of learning disabilities*. San Diego, CA: Elsevier.

Yuen, M., P. Westwood and G. Wong. 2005. 'Meeting the needs of students with specific learning difficulties in the mainstream education system: data from primary school teachers in Hong Kong.' *International Journal of Special Education* 20 (1): 67–76.

Chapter 8

Learning that lasts

Intended learning outcomes

Engagement with the text in this chapter will enable readers to do the following:

- know how to facilitate effective transitions between home and school for all students, and especially for students with disabilities and learning difficulties

- consider how action research underpins learning that lasts for teachers

- constructively critique the model of professional learning described

- analyse and add to the strategies presented for addressing learning difficulties

- access information about assistive technologies available to support students with disabilities and learning difficulties

Big ideas

- Learning that lasts is meaningful, intentional and future directed.
- Future-directed learning is focused on transitions *to* educational settings, *between* educational settings and *from* school to work.
- Action research cycles grow out of the RTF and can guide professional practice to foster teacher learning that lasts.
- A promising model of professional development involves exploring how different professionals create connections and how artefacts from one community are introduced into another.
- Literacy, numeracy and ICT competencies provide a foundation for lifelong learning.
- Individual, context and technology factors must be considered when matching individuals with assistive technology.

Introduction

Learning that lasts is learning that underpins lifelong development and active engagement in society. It dynamically embodies the **ATRiUM** capabilities in the independent and social activities of living. Specifically, it is learning stemming from the application of individuals' capabilities in current and new learning situations. Active learners apply their thinking skills, practise self-regulation and self-management skills and develop and maintain positive attitudes to learning throughout their lives. They also initiate their own learning opportunities and use flexible problem-solving strategies in response to novel situations.

> **ATRiUM** Active learning; Thinking; Relating to others; Using language, symbols and ICT; and Managing self.

For example, lifelong learners are not 'stuck' using only one level of thinking, so utilise all the SOLO taxonomy's thinking levels as required, pushing themselves from multi-structural to relational and extended abstract as needed. Such learners also relate to others and work together to function well in classrooms, families, workplaces and society. Being able to competently use the tools of learning – literacy, numeracy and ICT – is essential for lifelong learning, because mastery of these foundational skills allows individuals to continue learning throughout their lives. While it must be acknowledged that literacy, numeracy and ICT practices are culturally defined and bound, they are the tools of lifelong learning – of learning that lasts.

This chapter looks at sustainable learning in terms of life journeys. Formal learning includes the 13 years that learners are engaged in schools as well as their preschool and early childhood educational experiences and tertiary and workplace educational contexts. Learning is not confined to these formal educational phases, however; learning is lifelong and happens in response to the phenomenally dynamic and volatile world in which we live. The first part of this chapter examines teachers' lives and emphasises the perpetual learning that is inherent in being a teacher. The second part focuses on transition points experienced during the years of formal education – the times when the settings or demands change – and the different responses required by these changes, articulating the considerations necessary for teachers to support their learners. The final section provides a focused discussion and then summaries of useful instructional responses to students' affective and academic challenges.

Lifelong learning

Teachers can spend 13 years at school, four or more years at university and then 30 or so back in schools and never stop learning. They can always learn more about their students, themselves, their communities and the relationships that underpin teaching and learning in educational settings. Teachers also have the constant opportunity to familiarise themselves with new learning, teaching and information-sharing tools. Early in their careers, young teachers tend to be enthusiastic and largely optimistic individuals. As their careers progress, teachers who experience continuing renewal keep finding opportunities that challenge them beyond, as well as within, their own classrooms.

According to Hargreaves' (2005, 974) ideas about facilitating sustainable educational change, the most productive teachers are 'positive focusers', who concentrate improvement efforts on their classrooms and students. Teachers can make sense of how effective they are by comparing themselves to their peers, who they see as either positive or negative examples. Positive focusers tend to be lifelong learners who use their combination of knowledge, skills and attitudes to extend their spheres of influence and enhance the quality of their work throughout their careers.

The cycle used in action research echoes the responsive teaching model used throughout this book. In its simplest form, action research is a cycle of planning, action, observation and reflection followed by revisions of the initial plan that are informed by data and lead to subsequent cycles of action, observation and reflection. Important aspects of action research include the need for planning, which covers data-gathering and the use of formative assessment practices; consideration of strategies for sharing the research outcomes; and feedback analysis that it informs both future teaching decisions and provides information to students about instances of successful learning.

The process of professional practice supported by the RTF becomes action research as multiple cycles are generated. The four tenets of action research are equivalent to planning, teaching, assessment and feedback, and evaluation and reflection. In figure 8.1, three cycles of responsive teaching are represented, with planning (P) the entry to each cycle, followed by the action of teaching, learning, assessment and feedback (T) and then evaluation and reflection (E). A series of responsive teaching cycles becomes action research, as teachers' actions in subsequent cycles are informed by evidence from the previous cycles (see figure 3.1). In this way, teacher practice using the RTF becomes evidence based.

Reflection 8.1: Definitions of lifelong learning

The European Parliament, Council of the European Union (2006, 13) defines eight key competences (also termed '21st-century skills') that underpin individuals' ability to remain flexible learners throughout their lives:

1) Communication in the mother tongue;

2) Communication in foreign languages;

3) Mathematical competence and basic competencies in science and technology;

4) Digital competence;

5) Learning to learn;

6) Social and civic competences;

7) Initiative and entrepreneurship; and

8) Cultural awareness and expression.

Similarly, Mayer (1992) defines the following seven key Australian competencies:

- collecting, analysing and organising information
- communicating ideas and information
- planning and organising activities
- working with others and in teams
- using mathematical ideas and techniques
- solving problems
- using technology

New Zealand has extended the range of key competencies identified across all educational sectors based on the rationale that these competencies (acting autonomously, operating in social groups, using tools interactively and thinking) are key to supporting lifelong learning in our changing world (Ministry of Education 2005). It is important to note how closely the competencies listed here align with the ATRiUM capabilities.

Teachers never stop learning; they set up a process of perpetual learning by seeking evidence on which to base their professional organisation and activity. Teachers, as professionals, never reach a point where they know all there is to know about teaching and learning, simply because learners change and bring individual differences to their learning, and the teachers change in light of experience, new professional learning and engaging with new students.

Ongoing professional learning is part of all teacher-accreditation frameworks in Australia and New Zealand and is also, of course, important in terms of learning that lasts. Ideally, teachers monitor their own professional learning needs, align them to the learning needs of their students and actively engage in the kind of professional

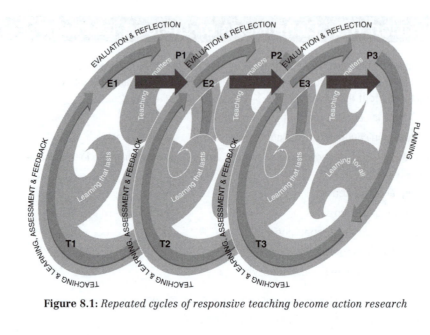

Figure 8.1: *Repeated cycles of responsive teaching become action research*

development that improves their practice in a targeted and collaborative way (AITSL 2012).

In 2014, the Australian Institute of Teaching and School Leadership released the report 'Global trends in professional learning and performance and development: some implications and ideas for the Australian education system', which presented findings from a worldwide scan of professional learning programs and practices in terms of whether they used contemporary learning principles and offered efficient low-cost solutions to complex challenges. This report determined that innovation in professional learning:

- taps into passions of and is owned by participants
- engages with external partners ... who offer a fresh perspective
- uses technology to support collaboration
- draws on new or existing data ... [in new ways]
- enables participants to rethink their use of resources (AITSL 2014, 29)

Sharing the information and insights gained from applying the frameworks used throughout this book to classroom contexts and reflecting on their application can be assisted by using technology like wikis and learning management systems that support the sharing of appropriate resources, collaborative effort and professional communication.

In their review of professional development research for inclusive education, Waitoller and Artiles (2013) note that, of late, effective professional development in inclusive education has mostly focused on the learning associated with specific action research projects that offer ongoing opportunities for problem-solving, generation of knowledge focusing on practice, reflection and engagement with inquiry and feedback and collaborations with peers. For example, the *QuickSmart* professional development model fits this description (Pegg and Graham 2013). However, we predict that the impetus for professional development in the future is likely to lie with schools and universities negotiating the content and form of professional learning and then expanding their shared artefacts (for example, understandings of action research and inclusive education, shared products, proformas and scaffolds) in order to examine how learning occurs around the use of 'boundary practices' and how this affects teacher learning.

A boundary practice is defined as a practice that provides an ongoing forum for mutual engagement between two communities of practice. Boundary practices facilitate learning because they are practices that both communities can examine with the aim of improving the educational experiences of all students. Boundary brokers – faculty members and teachers with different expertise – play a key role in connecting practices and tools across overlapping communities and facilitating transactions and joint work. How university faculty and school professionals create connections and how artefacts from one community are introduced into another is the stuff of professional learning with promise.

Think and do 8.1: Professional learning

Interview one or more experienced teachers about their professional learning. Ask them about how teaching has changed during their careers and how they have kept up with the evolution of the curriculum, pedagogy, social expectations, cultural changes and technological developments. What other aspects of their journey have contributed to their professional learning and practice habits?

Teachers observe the learning journeys of many young people as they become increasingly able to manage their lives' complex demands. Teachers can assist in the development of students' self-awareness and self-management skills by helping them make sense of their learning experiences through metaphor. Metaphors allow people to understand new information, ideas and concepts through a scaffolded description anchored in what they already understand. By associating new ideas and processes with what is already well known, learners gain insight into complex meaning. In this way, the complicated ideas and processes that constitute our understanding of learning can make more sense.

Durie's (1998) human health model, 'Te whare tapa wha', as represented by a Māori meeting house (*wharenui*) provides an example of how metaphors are used to illuminate complex ideas (see figure 8.2). The underlying meaning of this metaphor is that it is important to consider all dimensions of wellbeing when providing education.

This same message is contained in a very different metaphor, 'The dance of life' (see figure 4.1), which is consistent with an Aboriginal perspective that emphasises the need for wellbeing across all five dimensions (physical, spiritual, psychological, social and cultural) in order for an individual to be whole and dance through life. Both metaphors emphasise the need for all dimensions to be considered in any growth-focused support activity, such as education.

include changing school enrolments as students' learning needs and family circumstances alter.

Prior to the 1980s, many children who displayed delays or disorders in development were automatically placed in special educational facilities and thereby excluded from most local community schools. There was little choice for their families. Today, although most families choose local schools for their children with and without disabilities, there are still some special educational options available in parts of Australia and New Zealand, particularly in urban areas. Depending on the educational system and geographical area, there may be a range of schools available for students. As well as local schools, there are sometimes support or special classes (most often for children who have a diagnosis of ASD, intellectual disability, behavioural difficulties, language delay or sensory impairment) and some special schools or schools for specific purposes. These educational options are usually available only for students who have specific, complex disabilities. Each facility has an eligibility criteria with the assessment process and eligibility determination carried out by a team of educational and assessment professionals. In regional areas, special schools are rare, with support classes in local schools being more common. Families may have the option of educational placement in a special or support class, full time in the regular classroom or a tailored mix of inclusion in both settings. It is usual for students with a disability to move between different types of settings during their school years.

Deciding on the right school setting for a child with disabilities can be a complex process, with the transition to school taking two years or longer for some families. In these cases, students have most likely been diagnosed with a significant disability requiring intensive early intervention, structured preschool experiences and therapy services and support throughout the process of preparation for school, including a specific **transition plan**. There are many issues to consider when organising the transition to school for a child with significant disabilities; however, the same basic conditions are sought by all families: a safe, valuing, welcoming school where children's learning needs are met by effective, caring and responsive teachers.

> **Transition plans** coordinate support options for students moving to, between and from educational settings.

Transition between schools

Most children make one or two transitions between school settings as they move with their peers from primary to intermediate or middle school and then on to high school. Such transitions are usually full of excitement, anticipation and optimism: they are expected, experienced as a member of a group and considered a sign of growing maturity and development. Some children, however, move between school settings more often, because of their family circumstances. Such moves have the potential to exacerbate learning problems, so responsive teachers need to monitor closely how well new students manage transitions. This can be difficult if the student arrives with little accompanying information. There are some practical things teachers can do, however, that focus on efficiently gathering information about what skills students bring to their new schools and how their current learning needs can be defined. Again, an active mindset leads responsive teachers to ask, 'What are my students' learning needs?' Relevant information can be gathered from a number of sources, such as those listed below:

Previous schools, teachers, records: Most schools have procedures for contacting new students' previous schools. These are often linked to the paperwork needed for enrolment.

Family contact: Teachers can make sure they make personal contact with new families to welcome them and inquire whether their child has any particular strengths or weaknesses.

Students: A personal talk with students can uncover more about what they bring to the classroom, such as what attitudes they have to learning and how skilled they are at settling in and making friends.

Family and community links: It is not unusual to find out that new students have family links with others at the same school. This can be useful information for teachers to build on to help students settle in.

Indications of learning difficulties: Teachers need to know who in their school investigates whether new students have a documented disability. This may be the principal, school psychologist, special educational needs coordinator or learning assistance support teacher. It is most important to find out which teaching strategies have been successful with new students and which ones are not appropriate.

Because communication between schools may be delayed, it is imperative that teachers make sense of what each new student brings to their classroom in order to minimise the gaps that can accompany changing schools and missing classroom time. The key action for teachers at each transition point is to share knowledge about students' learning needs, so that what is already working well can be used as the foundation from which students can embrace the opportunities of their new setting.

Ideally, each educational setting gradually prepares students to transition to their next setting. All contexts and transitions are related and cannot really be considered separately. They are part of students' total school experiences. The following list shows some key questions for teachers to ask that can guide students' transitions within and between educational settings:

- What skills and knowledge are needed in the next (or will be brought from the previous) setting?
- What transition processes and activities will be appropriate?

- What can I share with the next (or find out from the previous) teachers? What works well (supports learning)? What should be avoided (hinders learning)?
- Are there any students or families who may need different or additional transition preparation?

Transition from school

A smooth transition from the formal school system to tertiary education or the workforce is important for all students. It can be facilitated by family (*whānau*), teachers and other school personnel considering the same key questions as for other school transitions:

- What skills and knowledge are needed in the next setting?
- What transition processes and activities are appropriate?
- What can be shared with the next teachers or professionals who will provide support?
- What works well to support learning and living?
- What should be avoided because it hinders learning and living?

For students who do not have the capability level required for making this transition into the world independently, school systems may provide extensions of time at school. With the trend of having all students progress through their school years alongside their age peers, however, this option has been largely replaced with transition-to-work programs. In New Zealand, an extension of time in school settings was still available in 2014, based on the idea that students who have an intellectual disability will benefit from further time to consolidate and practise their skills.

Part of the process of coming to terms with being the family (*whānau*) of a child with a disability is the consideration of what life may be like for them after school. Sometimes, this is hard to envisage. For many families, the process of grieving over the losses experienced by their child continues throughout their life and becomes prominent at times of transition. Positive options may be full-time care, supported workplaces or part-time supported work. Families require assistance to make informed decisions about their child's direction, as well as support for the emotional consequences of ongoing responsibility.

For example, for students who have sensory, physical or intellectual disabilities, an extended transition process needs to be planned, which in some cases will be the focus of these students' entire high-school program. Such a transition plan includes work experience and practice of authentic everyday life skills. Some schools set up commercial workplaces to provide students with opportunities for supervised skills development. Other schools negotiate jointly supervised work placements within local businesses. Government funding can be accessed to support employment for people with disabilities (in Australia, see Australian Government, n.d., and in New Zealand, Ministry of Social Development, n.d.).

Think and do 8.3: Teachers' impacts

While teachers often have only one year with any particular student, or a limited number of lessons depending on high-school subject choices, it is important to recognise how meaningful each teacher's input can be for every learner. This is especially so for learners with disabilities and learning difficulties, who depend on their teachers to ensure some level of authentic learning success. Most pre-service teachers can also point to at least one teacher who made a profound difference to them. Often, that teacher is the reason they subsequently decided to become teachers themselves.

Consider this question: What was it about an inspirational teacher in your life that made a difference to you? (You could be such a teacher for your students and make a profound and positive impact on their lives during their school years and after they begin their adult lives.)

Strategies for enhancing learning

The discussion in this chapter so far has focused on transitions to, between and from educational settings. While contexts are important in learning that lasts, so is establishing a foundation for lifelong learning through teaching that matters and teaching *what* matters. While literacy, numeracy and ICT competencies are skill sets that are foundational to sustainable learning, it is beyond the scope of this text to look at all of the issues involved in teaching these areas in detail. What can be offered instead is a focused discussion and then summaries of some key instructional responses to the affective and academic challenges students often experience.

Social and emotional factors, general learning behaviours, thinking strategies and literacy, numeracy and ICT competencies are all core to learning, primarily because proficiency in these areas allows learners to continue learning after teaching stops; capability in these areas represents a good chance at learning that lasts throughout life. As soon as a learner is seen to be responding differently from the way teachers may anticipate, adaptations within inclusive classrooms can begin. Much research has produced evidence about effective strategies for specific aspects of learning that can be drawn on in response to individual students' learning patterns. The following sections (based on Bellert 2012) list strategies that can be used as different learning needs are observed and taken into account during instruction.

Social and emotional factors that affect learning

A necessary focus on some of the social and emotional factors that support learning is now evident in many schools. For example, the five 'You can do it' keys to success is a program being used across Australia and New Zealand to address the social and emotional conditions that can support or hinder learning (PNINS, n.d.; Drummond Memorial Public School, n.d.; see figure 8.3).

The five keys to success have a focus on social (interpersonal) and emotional (intrapersonal) learning. These capabilities are inherent in ATRiUM through relating to

Figure 8.3: *Sculptures of 'You can do it' pencils showing the five keys to school success*
Source: Danthonia. Photograph J. Berman.

others and managing self and are relevant both at school and throughout life. In fact, ATRiUM is a combination of capabilities and includes attention to ways of managing interpersonal and intrapersonal functioning so that students are confident, persistent, resilient, organised and can get on with others. Approaches such as 'You can do it' in schools provide explicit language for talking about social and emotional function-ing and direct students and teachers to consciously notice and develop processes and strategies for competently relating to others and managing self, as well as reflecting on that competence. Such functioning lays the groundwork for the development of self-reflection, not only about social and emotional aspects of living and learning but also potentially about the other ATRiUM capabilities.

Strategies for supporting social and emotional aspects of learning

Social competence

- Carefully plan cooperative learning activities.
- Consider seating and placement.
- Use careful groupings to facilitate good peer modelling.

- Tell students about the structure of the lesson – for example, 'First we will be doing … then …'
- Display classroom rules clearly, refer to them regularly and consistently and enforce them fairly.
- Clarify the consequences of non-compliance in advance and where possible ensure that they are logical with regard to the undesired behaviour.

Self-esteem regarding learning
- Adjust the task difficulty level to ensure the work is at an appropriate level for students' capabilities and skills.
- Avoid failure situations – for example, asking students to answer questions unexpectedly, to read aloud without prior warning or to complete assignments or assessments without adjustments.
- Reward effort more than achievement.
- Measure progress against previous achievement where possible rather than standards-referenced benchmarks.

Self-efficacy and confidence
- Provide time for student reflection about learning and to examine attributions – explanations about success and failure, like effort, luck and strategy use.
- Focus teacher feedback to students on strategies used, persistence and effort.
- Encourage realistic pre-task expectations of performance.
- Model and use 'think alouds' from targeted and other students to show a range of attributions regarding why individuals considered they were able to succeed at a task.

General learning and thinking strategies
Students' thinking capabilities can change and develop with attention, effort and appropriate strategy use. Teachers' efforts can usefully focus on consolidating their students' general learning behaviours and thinking skills (see table 8.1).

Strategies for developing thinking capabilities
Appropriate and efficient use of strategies
- Model efficient strategies in a supportive environment.
- Use teacher and peer 'think alouds'.
- Teach by showing, demonstrating and peer modelling.
- Encourage reflection and talk about learning processes. (Graham et al. 2007)

Recalling previously encountered knowledge
- Provide explicit repeated reviews and practice.
- Begin every lesson with a review of prior content.

Table 8.1: *Strategies for supporting effective general learning behaviours*

LEARNING DIMENSIONS	BEHAVIOURS	SUPPORTS
Approaches to learning	Inefficient strategy use Inappropriate strategy use Difficulty implementing new strategies	Teacher and peer modelling Use of 'think alouds' as demonstration Explicit strategy instruction
Attention	Difficulty attending to task Poor concentration Distractibility Lack of persistence	Short, fast-paced learning activities A prescribed sequence of lesson activities Consistent teacher expectations Hands-on activities, timed activities
Work habits	Difficulty commencing a task Lack of persistence Poor task completion	Established work routines Pre-teaching and rehearsal Rewarding effort as well as achievement
Memory	Inconsistent recall Incorrect recall Forgetting Slow recall	Repeated practice of the same content Frequent review of previously encountered content Linking new learning to prior knowledge
Impact of affective factors	Social difficulties Lack of confidence in self as a learner Anxiety about learning or performing Fear of failure	Small-group instruction Supportive learning environment Established work routines Experiencing success

Source: Bellert 2012.

- Make strong connections with prior knowledge and current interests.
- Use mnemonics and other memory aids.
- Provide visual cues and supports to aid retention and recall. (Graham et al. 2007)

Working memory

- Teach cognitive strategies and procedures repeatedly.
- Use advanced organisers (preview and pre-teach).
- Break down content and tasks into achievable steps.
- Use graphic organisers.
- Provide scaffolds and proformas – for example, proformas for text types and subject-specific reports and scaffolds for assignment responses. (Graham et al. 2007)

Attention and task persistence

- Ensure the task set is within the students' capabilities.
- Reward effort more than achievement.
- Break tasks up into step-by-step procedures.
- Provide short lesson breaks.
- Focus feedback on effort and strategies used.
- Use individual goal-setting and reward schedules.

Strategies for using literacy, numeracy and ICT tools for learning

Being able to use the sociocultural learning tools (that is, oral and written language systems, the number system and ICT systems) efficiently not only supports school performance but also prepares learners for the dynamic world after school. Responsive teachers know how to teach learners the skills necessary to 'learn how to learn'. As the adage goes, 'learn to read, so you can read to learn'. This orientation is pertinent for all learning tools. The language, literacy and numeracy and ICT skills required for independent learning must be explicitly taught, especially to students who are less likely to learn them easily without this kind of instruction. Some students do not have access to enriching environments outside school in which to practise and build their basic academic skills. Alternatively, some students do not use these culturally defined skills regularly outside their formal school and classroom experiences because they are different from those used in their home cultures.

Literacy is evident across all aspects of the curriculum. Teachers need to ask themselves in what ways the development and application of literacy is supporting or hindering students' learning with regard to any particular curriculum domain. For example, an analysis of a student's performance on mathematical word problems could uncover that the barriers to success relate to the literacy and language demands of the problem rather than the mathematical reasoning it requires.

Strategies for supporting reading

Word reading and automaticity

- Provide frequent reviews and revisions of basic words (common words and sight words), with some reference to phonics. Practise these in a variety of ways to the point of automaticity.
- Pre-teach and frequently practise relevant vocabulary for every new content area.
- Display each keyword with a visual cue.
- Explicitly teach decoding strategies such as the following:
  - breaking words into parts – for example, onset and rime or syllables

- sounding out parts of words then blending parts together
- seeing small words or blends in big words
- thinking of similar-looking words
- Develop students' knowledge of parts of words: prefixes, suffixes, root words, vowel blends.
- Practise using the repeated reading of familiar texts with a focus on fluency.
- Provide peer reading, guided reading and readers' theatre experiences.
- Incorporate use of appropriate technology – for example, software and applications that provide varied practice experiences.

Reading comprehension
- Preview the content before reading to set the context and to help activate background knowledge.
- Encourage students to make predictions prior to reading.
- Use a highlighter to mark out important parts of the passage, unknown words, parts where meaning is unclear and so on.
- Slow down the pace of reading so focus can shift to meaning.
- Construct an overview of the text.
- Fill in a graphic organiser after reading.
- Teach question–answer relationship strategies such as 'Here, hidden, in my head'. (Graham and Wong 1993)

Numeracy demands are also important to consider across the curriculum. Many of our basic concepts of size, quantity, position and relationships between items are mathematical. It is very demanding for beginning students to follow instructions in the first years of schooling without well-developed understandings of these concepts. The curriculum content in higher school years relies on assumptions related to what mathematical terms and relationships mean. For example, statistics is central to many disciplines, from social studies and geography to science and history. Spatial mathematics is inherent in geography, design studies and physical disciplines including sport. Any exploration of financial literacy, from home finances to world economics, rests on knowledge and skills with quantities. Effective teachers are able to identify what assumptions are problematic for their students and provide opportunities for clarifying and practising the appropriate skills (Graham, Bellert and Pegg 2007).

Strategies for mathematical learning

Basic maths skills
- Provide opportunities for frequent reviews and practice of basic facts.
- Teach and practise similar facts together (plus, minus and multiply, divide).

- Maintain focus on practice activities over an extended period of time.
- Use timed practice activities so students can beat their personal best times.
- Give preference to frequent, intense, short bursts of practice.
- Use a variety of practice approaches – for example, flashcards, speed sheets, games, repeated and timed practice on appropriate worksheets, peer activities.
- Teach repeatedly and model counting and grouping strategies.
- Relate basic math facts to basic living skills, such as money, measurement, card games and cooking.
- Explicitly teach the language of mathematics, especially key vocabulary relevant to the current topic.
- Incorporate use of appropriate technology – for example, software and applications that provide varied practice experiences.

Mathematics problem-solving

- Consistently teach and demonstrate a step-by-step approach to problem-solving, an example of which is below:
    - Identify the problem.
    - Draw the scenario.
    - Select a strategy to solve the problem.
    - Put the information into an algorithm.
    - Calculate.
    - Evaluate.
- Provide teacher and peer modelling followed by guided and independent practice.
- Pre-teach and frequently practise keywords for each new mathematics topic as well as generic mathematics prefixes and suffixes – for example, 'deci-', 'centi-', 'milli-', '-meter', '-gram'.
- Provide graphic representation of problems – for example, diagrams, graphic organisers, use of symbols, arrows.
- Explicitly teach strategies such as those listed below:
    - Use models, number lines or concrete materials.
    - Look for keywords.
    - Make a drawing or diagram.
    - Act or visualise.
    - Remove irrelevant detail.
    - Construct a table or graph. (Graham et al. 2007)

Assistive technology

Being competent with ICT is a way of thinking and problem-solving, as well as an opportunity for skill development. It is about flexibly adapting and transferring understandings to new technologies – learning new ways to search for and access information, collect and organise material and present, share and discuss information. Assistive technology is a particular use of ICT that is relevant for learners who have sensory or physical impairments or other complex disabilities or learning difficulties. It is used to provide access to the basic processes of communicating and electronic information. Such access is now almost essential for learning and for everyday living. As technology has advanced, many programs that were developed for people with disabilities have become commonplace and are used universally. For example, voice-to-text programs, which allow speech to be turned into text, were once available only on special request or at extra cost. These, and many text-to-voice programs, which allow text to be heard, are now generally available.

Responsive teachers in contemporary classrooms do not have to know everything about the specific technology available for students with disabilities. They do, however, need to know where to go to discover technology options and how to support students who rely on assistive devices. In general terms, the first source of information is the student and their family, which can be backed up by the literature related to a particular device and other professionals who work with similar situations.

Think and do 8.4: Matching models

Scherer (2005) has developed the matching person and technology model to clarify the factors that are important in selecting, using and evaluating assistive technologies. Some of the main areas considered by the model are the environments where the individual will use the technology, the person's characteristics and preferences, and the technology's functions and features (see Bruce 2000; IMPT 2014).

Create a series of questions based on these areas of importance to the matching person and technology model that could help matching individuals and assistive technologies.

Summary

Teachers are lifelong learners who become active researchers as they implement the RTF to guide their teaching. Responsive teachers contribute positively to their students' learning journeys with the aim of supporting strong foundations for learning that lasts a lifetime. The children in our schools come from a wide range of life situations and experiential backgrounds. They go on to experience the rest of their lives in many different ways and with many different opportunities and supports. Transitions between elements of the school journey and then into life after school are important times when extra support may be needed to ensure that the benefits of the current setting are extended to new settings. The final section of this chapter presented summaries of key considerations for enhancing learning, developing thinking, improving literacy and numeracy skills and selecting assistive technology. Developing capabilities in these areas provides a foundation for all students' independent and lifelong learning.

Further reading

ACT Government. n.d. 'Early years assessment.' ACT Government. www.det.act.gov.au/teaching_and_learning/assessment_and_reporting/early_years_assessment.

Department of Education and Communities. n.d. 'Kindergarten assessment.' NSW Government. www.curriculumsupport.education.nsw.gov.au/beststart/assess.htm.

Drummond Memorial Public School. n.d. 'You can do it.' Drummond Memorial Public School. www.drummondm-p.schools.nsw.edu.au/curriculum-activities/you-can-do-it.

Far from the Tree website: www.farfromthetree.com/.

Ministry of Education. 2005. 'Key competencies in tertiary education: developing a New Zealand framework.' New Zealand Government. www.minedu.govt.nz/~/media/MinEdu/Files/EducationSectors/TertiaryEducation/KeyCompetencies.pdf.

PNINS (Palmerston North Intermediate Normal School). n.d. 'YCDI! 5 keys to school success.' PNINS. www.pnins.school.nz/index.php/5-keys-culture.

Te Kete Ipurangi. n.d. 'Assessment details.' New Zealand Government. http://toolselector.tki.org.nz/Assessment-areas/Cross-curricular/School-Entry-Assessment-SEA.

References

AITSL (Australian Institute of Teaching and School Leadership). 2012. 'Certification of highly accomplished and lead teachers: principles and processes.' Available at Council of Education Associations of South Australia. www.ceasa.asn.au/assets/Word_documents/AITSL/Teacher-performance/20120430Certification-of-Highly-Accomplished-and-Lead-Teachers-Principles-and-processes.pdf.

——. 2014. 'Global trends in professional learning and performance and development: some implications and ideas for the Australian education system.' AITSL. www.aitsl.edu.au/docs/default-source/default-document-library/horizon_scan_report.pdf?sfvrsn=.

Australian Government. n.d. 'Employment assistance for people with disabilities.' Australian Government. http://australia.gov.au/topics/employment-and-workplace/employment-assistance-for-people-with-disabilities.

Bellert, A. 2012. 'The effects of improved automaticity in basic academic skills on test performance: a study of learning difficulties in the middle-school years.' PhD thesis, University of New England.

Bruce, B. C. 2000. 'Access points on the digital river.' *Journal of Adolescent & Adult Literacy* 44 (3): 262–7.

Cockram, J. 2005. 'People with an intellectual disability in the prisons.' *Psychiatry, Psychology and Law* 12 (1): 163–73.

Drummond Memorial Public School. n.d. 'You can do it.' Drummond Memorial Public School. www.drummondm-p.schools.nsw.edu.au/curriculum-activities/you-can-do-it.

Durie, M. 1998. *Whaiora: Maori health development.* Auckland: Oxford University Press.

European Parliament, Council of the European Union. 2006. 'Recommendation of the European Parliament and of the council of 18 December 2006 on key competences for lifelong learning ' *Official Journal of the European Union*, series L, no. 394: 10–18. EUR-Lex. http://eur-lex.europa.eu/LexUriServ/LexUriServ.do?uri=OJ:L:2006:394:0010:0018:EN:PDF.

Graham, L. and B. Y. L. Wong. 1993. 'Comparing two modes in teaching a question-answering strategy for enhancing reading comprehension: didactic and self-instructional training.' *Journal of Learning Disabilities* 26 (4): 270–9.

Graham, L. and D. Paterson. 2011. 'Using metaphors of teaching to explore inclusive practice with pre-service teachers.' *Asian Journal of Educational Research and Synergy* 3 (1): 31–43.

Graham, L., A. Bellert and J. Pegg. 2007. 'Supporting students in the middle school years with learning difficulties in mathematics: research into classroom practice.' *Australasian Journal of Special Education* 31 (2): 171–82.

Greenberg, G. and R. Rosenheck. 2008. 'Jail incarceration, homelessness, and mental health: a national study.' *Psychiatric Services* 59 (2), 170–7.

Hargreaves, A. 2005. 'Educational change takes ages: life, career and generational factors in teachers' emotional responses to educational change.' *Teaching and Teacher Education* 21 (8): 967–83.

Hattie, J. 2012. *Visible learning for teachers: maximising impact on learning.* New York: Routledge.

Holland, T., I. C. H. Clare and T. Mukhopadhyay. 2002. 'Prevalence of "criminal offending" by men and women with intellectual disability and the characteristics of "offenders": implications for research and service development.' *Journal of Intellectual Disability Research* 46 (Supplement s1): 6–20.

IMPT (Institute for Matching Person and Technology). 2014. 'Matching person and technology (MPT) assessment process.' IMPT. www.matchingpersonandtechnology.com/mptdesc.html.

Mayer, E. 1992. *Key competencies: report of the committee to advise the Australian Education Council and ministers of Vocational Education, Employment and Training on employment-related key competencies for post compulsory education and training.* Canberra: Australaian Education Council and Ministers of Vocational Education, Employment and Training.

Ministry of Education. 2005. 'Key competencies in tertiary education: developing a New Zealand framework.' New Zealand Government. www.minedu.govt.nz/~/media/MinEdu/Files/EducationSectors/TertiaryEducation/KeyCompetencies.pdf.

Ministry of Social Development. n.d. 'Mainstream employment programme.' New Zealand Government. www.msd.govt.nz/what-we-can-do/disability-services/mainstream/index.html.

NSW Public Schools. n.d. 'Disability, learning and support.' NSW Government. www.schools.nsw.edu.au/studentsupport/programs/disability.php.

Pegg, J. and L. Graham. 2013. 'A three-level intervention pedagogy to enhance the academic achievement of Indigenous students: evidence from *QuickSmart* mathematics research relevant to Indigenous populations; evidence-based practice (123–138).' In R. Jorgenson, P. Sullivan and P. Grootenboer, eds. *Pedagogies to enhance learning for Indigenous students*, Singapore: Springer.

PNINS (Palmerston North Intermediate Normal School). n.d. 'YCDI! 5 keys to school success.' PNINS. www.pnins.school.nz/index.php/5-keys-culture.

Scherer, M. J. 2005. *Living in the state of stuck: how assistive technology impacts the lives of people with disabilities*, 4th edn. Cambridge, MA: Brookline Books.

Waitoller, F and A. Artiles. 2013. 'A decade of professional development research for inclusive education: a critical review and notes for a research program.' *Review of Educational Research* 83 (3): 319–56.

Inclusive practices for 21st century classrooms

Sustainable learning is flexible and adaptable, with a focus on responsive action attuned to students' needs, the valid assessment of learning progress and the evaluation of teaching effectiveness. In this book we have presented learning for all, teaching that matters and learning that lasts as major considerations for shaping, planning and implementing contemporary inclusive practice. The RTF and its reiterative set of questions introduce an approach to inclusive practice that is strengths based and concerned with orchestrating classroom organisation and teaching actions in order to facilitate student learning. In keeping with the ATRiUM metaphor, this approach to inclusion suggests that learners have the space and light required to learn and can use and develop knowledge and skills to a higher level, given the right conditions.

Good teaching does not follow a one-size-fits-all approach but acknowledges that students have different learning needs. Responsive teachers have knowledge about learning trajectories that are typical within curriculum domains and use this knowledge to plan and differentiate their teaching in response to learning contexts and their students' learning needs. Importantly, responsive teachers also understand that some learners have complex profiles that do not fit expected learning and development trajectories. Valid assessment is vital as a foundation for responsive teaching, because it focuses on gathering information about all students' thinking and understanding and about the effectiveness of teaching.

Sustainable learning depends on effective, responsive teachers implementing differentiated teaching, learning and assessment, with a particular focus on ensuring that students with disabilities or learning difficulties participate and progress. As an example, consider a learner who has difficulties with written language but well-developed higher-order thinking abilities. For such a student, responsive teachers would find alternative ways to provide access to written information and for the learner to demonstrate their thinking. This allows the separation of relevant learning dimensions and rests on the clarification of the purpose of learning tasks. As a further example, consider a learner who is intellectually gifted but does not have well-developed basic academic skills because of learning difficulties associated with ASD. In response to this scenario, responsive teachers would avoid constantly expecting the demonstration of lower-order skills prior to fostering opportunities for the student's higher-order thinking and would take into account the student's learning capabilities and provide enriching chances for in-depth problem-solving. The development of lower-order skills would still be supported, but through explicit writing lessons or an intervention program. These approaches are individually focused and counter to the 'usual' way of teaching typically developing learners.

A significant challenge, and opportunity, for teachers in the 21st century is to work within a context of evolving societal change and fast-developing technologies.

Teachers now need to deliver teaching and learning that equip students to live, learn and continue to learn in future schools, society and workplaces that, due to the pace of change, were almost unimaginable even as little as 10 years ago. To support sustainable learning in this context, ongoing teacher professional learning and collaboration are essential.

Ideally, teachers monitor their own professional learning needs, align them to the learning needs of their students and actively engage in the kind of professional development that improves their practice in targeted and collaborative ways (AITSL 2012). The models, protocols, scaffolds and frameworks presented in this book aim to provide the stimuli for just this kind of professional learning. In fact, the future of professional learning is likely to lie in how school professionals and university faculties negotiate the sharing of artefacts that span their communities of practice and provide an ongoing forum for mutual engagement. Boundary practices facilitate learning because they are practices that both communities can examine with the aim of improving the educational experiences of all students. Readers are urged to explore their own inclusive practices by using these artefacts to examine, analyse and reflect on their teaching. The use, modification, further development, sharing of and discussion about these artefacts are important to the evolution of sustainable learning as learning for all, teaching that matters and learning that lasts.

As Leonardo (2010) notes, teachers have a unique opportunity to act as change agents and to transform education. This is because teachers not only implement and innovate instructional approaches but can provide access to opportunities to learn, to recognise and value student differences and to influence student thinking about issues of global importance that affect their lives, like sustainability and inclusion.

Further reading

Australian Institute of Teaching and School Leadership. n.d. 'Horizon scan of global trends.' AISTL. www.aitsl.edu.au/professional-growth/research/horizon-scan.

New Zealand Teachers Council. n.d. 'Your professional practice.' New Zealand Teachers Council. www.teacherscouncil.govt.nz/practising-as-a-teacher.

References

AITSL (Australian Institute of Teaching and School Leadership). 2012. 'Certification of highly accomplished and lead teachers: principles and processes.' Available at Council of Education Associations of South Australia. www.ceasa.asn.au/assets/Word_documents/AITSL/Teacher-performance/20120430Certification-of-Highly-Accomplished-and-Lead-Teachers-Principles-and-processes.pdf.

Leonardo, Z. 2010. 'Affirming ambivalence: introduction to cultural politics and education.' In Z. Leonardo, ed. Handbook of cultural politics and education, 1–45. Rotterdam: Sense Publishers.

Index